Practical 3D Printers

Brian Evans

Apress

1/14

Practical 3D Printers

ISBN-13 (pbk): 978-1-4302-4392-2

ISBN-13 (electronic): 978-1-4302-4393-9

Trademarked names, logos, and images may appear in this book. Rather than use a trademark symbol with every occurrence of a trademarked name, logo, or image we use the names, logos, and images only in an editorial fashion and to the benefit of the trademark owner, with no intention of infringement of the trademark. The use in this publication of trade names, trademarks, service marks, and similar terms, even if they are not identified as such, is not to be taken as an expression of opinion as to whether or not they are subject to proprietary rights.

Distributed to the book trade worldwide by Springer Science+Business Media New York, 233 Spring Street, 6th Floor, New York, NY 10013. Phone 1-800-SPRINGER, fax (201) 348-4505, e-mail orders-ny@springer-sbm.com, or visit www.springeronline.com.

For information on translations, please e-mail rights@apress.com, or visit www.apress.com.

Apress and friends of ED books may be purchased in bulk for academic, corporate, or promotional use. eBook versions and licenses are also available for most titles. For more information, reference our Special Bulk Sales–eBook Licensing web page at www.apress.com/bulk-sales.

The information in this book is distributed on an "as is" basis, without warranty. Although every precaution has been taken in the preparation of this work, neither the author(s) nor Apress shall have any liability to any person or entity with respect to any loss or damage caused or alleged to be caused directly or indirectly by the information contained in this work

Any source code or other supplementary materials referenced by the author in this text is available to readers at www.apress.com. For detailed information about how to locate your book's source code, go to www.apress.com/source-code.

*For my father, who opened his garage and taught me
how to tinker at a very early age*

Contents at a Glance

Contents

About the Author

Brian Evans is an artist working in electronic media and Assistant Professor of Art at Metropolitan State University of Denver, where he teaches multidisciplinary courses in art on topics that include electronics and digital fabrication. Many of his classes use open-source hardware—including MakerBot or RepRap 3D printers and the Arduino electronics platform—to create new works in art and design.

He is the author of *Beginning Arduino Programming* (Apress, 2011) and contributed to *Arduino Projects to Save the World* (Apress, 2011) with Emery Premeaux. His work has been shown at the Los Angeles Municipal Art Gallery at Barnsdall Park, the Orange County Center for Contemporary Art, and the University Art Museum at California State University, Long Beach. In 2009, Evans was a resident and contributor to the Grounding Open Source Hardware residency and summit at the Banff New Media Institute in Alberta, Canada, and in 2011 a contributor to the Open Hardware Summit in New York. He received an MFA from California State University, Long Beach in 2008, and a BFA from Arizona State University in 2005.

About the Technical Reviewer

Tony Buser began his technology career in 1995 by writing HTML code. From there, he moved into web site and intranet application development and now works as a web developer for MakerBot Industries in Brooklyn, NY. Tony loves turning virtual digital information into physical reality, and he believes that the affordable and easy-to-use 3D printing and personal fabrication technology might very well be the most significant new technology since the World Wide Web. He is excited to be a part of its development at such an early stage and can typically be found spending untold hours in his basement workshop in Reading, PA with his four 3D printers: two Makerbots, a RepRap, and a whiteAnt. And he's always building more.

Acknowledgments

There are so many people that without whom this book could not exist. If anyone deserves my deepest appreciation the most, it's my loving wife and best friend, Susan, who was always there for me during the long hours of this project. To my daughter, Kori, I am so grateful for your unconditional love and support. Thanks also to the rest of my family for their continued encouragement.

A big thank you to my friends and colleagues at Metro State who provided unwavering enthusiasm for this project and gave me a lot of leeway this last semester. I promise I will be more human now. My deepest gratitude to Greg Watts, Chair of the Art Department and our fearless leader, for having confidence in my hair-brained ideas and investing in the department's first MakerBot Cupcake in 2009 just because I thought it would be cool. Greg, you are a big reason that this book was possible. I am also thankful for my hard-working and always inspiring students at Metro, who keep entrusting me as their guide through this world of open-source art and design, and especially to Oliver and Rachel—the best teaching assistants ever.

To the technical reviewer, Tony Buser, I will never be able to thank you enough for what you have done. It was a privilege and honor to have such an enigmatic pillar of Thingiverse working with me on this project. I am also greatly indebted to the team at Apress: Michelle, my editorial champion; James, for knocking me around a bit; Jessica and Brigid, for keeping track of things; Kim, for running the whole thing through the ringer; and everybody else that worked on this project—it was a pleasure to work with all of you again.

Finally I want to acknowledge the vast multitude of talented artists, designers, engineers, tinkerers, and makers everywhere that have created such a rich and diverse 3D printing community for which this book extensively draws from. While too numerous to name everyone here, I would like to thank each and every one of you that generously contributed directly to this book by sharing images of the things you have made, or indirectly by advancing some truly great ideas and engineering genius. Thank you all.

Introduction

Wired, The New York Times, The Economist, The Wall Street Journal, BBC, and even *The Colbert Report*, yes—personal 3D printing is everywhere. 3D printing, sometimes called *additive manufacturing* or *rapid prototyping*, is all about building 3D objects using plastic and other materials from a digital design. As a technology, it has actually been around and in use by engineers and designers for more than 25 years. It hasn't been until the last five years, though, that *personal* 3D printing has begun to make such an impact—where objects made on a machine that might cost $30,000 in the industry can now be made with nearly the same quality on a machine that fits at home on your desk for less than $2,000.

Better yet, it doesn't take a trained designer or engineer to design and print 3D objects on this new breed of personal 3D printers. In fact, these machines are actively used throughout K-12 education right now, and the technology is becoming increasingly more popular every year. All it takes is an insatiable curiosity about things, the desire to tinker and experiment, and a willingness to learn a handful of different applications that can be used to design and print 3D objects. The things people make with their 3D printer range from as simple and practical as a clothespin to as ridiculous and wonderful as an entire robotic petting zoo.

This book assumes that you are as deeply inspired by the idea of personal 3D manufacturing as I am. Maybe you are just now considering buying your own 3D printer to see what it's all about. Or maybe you have already bought your first 3D printer and are now trying to figure out what exactly to do with it. Either way, this book will be your guide as you learn the ins and outs of both your 3D printer and how to design objects to be made with it.

Why Own a 3D Printer?

Why own a 3D printer? Because it's fun! While many might rave about the economic benefits of owning a 3D printer or the way in which personal 3D printing will revolutionize our world, these viewpoints are all just a bit too hyperbolic for me—and miss the fundamental point. Sure, you might be able to make a few dollars printing things and selling them on sites like Etsy or Ebay. And sure, once you have a 3D printer, you start to look at things around the house a little bit differently. Above all else, though, you should want to own a 3D printer and learn how to use it because it can really be a lot of fun. My students and I spend countless hours watching things emerge from our 3D printer—it's amazingly mesmerizing.

You might be a designer looking to integrate this technology into your professional practice. Or an artist exploring the realms of a relatively new media. Maybe you're an inventor and need your own desktop assembly line. On the other hand, maybe you want to explore the possibility of creating 3D printed jewelry. Or you happen to like trains. Or robots. Whatever you're into, above all you should probably enjoy the simple act of tinkering. If you are buying your very own personal 3D printer, then I can assure you it will not "just work" like the document printer that you most likely already own. It's just not that simple, and that should be considered a good thing. It might be challenging at times to make your 3D printer do exactly what you want of it, but that is a big part of the fun.

It's a Big World of 3D Printers

In the last five years, we have gone from a single personal 3D printer to hundreds of them. From RepRaps to MakerBots; Printrbots to Mosaics. There's a bunch of them out there and every week it seems there is a brand-new 3D printer that someone has designed and is putting out into the world. So how can one single book encompass all of these 3D printers? In some ways, it can't. There are just too many personal 3D printers out there and simply no way to cover them all in sufficient detail.

Although we can talk about all the ways these many different printers are alike. We can also look at how to use 3D printers in general and how to design objects to be printed on them. We will discuss specifically a handful of different 3D printers, and the software and electronics that make them work. We might have missed your favorite printer, but it's a big world out there and the best thing we can do is build on what the printers have in common to get you started with 3D printing the right way.

Find a 3D printer that makes you happy, and let's figure out how to use it.

About This Book

This book is roughly divided into three sections: hardware, software, and upgrades. The first three chapters cover the hardware side of things by starting with the big picture of how 3D printers work and digging down to the specifics of a 3D printer's toolchain, before wrapping up with some useful tips for making your first 3D prints and calibrating your machine. The largest part of this book covers all the different sorts of software that can be used to design and print 3D objects, with projects that include a diverse range of topics— from 3D text, multipart models, robotics, and 3D memes. We wrap up the book with some helpful upgrades and resources for working with and improving your 3D printer.

This book is designed both as a how-to manual and as a reference. As a manual, starting with Chapter 1 and working all the way to the end, we walk through the process of buying a 3D printer, learning how it works, calibrating the printer, designing objects for printing, and then ending with how to improve the printer after we've given it a good run. If you already have a little knowledge of 3D printing or design, then this book provides a useful reference to support those things that you might want to learn more about. This might include designing shapes in an illustration application and then extruding it into three-dimensions, learning more about parametric computer-aided design (CAD), or even how to process and prepare 3D models for printing.

This book is not an instruction booklet for how to build a Model X 3D printer. If we were to do that, then the book would be obsolete before it were published. Even as I write this now that the book is finished, a few changes in the available models of 3D printers are already underway. Instead, we will assume that once you make your 3D printer purchase you'll be able to figure out how to put it together and get started. We will pick up again at that point, guiding you along the way of breaking in the new printer and making new things with it. The 3D printer enthusiasts are an amazingly active community of makers who go out of their way to share information with the world. Rely on the many forums, wikis, blogs, and other sources of online knowledge to get your 3D printer up and running—many of these resources are listed at the back of this book in Appendix B.

Our design projects in Chapters 4 through 9 take a thematic approach to our project considerations and the type of software used in their creation. The intent is that these projects will give you a broad range of real-world, dare we say practical applications for designing and building 3D objects with your new 3D printer. We will introduce a handful of software applications this way, which can be used in various capacities to model 3D objects. There is not "The One" 3D application that can do everything that we might want, and that diversity makes things interesting. Every reader will have their own personal style and what works best, or doesn't, for them. If I did my job right, then this book should have a little something for everyone.

Learning by Making

The best lesson I can give to my students is that you learn best by making something. The projects in this book might at first seem, at least to a few, limited to some way-out-there or even goofy ideas, but everything we make in this book should be directly applicable to many of the things you would want to make every day if you only knew how. You are really only limited by your own imagination. But first, start with these projects, give them a try, tinker with them to see what happens, and use them as a jumping off point for your own creations.

Not only do you learn by making, but making mistakes is also a very important part of the process. This is called *iterative design*: make one thing, see what works and what doesn't, make a new version, see how it can be improved, and make another new version. Iteration and experimentation are ways to learn those types of things that we can't really teach you in this book. How does the material hold up to repeated stress, to sunlight, or to water? What does it feel like and how quickly will it wear out? By having your very own desktop factory (well, almost), you have the power to make an infinite number of iterations to improve your designs and share those with the world.

Sharing Things

Sharing things is a very important aspect of this whole 3D printing community. All of the designs in this book are licensed under a Creative Commons Attribution-ShareAlike license (`www.creativecommons.org/licenses/by-sa/3.0`). Each design can be easily downloaded from the thing-sharing site, Thingiverse (`www.thingiverse.com`), by searching for my user profile, bwevans, or for the tag `Practical 3D Printers`. My hope is that everyone who picks up this book will make many, if not all, of the projects and create even more new designs from the lessons learned here.

I desperately want to see each and every one of them, so if you make something from this book, be sure to use the I Made One button from that project's page on Thingiverse, discussed in Chapters 3 and 4, and post a photo of your thing. If you make a new derivative or something inspired by this book, then be sure to either post your thing on Thingiverse as a derivative of the project or use the `Practical 3D Printers` tag so that others can find it, including me. Hopefully, I will come to know everyone that reads this book through the things that you make.

CHAPTER 1

A World of 3D Printers

If you've picked up this book, then you are as captivated by the possibilities of 3D printing as much as I am. Maybe you've seen one of the many personal 3D printers in the media and you want to know more; maybe you are an artist, designer, engineer, inventor, or a maker of things and want to know how to get started 3D printing your designs; or maybe you have already purchased your 3D printer and now just need some help in learning what to do with it. This chapter begins our journey with 3D printers, starting with a general overview of how 3D printers work. We then take a look at many of the current DIY 3D printers on the market today for under $2,000 to serve as a buyer's guide for picking up a new printer, or simply just to give you an idea for where the 3D printer you might already own fits in. We will then wrap up the chapter with a discussion of the materials and supplies that you will need to successfully complete the projects in this book.

In this chapter, we will do the following:

- Find out what a personal 3D printer is and how it works

- Survey many of the different types of DIY 3D printers available today

- Review the different materials that are available to print objects with

- Discuss the various tools and supplies needed to successfully make 3D prints

Let's begin by trying to separate the science fiction of 3D printing from the reality of making objects with a 3D printer.

Tea. Earl Grey. Hot.

These words should sound familiar to many of you. The character Captain Jean-Luc Piccard from TV's *Star Trek: The Next Generation* would say these words to a terminal in the wall and his beverage of choice would materialize in front of him within mere seconds. This fictional device was called a "replicator," a machine that reorganized the atoms of basic materials to create all manner of new things at the instant of a request. Just to be clear with the current state of 3D printers: we are not there yet. The advances that a community of industrious developers have heralded into place over the last few years has been nothing but astonishing; however, we are a long way from reforming molecular structures to make things from thin air.

Instead, the personal 3D printers of today most often build things from plastic using a process called fused filament fabrication (FFF). Plastic filament is heated and extruded from a nozzle like a tiny and precise hot glue gun while the machine draws out 3D objects layer by layer. As one layer of plastic is laid on top of another, they fuse together, and, when cooled, form a solid and durable plastic part. This technology has been around for about 25 years and used in the design and engineering industries for everything from designing parts for cars to designing toaster ovens.

Because today's industrial printers cost in the tens to hundreds of thousands of dollars to start, a few brave souls dared to ask that fateful question, "How hard could it be to build our own 3D printer?" The answer, at least initially, was something along the lines of very hard; however, over the last five years (since the first DIY 3D printer was assembled), many advances in the technology have been made through the combined efforts of developers that have made the many thousands of 3D printers worldwide. To see the ever-evolving taxonomy of 3D printers, be sure to visit the RepRap Family Tree at `http://reprap.org/wiki/RepRap_Family_Tree`. For now, let's take a broader look at how these printers work.

How a 3D Printer Works

All of the personal 3D printers that we will look at in this chapter share many similarities with one another, at least in principle, although they might each approach things a little differently. Let's take a closer look at how these 3D printers work using the example shown in Figure 1-1.

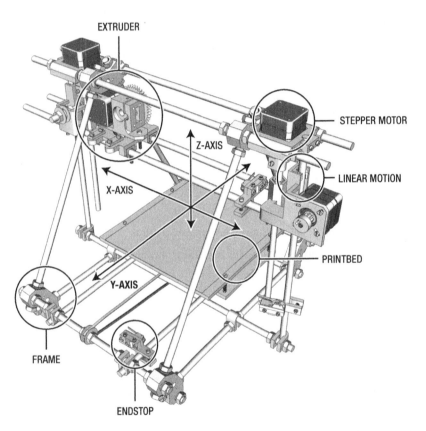

Figure 1-1. How a 3D printer works (original model courtesy Gary Hodgson, 2011)

Cartesian Robot

Central to a 3D printer is the idea of a Cartesian robot. This is a machine that can move in three linear directions, along the x-, y-, and z-axes, also known as the Cartesian coordinates. To do this, these 3D printers use small stepper motors that can move with great precision and accuracy—usually 1.8 degrees per step, which translates to resolutions in the fractions of a millimeter range through the unique way that these stepper motors are controlled. The three-axis robot is like any other computer numerically controlled (CNC) robot and is able to position its thermoplastic extruder along each of these linear axes of movement to lay down layer upon layer of hot plastic. All of the 3D printers in the book use timing belts and pulleys along their x- and y-axes to provide fast yet accurate positioning, and most use threaded rod, or lead screws, to position the z-axis with even greater precision.

While it might all sound complex, it is really not all that complicated, as nearly all of these DIY 3D printers use standardized off-the-shelf components that are put to use in many different industries. In part, it took a lot of hard work over the years to figure out what worked well and what didn't to end up with such outstanding printers today. Thanks to an open and sharing community, these designs and improvements have been shared freely, further improving the technology.

Thermoplastic Extruder

With our Cartesian system providing accurate linear positioning, we need an extruder capable of laying down thin strands of thermoplastic—a type of plastic that will soften to a semiliquid state when heated. The extruder (see Figure 1-2), arguably the most complex part of a 3D printer that is still seeing intense development, is actually the marriage of two key elements: the filament drive and the thermal hot end.

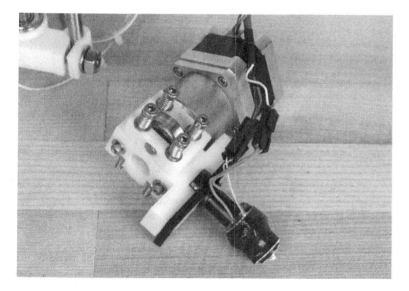

Figure 1-2. Complete extruder with filament driver and hot end

The filament drive pulls in plastic filament often bundled in spools of either 3mm or 1.75mm diameter filament using a geared driver mechanism. Most, if not all, contemporary filament drivers use a stepper motor to better control the flow of plastic into the hot end. These motors are often geared down with printed gears or an integral gearbox, as shown in Figure 1-2, to give the filament driver the strength needed for continued extrusion.

The filament, after being pulled into the extruder by the filament driver, is then fed to the heater chamber or hot end. The hot end usually is thermally insulated from the rest of the extruder and is made up of either a large block of aluminum with an embedded heater or some other heater core, along with a temperature sensor. When the plastic reaches the hot end, it is heated to somewhere around 170°C to 220°C, depending on the plastic to be extruded. Once in a semiliquid state, the plastic is forced through a print nozzle—with an opening somewhere in the vicinity of 0.35 millimeters to 0.5 millimeters in diameter—before laying this thin hot extrusion onto the printbed drawing lines that outline that layer of the shape to be printed or fill that layer using some type of infill pattern.

Printbed

The printbed is the surface that your 3D prints are built on. The size of a printer's printbed will vary from one printer to the next, ranging from 100mm² to 200mm², somewhere between 4 inches and 8 inches or larger. Most, although not all, personal 3D printers on the market offer a heated printbed (see Figure 1-3), either as standard or as an option, although it is also easy to build one from scratch if needed. The printbed is used to prevent warping or cracking of prints as they cool and to create better adhesion between the first layers of the print and the printbed surface.

Figure 1-3. *Heated printbed*

The surface of the printbed is often made from either glass or aluminum to better spread the heat across the area and to make for a smooth and level surface. Glass provides the smoothest surface to print on while aluminum conducts heat better for a heated platform. To prevent the object from lifting off the surface in mid-print, these surfaces are often covered in one kind of tape or another to provide a surface that is inexpensive to replace periodically. These materials include Kapton or polyimide tape, PET or polyester silicon tape, or even hardware store–variety blue painter's tape, depending on the type of filament used.

Linear Motion

The type of linear motion system (or the mechanical assembly that allows each axis to move) that is used by the 3D printer will often determine how accurate the printer is, how fast the printer can print, and how much or how little maintenance will be needed by the printer over the long term. Most personal 3D printers use smooth, precision ground rods for each axis, and either plastic, bronze, or linear ball bearings to glide across each rod. Linear ball bearing systems have gained a lot of popularity lately for their longevity and smoother operation over the life of the printer; although they are often louder during operation than bronze bushings like the self-aligning variety shown in Figure 1-4, which are generally quieter but often require a little more work to align during the build process.

Figure 1-4. Self-aligning bronze bearings on a Prusa Mendel

The "best" type of linear motion system for a 3D printer is about as personal a decision as the kind of car you drive. 3D printed bushings are very cheap, but don't last that long. Machined plastic bushings (called Igus bushings) are very smooth and work well for the slow-moving z-axis, but they tend to deform under heavier use. On the other hand, the reliability of linear bearings discussed earlier depends on the quality of the smooth rails they ride on and they cost more. Other, more exotic materials, like felt, have also been tried with mixed results. Some printers even use industrial linear glides that have the potential for greater accuracy and longevity at increased cost and mechanical complexity.

Endstops

The length of travel for each linear axis is limited by usually mechanical or optical endstops (see Figure 1-5). Basically, these are switches that tell the printer's controller electronics when it has reached a limit in one direction of movement in order to prevent the axis from moving past its limits.

Figure 1-5. *Mechanical endstop on y-axis*

While endstops are not strictly needed for operation, having at the very least one endstop in the minimum position on each axis will allow the printer to home itself at the beginning of each print for repeatable and accurate prints every time. We will discuss the electronics in greater detail in Chapter 2.

Frame

Holding everything together is the 3D printer's frame. This frame forms the structural element of your 3D printer and its material and construction determine a lot about the final accuracy of your printer. All of the RepRap style designs will use 3D-printed components along with threaded rod and other hardware to make the frame structure. On the other hand, Box Bots like the MakerBot or the MakerGear Mosaic use laser-cut plywood that is bolted together to make the frame, as shown in Figure 1-6.

Figure 1-6. *MakerGear Mosaic plywood frame*

A laser-cut plywood frame uses slot-and-tab construction, where two pieces of plywood are held together with tabs from one piece fitting into slots in the other, and connected with nuts and bolts. This type of frame is generally easier to assemble and offers better up-front precision so that printer calibration is easier; however, these frames are often louder during operation and all those screws will eventually need retightening later. Conversely, threaded rod frames make for quieter robots, but add to an even more complex assembly and calibration. If you are sourcing all the parts for your 3D printer, then you will often need to cut the various lengths of threaded and smooth rod again, adding to the complexity of the overall build. Finally, some of the more recent printer designs are using commercial aluminum extrusions to build a frame that is rigid and easy to assemble, although it can cost as much as $100 to $200 more.

So that's a brief overview of the main components in a 3D printer. We will look at the workflow of moving from a digital 3D model to printing a 3D design in the next couple of chapters; but for now let's talk about some of the more popular and affordable 3D printers on the market today and how they compare with one another.

A Survey of 3D Printers

There is a diverse and rapidly expanding field of 3D printers—so big, in fact, that to give all of the available printers ample coverage, it would take a book just on that alone. We can't cover everything here, but what we can do is to provide a brief survey of some of the most popular printers available right now. These printers can be roughly categorized into four main groups: the RepRaps, the Box Bots, RepStraps, and the Upstarts. All of the printers discussed here can be purchased for $2,000 or less in a kit form or sourced from individual parts and suppliers. Each of these 3D printer designs has been proven through extensive testing and development, and if available through a retailer, the company has proven to be reliable and consistent. If you choose to build a 3D printer yourself instead of buying a preassembled one, you will find that it is generally not that much more difficult than building your own personal computer—although being handy with the business end of a wrench is helpful.

RepRaps

The RepRap, developed by Dr. Adrian Bowyer at Bath University, is the 3D printer that started it all in 2007. The first RepRap (short for "replicating rapid-prototyper") named Darwin, was a 3D printer capable (at least in theory) of reproducing itself by printing the parts needed to make a new one. By designing a working 3D printer using 3D printed parts (albeit parts printed on an expensive industrial machine in the beginning) along with off-the-shelf hardware, the RepRap broke through the price barrier of industrial 3D printers. With the Darwin, RepRap started the DIY 3D printer revolution that has been evolving ever since.

RepRap Mendel

Darwin was eventually replaced by a second-generation RepRap named Mendel, which was further refined in 2010 by Josef Prusa to require fewer parts, both printed and hardware, while retaining most of the functionality. This new stripped-down design has been called the Model T of 3D printers and for good reason: it operates under the mantra of function over form and it can be very affordable. One of the highest quality Prusa Mendel kits available on the market today, shown in Figure 1-7, is produced by the Ohio-based company MakerGear (www.makergear.com).

Figure 1-7. *MakerGear Prusa Mendel*

The Prusa Mendel is a low-cost, low part-count 3D printer that has a useable build volume of 200mm × 200mm × 110mm (roughly 8" × 8" × 4.5") with a frame built using a combination of printed parts, threaded rod, and other hardware. Prusa Mendels use two motors for the z-axis wired in parallel to reduce the amount of manufactured parts like pulleys and timing belts. MakerGear improves on the basic design by using stainless-steel hardware, self-aligning bronze bushings for linear motion, a heated printbed, and a laser-cut sled for the y-axis.

If you are more interested in saving a few pennies than getting all the bells and whistles, the Prusa Mendel can be one of the least expensive printers to obtain—if you source all of your own hardware and have a friend or hackerspace nearby that can print the plastic components for you. For more information, head over to the

RepRap wiki at http://reprap.org. These printers take significantly more time than others to build and get properly calibrated, especially if you are sourcing all of your own parts; however, there is a large group of Prusa Mendel owners that are willing to share their knowledge, advice, and improvements for the design.

The following are some of the highlights of the Prusa Mendel:

- Mid-range build volume

- With some work, can obtain quick print speeds

- Very affordable if sourcing your own parts

- Takes quite a lot of time to build and properly dial in

RepRap Huxley

The Huxley design is the smaller, more portable brother of the RepRap Mendel. Currently, the Huxley design of choice, shown in Figure 1-8, is made by RepRapPro, Ltd. (http://reprappro.com), lead by RepRap's primogenitor, Dr. Adrian Bowyer, and eMAKER's Jean-Marc Giacalone.

Figure 1-8. *eMAKER Huxley (courtesy Johannes Heberlein, 2011)*

The Huxley is a little cheaper than the Prusa Mendel, depending on whether you source it yourself or if you buy a kit, although size and portability is more important to this design than price. The Huxley features a modest, build volume of 140mm × 140mm × 110mm (about 5.5" × 5.5" × 4.5")—in one of the smallest 3D printers in overall size. Through a combination of linear bearings on the x- and y-axes and fine pitch threaded rod on the z-axis, the Huxley is capable of some astonishingly detailed prints.

Because of the smaller size of the printer, the filament driver portion of the extruder that normally rides on the x-axis carriage has to be separated from the hot end and relocated to the frame of the printer. To link the filament driver and the hot end, the designers use something called a Bowden cable, basically a plastic tube that connects the filament driver to the smaller hot end on the x-axis carriage. This can be seen as a good or bad thing, depending on your point of view. Either this design offloads much of the bulk of the extruder from the x-axis, allowing it to move more quickly and with greater accuracy, or it might present problems with the actual plastic extrusion because of the added complexity of this arrangement and the increased friction of the tube, causing prints that look stringy in appearance.

The following are some of the highlights of the RepRap Huxley:

- One of the smallest available printers with a modest build volume

- More accurate and reliable linear motion system

- Bowden cable extruder is either a pro or con

- Takes almost as long to build and set up as a Prusa Mendel

Box Bots

Where the RepRaps are unified by their basic design premise and a loose affiliation with the reprap.org web site, Box Bots can only be easily grouped together because of their use of plywood frames, built from bolted-together, precision, laser-cut panels. Because of this, and unlike the RepRap printers, a 3D printer is not needed to produce one of these kits, making them easier and faster to distribute. Additionally, the printer's assembly is often much easier than the RepRaps', making the printer more precise and easier to calibrate. This section looks at three different printers made by three different companies that are attempting to make 3D printers for the masses.

MakerBot

MakerBot Industries (http://store.makerbot.com) was the first post-RepRap 3D printer to introduce an easy-to-assemble, low-cost 3D printer kit with their Cupcake CNC in 2009, which, while inspired by the RepRap Darwin, used a laser-cut plywood frame and structural components along with off-the-shelf hardware. MakerBot's second-generation Thing-O-Matic, shown in Figure 1-9, featured numerous advancements in their linear motion control and extruder technology.

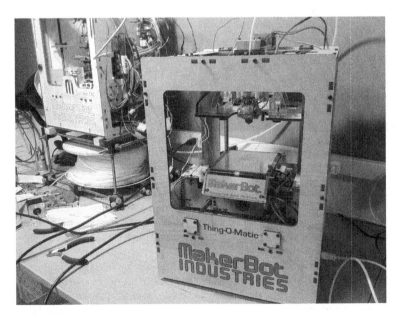

Figure 1-9. MakerBot Thing-O-Matic (foreground, courtesy Tony Buser, 2011)

The Thing-O-Matic has one of the smallest build volumes at 120mm x 120mm x 115mm (or 4.7" × 4.7" × 4.5"). MakerBot's recently introduced third-generation printer, called the Replicator, will feature a larger 225mm × 145mm × 150mm build volume (roughly 8.9" × 5.7" × 5.9"). Where the Cupcake and Thing-O-Matic were offered as kits that could be built in about a weekend, the Replicator will be the first of the Box Bots to come fully assembled directly from the manufacturer as standard, with a heated build platform. While it has the potential of being the easiest 3D printer to set up and get printing, the cost of assembly places the Replicator at the top of our $2,000 price range.

Not only does the Replicator ship preassembled, it is also the only low-cost 3D printer that comes with a standard option for dual extruders. This means that it is now possible to print using two different colors of filament or, while still experimental, to print very intricate parts or unsupported overhangs using a water-soluble support material in addition to the standard plastic filament. While other printers have had dual extruders on their radar for some time now (and some even have the electronics to do this), the MakerBot Replicator is the first and only printer to the market with this capability as standard at or below our price range.

With the Thing-O-Matic discontinued and the Replicator only just now shipping, the following summary for the MakerBot is a little speculative:

- Prebuilt at the factory, giving it a fast out-of-box to printing time

- Little to no initial calibration, although long-term reliability is unknown

- Dual extruder option for two-color or support printing

- Most expensive printer in our survey, and not as gratifying as building it yourself

MakerGear Mosaic M1

In addition to the Prusa Mendel kit pictured earlier, MakerGear also produces their easy to use and set up Box Bot, the Mosaic, available at www.makergear.com/products/m-series-3d-printers and shown in Figure 1-10.

Figure 1-10. MakerGear Mosaic M1

Even though the Mosaic is not a box in the strictest sense, it uses laser-cut plywood as a structural element while featuring an interesting take on the 3D printer formula by having the printbed move on both the y- and z-axes, with the z-axis lowering as the object is printed. Its build volume sits nearer to the smaller end of the spectrum at 127mm × 127mm × 127mm (exactly 5" × 5" × 5") although it includes a heated printbed as standard. What makes the Mosaic unique, besides its unusual form, is the use of precision-machined linear guides and rails for the x- and y-axes, and Teflon-coated lead screws and antibacklash nuts specifically designed for CNC machines. This creates a machine that is reasonably easy to assemble and calibrate, and fairly precise at the same time.

To make the assembly of the Mosaic as painless as possible while still catering to us DIYers, MakerGear has preassembled some components of the kit and have also prewired all of the electronics so that you can quickly assemble the printer, connect the electronics, and get to printing—all in a single afternoon. Compared to some of the other 3D printers in this chapter, calibration is reasonably painless and it holds its calibration longer, requiring less long-term maintenance—and all of this in a printer that retails for about half of the newest MakerBot and is second only to the Huxley in its small size.

The following are some of the highlights of the MakerGear Mosaic:

- Fastest out-of-box to printing time of the kit-based printers

- Unique precision hardware for painless calibration and long-term reliability

- One of the more accurate linear motion systems

- Most affordable Box Bot kit

Ultimaker

Even though Ultimaker (https://shop.ultimaker.com) has not been around as long as MakerBot and MakerGear, the company makes one of the fastest DIY 3D printers on the market, shown in Figure 1-11.

Figure 1-11. Ultimaker (courtesy Dave Durant, 2011)

At 210mm × 210mm × 220mm (or 8.25" × 8.25" × 8.5") the Ultimaker has the largest build area of any of the 3D printers covered in this chapter, although a heated printbed is not included in the design. Unique to this Box Bot is a flying gantry-based thermal printhead that can move at amazing speeds on both the x- and y-axes. To limit the weight of the printhead, the Ultimaker also uses a Bowden cable to decouple the filament pusher from the hot end, resulting in some of the same problems that the RepRap Huxley suffer from, namely stringy prints where the filament doesn't retract quickly enough when the printhead moves from one location to the next. Mechanically, the Ultimaker features a veritable plethora of linear bearings on every axis, which lends to this printer's fast speeds and overall reliability.

While the Ultimaker's feat of engineering provides for some great accuracy, it comes at price—it is one of the most expensive 3D printers on the market, second only to the MakerBot Replicator—and the kit is a little harder to assemble than the others, as well. Once assembled, though, the Ultimaker makes for a very reliable 3D printer with minimal maintenance over the long term. The prints that Ultimaker owners have shared online are simply awe-inspiring, albeit most of these higher-quality prints use an optional, closed-source printer application that costs about $200; even so, the Ultimaker has a devoted following among its community of owners.

Highlights of the Ultimaker 3D printer include the following:

- Best print speed and highest precision of any kit printer with excellent print quality

- Largest available print area in a relatively small footprint

- Lack of an option for heated printbed limits the materials or kinds of prints

- Cost and complexity limit this printer to the dedicated-enthusiast level

RepStraps

When the RepRap was just getting started, the printed components of the Darwin were printed using expensive, industrial 3D printers—limiting the early adoption of personal 3D printers. To get around this chicken-and-egg problem, the community developed the RepStrap—a mashed-up name for a bootstrapped RepRap. These machines were simple CNCs made in home workshops, coupled with some form of a thermoplastic extruder that was capable of printing the parts to make a RepRap printer.

whiteAnt CNC

While many RepStraps have come and gone, the whiteAnt CNC, shown in Figure 1-12 and featured in the book *Printing in Plastic* by Patrick Hood-Daniel and James Floyd Kelly (Apress, 2011), is the only design, currently in development, with plans that are easily accessible and has hardware that is available.

Figure 1-12. whiteAnt CNC (courtesy James Floyd Kelly and Patrick Hood-Daniel, 2011)

The RepStraps are a tinkerer's wildest dream. With little more than a home woodshop, some base materials like plywood and simple hardware, some electronics and motors that you might have lying around, as well as a few open weekends, and you're set to build one of these 3D printers on your own at a potential savings. The whiteAnt (`http://buildyourcnc.com`) design has a build area of 160mm × 190mm × 125mm (roughly 6.25" × 7.5" × 5"), although there is little reason why this couldn't be modified to fill any need you might have. The real attraction of this design is that it's made for someone who values the journey even more than the destination.

Some of the highlights of the whiteAnt CNC include the following:

- Very DIY-friendly design allows for endless customization

- Provides a good excuse to spend hours in the woodshop on weekends

- Middle-of-the-pack build volume, but easily expandable

- Takes the most amount of time to calibrate and get up and running

Upstarts

With all the development that has ramped up in the world of personal 3D printers, it wouldn't be fair to exclude some of the newest designs that are gathering steam as I write this chapter. This section affectionately calls these designs the "upstarts" because they offer a lot of promise; but only time will tell how lasting their designs hold up in the end.

MendelMax and AO-100

Where the RepRap printers generally use threaded rods for the structural frame, making the printer harder to build and properly calibrate, a new breed of 3D printers are turning to square, aluminum extrusions to replace the threaded rod. These printers include the new AO-100 from Aleph Objects (`http://alephobjects.com/AO_100.html`), shown in Figure 1-13, and the MendelMax designed by Maxbots (`http://mendelmax.com`).

Figure 1-13. *Aleph Objects AO-100 (courtesy Aleph Objects, Inc., 2012)*

These aluminum extrusions measure 20mm², with lengths cut to order from the manufacturer. They feature T-slots that run down the length of the extrusion, allowing for special nuts that fit into these slots that parts can be bolted to. These extrusions are often used in structural machine components, providing the printer with much greater structural rigidity, and generally making the printer easier to assemble. While this new material adds anywhere from $100 to $200 to the cost of a standard Prusa Mendel, these printers offer increased printing precision and faster print speeds. Print volumes vary, with the AO-100 coming preassembled with a build area of 200mm × 190mm × 100mm. The MendelMax is available as a kit with a maximum print area of 250mm × 250mm × 200mm. The AO-100 is one of the easier printers to set up and get printing because it ships preassembled. The MendelMax still caters to the tinkerers that enjoy the added challenges that come with the larger print volumes; it is available in either kit form or needs to be self-sourced.

Some of the highlights of the extrusion-frame printers include the following:

- Greater printbed sizes than the standard Prusa Mendel are possible

- Theoretically more precise prints from a more rigid and symmetrical frame

- Aluminum extrusion frames is more expensive than a standard Prusa Mendel

- Quicker assembly than a Prusa Mendel, with prebuilt versions available

RepRap Wallace and Printrbot

One of the defining traits of the RepRap and Box Bot printers is the large angular or boxy frame that supports the three separate axes. The RepRap Wallace (`http://reprap.org/wiki/Wallace`), shown in Figure 1-14, and the Printrbot (`http://printrbot.com/shop/printrbot`) are two up-and-coming printers that fundamentally redefine what a 3D printer looks like.

Figure 1-14. RepRap Wallace (courtesy Whosawhatsis, 2012)

What makes these 3D printers so unique are their pseudo-frameless design and extremely low part-count. By using two z-axis motors like the Prusa Mendel—except inverting the placement of these motors, placing them at the bottom of the printer, and attaching the y-axis smooth rods to the printbed platform—there became no real need for the trapezoidal or box-like frame of other printers. The drawback to this design is that without the added support, these printers need to run much more slowly than other printers to maintain reasonable print quality. The entry-level Printrbot comes with a heated printbed for a build volume of about 150mm × 150mm × 150mm (or 6" × 6" × 6"), while the standard RepRap Wallace design fits the Prusa Mendel heated printbed with a volume of 200mm × 200mm × 200mm (8" × 8" × 8"), although this latter design is parametric and can be changed to create other sizes of printers, both large and small. Where the Printrbot is sold as a kit, parts for the Wallace need to be purchased from various suppliers; and the printed parts will need to be made by a friend with another printer. If the promise of these designs holds up though, we are looking at the new crop of low-cost 3D printers for the masses, which might put 3D printers in kitchens everywhere.

While still somewhat speculative, the following are the highlights for these frameless printers:

- Extremely efficient design makes for a very low-cost 3D printer kit

- Easily hackable designs allow for a variety of shapes and sizes

- low part-count means that these printers can be built very quickly

- At this point, a somewhat untested and unproven design

Choosing the Right 3D Printer

We just finished looking at a handful of the many DIY 3D printers in common use today that can be purchased for less than a new laptop computer. So how does anyone choose a printer that is just right? First of all, choosing the right 3D printer is a very personal choice and you should consider what printer seems best for you, what kinds of things you want to make with your printer, as well as the time you wish to invest in buying or building your printer. To help with this decision, let's first summarize the printers, comparing their speed, resolution, preferred material, and price. Then we can compare their relative print volumes and finally decide between buying a kit or building our own.

3D Printer Summary

With so many options and design philosophies across a vast number of personal 3D printers, choosing one 3D printer can be a little difficult. To make this simpler, we will compare the different technical specifications of each of these printers to see how they stack up. Table 1-1, originally compiled by Luke Chilson and Alex English at ProtoParadigm (www.protoparadigm.com/2012/02/comparing-3d-printers), provides a rundown of the technical specifications of some of the printers discussed earlier in this chapter, including details for the print volume, or the maximum printable area of the printer; layer resolution, or the minimum layer height and smoothness of the prints; the print speed; preferred material of choice; and the approximate price of each printer if available as a kit.

Table 1-1. *Printer Specifications Comparison*

Printer	Print Volume (mm)	Resolution	Print Speed	Pref. Material	Price
RepRap Mendel	200 × 200 × 110	0.1mm	150mm/s	3mm PLA	$830
RepRap Huxley	140 × 140 × 110	0.1mm	150mm/s	1.75mm PLA	$600
MakerBot Replicator	225 × 145 × 150	0.2mm	45mm/s	1.75mm ABS	$1,750
MakerGear Mosaic	127 × 127 × 127	0.15mm	75mm/s	1.75mm PLA	$900
Ultimaker	210 × 210 × 220	0.04mm	300mm/s	3mm PLA	$1,570
whiteAnt CNC	160 × 190 × 125	0.25mm	35mm/s	3mm ABS	NA
Aleph Objects AO-100	200 × 190 × 100	0.1mm	200mm/s	3mm PLA	$1,500
Printrbot	150 × 150 × 150	0.3mm	25mm/s	3mm ABS	$550

The layer resolutions and print speeds in Table 1-1 are based on reported results that can be achieved consistently with a well-tuned printer, although these numbers only partially represent the quality of the prints and the print times of any particular model. While many printers work well with ABS (acrylonitrile butadiene styrene) or PLA (polylactic acid), the preferred material represents arguably the best option for that particular model. This is due to either the lack of a heated build platform, or a build platform that fails to reach a high enough temperature to print ABS successfully; or an extruder whose design makes printing in PLA a little more challenging or will only fit one size of filament.

The listed print speeds should be taken with a grain of salt, although these figures do provide a sense of how fast the printer prints. So, for example, if print speed is at the top of your priorities, then consider the Ultimaker or Aleph Objects AO-100. If you place the cost of the printer over print speed, then the RepRap Wallace or Printrbot is probably the better choice. Lastly, you'll need to consider the layer resolution as an indication of the quality of prints possible with any of these printers. The best way to gauge the print quality of a printer is to see a printed object in person. Failing that, looking at the maximum layer height resolution might tell you that a Prusa Mendel or Ultimaker, if purchasing the optional software, are both generally the best options for print quality; while at the other end, the Printrbot design may not provide the most detailed prints.

Print Volume Comparison

One of the more significant differences and biggest feature of any of these personal 3D printers is the relative print volume of the printer, determined by the printer's printbed dimensions and the height of its z-axis. The print volume is, in essence, the largest-sized print possible on that printer, given ideal circumstances. However, with that bigger volume comes a bigger printer and some epically long prints for something that large. To show their relative sizes, Figure 1-15 provides a graphic illustration of four of the more common print volumes from our printer summary.

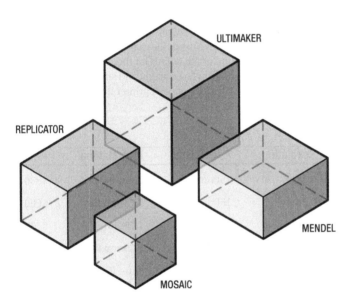

Figure 1-15. Comparative print volume

As the area increases from the Mosaic's 127mm³ print area to the Ultimaker's just over 210mm³ print area, the print volume increases exponentially. In this case, it's a difference of a 2-liter print volume for the MakerGear Mosaic compared to 9.7 liters with the Ultimaker. That makes a big difference in the types of things that you can print, although the Ultimaker is nearly 2.5 times the physical size of the Mosaic. When it comes to print volume and overall size of the printer, it becomes a choice between whether you prefer to print medium-sized objects one at a time or if you would prefer to print massive objects or multiple parts all at once at the cost of print times and desktop real estate.

Buying a Kit or Building Your Own

Apart from one or two of the printers that ship as preassembled printers, the last consideration to make often comes down to whether you should buy a kit or build your own. Most of these printers can be built by self-sourcing all of the different parts and components from a handful of suppliers to assemble the entire printer from scratch. On the other hand, many different vendors exist online that provide kits complete with all the parts you need to build a particular printer. To help make this decision, let's look at these two options.

Buying a Kit

If you are brand-new to 3D printing: buy a kit if you can. Getting your 3D-printing adventure started on the right foot ensures that you have a rewarding experience designing and printing new things in plastic. Starting the journey with sourcing your own 3D printer, however, might leave you lost in the bowels of a McMaster-Carr catalog, questioning the tensile strength and carbon composition of precision ground rods. Worse yet, you could end up spending a lot of money to have a pile of parts on your desk, when frustration finally overcomes your threshold for patience and you give up right then and there. We don't want that. Instead, we want happy 3D printer owners making new and cool things; so save yourself the frustration and consider buying a kit.

If you have a friendly rapport with your local hardware store, if you can wield the mighty soldering iron with reasonable precision, and if you've ever worked on your car on weekends, then you might consider one of the RepRap-style 3D printer kits—so long as you give yourself enough time to assemble and then fine-tune your new 3D printer. If you are looking for something with a little more finesse or something that might look at home on your office desk as opposed to your garage's workbench, consider one of the laser-cut Box Bots.

If you have very little experience building elaborate contraptions and just want to get on with designing and printing your digital creations, I recommend that you buy a MakerBot Replicator. If you don't have the budget for this printer or are looking for something a little cozier, then pick up the MakerGear Mosaic. These printers are equally good machines, with the Mosaic requiring only a modicum more assembly.

Building Your Own

If you are considering building your own, stop right now and buy a kit instead. Still reading? Okay, fine. Building your own 3D printer from a pile of parts that you bought from a half dozen retailers can actually be a very rewarding experience. Just as I'm sure building your own car, airplane, or house can be. Building a 3D printer is probably easier than building a car, airplane, or house, and you might even finish it in less time. While many people new to 3D printing will consider building their own printer from scratch, sourcing your own parts and building the printer will require navigating many conflicting sources of information and making a few improvisations along the way, but this process can teach you more about how the design of 3D printers actually works than putting together a semiassembled kit will. Expect mistakes and things to not necessarily work the first time, and give yourself enough time and a little extra budget to order replacement parts when you need them and to fix problems as they arise.

If you have a modest number of hand tools in your collection, consider a Prusa Mendel or a MendelMax. These printers require sourcing parts from a half dozen different places and a little trial and error to get things working. You will need to be able to cut threaded and smooth rods to the dimensions required by the design, so be sure to order extra just in case, and be ready to pick up some special tools for cutting and assembly if you don't already own or have access to them.

If you have a budding workshop in the garage and more than a few weekends to kill, you might consider the adventure that a RepStrap CNC can provide. The bonus here is you could just as easily build a large CNC router for cutting out large creations in sheets of plywood or other materials. This just means more weekends of fun projects in the workshop.

The Choice Is Yours

In the end, the choice is yours. 3D printing is a nascent pastime that, at times, can be a little frustrating; so there is little need to make life more difficult before you even have a working printer. In my experience, 9.5 out of 10 times a person frustrated with building a 3D printer should have bought a kit to begin with. When you are ready for your second printer (or third—yes, it happens all the time) you should then branch out into the untested, experimental wilds of the latest printer designs—just for the added challenge. But if you are just getting started, then my recommendation is to keep things as simple as possible and start with the easiest kit that you can find.

Choosing the Right Material

Once you have chosen a 3D printer, you don't get to sit back and wait for cool stuff to pop out of it. You first need to select some additional things to compliment your printer, beginning with the filament material shown in Figure 1-16.

Figure 1-16. Assorted filament on spools

Filament is like the ink or toner in a traditional printer except that it's, well, plastic. It is available in a variety of diameters, colors, and types of material, sold in long lengths, coils, or spools. There are some important things to consider in your filament buying decision, so let's look at some of the possibilities.

Filament Materials

Regarding the choice of filament materials, there are two very popular types of plastic in common use today: PLA and ABS. ABS, or acrylonitrile butadiene styrene, is essentially the same stuff that LEGO bricks are made of. It is a very durable thermoplastic that is slightly flexible and suitable for many purposes. It can be sanded, painted, and glues very well with plastic glue made for ABS; and it is dissolvable in the household chemical acetone (think fingernail polish remover). It is impact resistant and has a relatively high resistance to heat, extruding at temperatures around 210°C. When printing with ABS, a heated printbed covered in polyimide tape set to about 110°C is a near absolute necessity or otherwise the parts will curl as they cool and might even crack with larger prints. ABS has been the long-standing favorite material of the personal 3D-printer community, although the recent increase in the availability of PLA has changed that somewhat.

PLA, or polylactic acid, is a biopolymer plastic derived from cornstarch or sugar cane. It is not easily recyclable, but it is biodegradable in the right circumstances. PLA is a more environmentally friendly alternative to petrochemical plastics and it smells a little like maple syrup while extruding. It is a tough plastic when cooled, albeit a little on the brittle side, and it has a lower threshold for high temperatures than ABS, extruding at a temperature around 180°C. A heated printbed is not absolutely necessary; however, if you have one, printing with the printbed set to 60°C helps with the quality of the print. PLA can even be printed on a clean glass print surface as long as the surface is heated. This plastic is slow to cool, though, so having a secondary fan pointed at the recently extruded filament will make for better prints. Many suppliers of PLA filament offer PLA in very pleasing colors that range from bright semitranslucent to very dense and opaque.

Other, more exotic thermoplastics have had mixed results on most DIY 3D printers—including polycarbonate, high-density polyethylene (HDPE), and polyvinyl alcohol (PVA)—although the community continues to experiment with these plastics.

When choosing the right material, consider the environment that your 3D printer will be placed in. If you have an open place for your printer that is well ventilated, then ABS extrudes in most printers very well and gives you a lot of flexibility with the material after your object has been printed. On the other hand, if your 3D printer lives in a closed office or classroom, then PLA is a better choice for producing less toxic fumes, and the material contributes to more renewable green material practices. As a general rule of thumb, if your printer supports PLA, I recommend this material about 95 percent of the time.

Filament Diameter

Once you have chosen a material, you might need to decide on the diameter of the filament to use in your printer. Nearly half of the printers discussed in this chapter have moved to extruders that exclusively support 1.75mm diameter filament. Proponents of the smaller filament argue that it is easier to design filament drivers and hot ends because it requires less material to heat and is easier to feed into the extruder. Filament in 3mm diameter had been the de facto standard of the RepRap printers from the beginning. Proponents argue that it is easier to keep a steady extrusion with the larger filament and it is still possible to create really fine layer heights even with the larger filament.

Regardless of the theoretical views of which filament is best, you might not have much option in the filament that you choose depending on the 3D printer that you settle on. Instead, all you need to do is to choose the correct filament for the extruder of your printer. For example, the MakerGear Mosaic is exclusively a 1.75mm filament printer, while the Ultimaker uses only 3mm filament. It's not so much that one is better than the other, only that the designer decided on one size over the other and built their extruders to fit.

Buying Filament

For the most part, filament has been sold increasingly on 1kg or even 2.2kg spools (roughly 2 to 5 pounds) for easy feeding into your printer. All you need to do is make, print, or cobble together some form of spindle holder, and you will never need to worry about your filament again. Some suppliers, however, prefer to offer their filament in loose coils or sell it by the meter. While this might be less convenient than filament on spools, it is usually cheaper and gives you more options for exploring many different colors.

Whatever you do, buy from reputable suppliers of filament that have a proven track record as evidenced by positive comments by the community in forums, message groups, and web chat. Research any new supplier before blindly throwing money at them because not all filament is the same and it might cost you more in the long run. Some suppliers sell filament that is of inconsistent diameters over the length of the filament, or filament that is oval instead of round. Either of these conditions will jam your extruder in mid-print, causing unnecessary maintenance, repairs, and frustration. Some filament has even been reported with grainy, sand-like material inside of it that can destroy parts of your extruder, which will then need to be replaced. Other filament simply never prints very well, leaving you to think you have a bad printer when really it's just poor-quality filament.

Remember: choosing the right filament is at least as important as choosing the right printer. The following are a few vendors that have had very good track records of providing excellent-quality filament:

- MakerBot Industries (http://store.makerbot.com/plastic.html)

- Ultimaker (https://shop.ultimaker.com/en/consumables.html)

- ProtoParadigm (https://www.protoparadigm.com/products-page)

- Faberdashery (www.faberdashery.co.uk)

Once you have received your filament, don't leave it exposed to air and moisture for longer than is absolutely necessary. Instead, keep unused filament in sealed plastic bags, and if you have them around somewhere, toss in a small bag of desiccant to keep your filament dry.

Basic Tools and Supplies

Even if you are buying a fully assembled kit, there are a handful of tools and supplies that are essential to successful 3D printing. While some printers might require an exhaustive tool list, in this section we will look at just the bare essentials that you should have on hand regardless of the complexity of your 3D printer.

Hand Tools

If you bought a kit, then all you need to build and operate your 3D printer are some simple hand tools, as shown in Figure 1-17. If you are sourcing your own printer, then you will also need tools to cut steel rod and plywood.

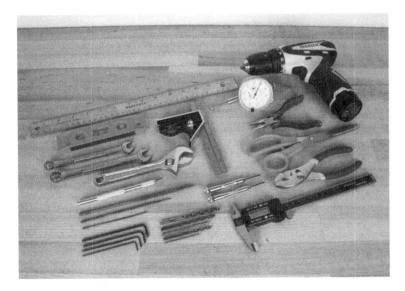

Figure 1-17. Some basic hand tools

Figure 1-17 shows the following tools (remember, this is not a definitive list but rather a good cross section of tools that are helpful to have on hand):

- Small, battery-powered hand drill (10.8V drill shown)

- Assorted drill bits

- Precision dial indicator

- Torpedo or spirit level

- Set of precision screwdrivers

- Set of metric hex keys, including 1.5mm, 2.5mm, and 3mm

- Metric wrenches, including 10mm and 13mm

- Adjustable wrench

- Flat and needle files

- Hobby knife

- Metric ruler

- Digital calipers

- Square

- Needle-nose pliers

- Slip-joint pliers

- Scissors

When cleaning the printed parts of your printer, you will probably use a drill and drill bits to clean out holes and the files, and a hobby knife to smooth edges. To build the printer's frame, you will need the ruler to ensure correct spacing, and the square and torpedo level to make things level and square. Wrenches, pliers, and hex keys are useful for tightening all the nuts and bolts, while scissors are useful for cutting any tape you use to attach to the hot end. Finally, the digital calipers and (though not entirely necessary) the dial indicator are used to calibrate your finished printer and will come in handy later for designing some of our projects.

Electronics Toolkit

If your electronics come preassembled, then you might not have much of an urgent need for these tools; but inevitably you will need to fix something, so having the tools shown in Figure 1-18 is just as helpful as having a good toolbox.

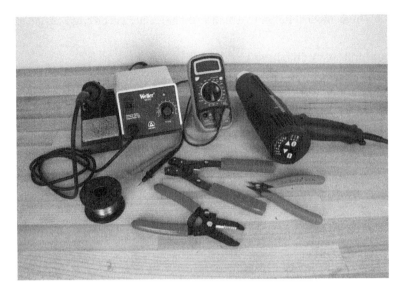

Figure 1-18. *A sample electronics toolkit*

Figure 1-18 shows the following equipment:

- Soldering iron
- Solder
- Digital multimeter
- Heat gun
- Flush cutters
- Wire strippers
- Crimping tool

The soldering iron and solder are useful for assembling the controller electronics, endstops, wires, and other electrical components. A wire stripper is the best tool for cleanly removing the wire insulation before soldering. Flush cutters are useful for tripping wires and the legs of electrical components, and wire crimpers might be used for connecting plugs on the ends of the wires. A heat gun or other heat source is useful for applying heat shrink to bare wires, and the digital multimeter comes in handy when troubleshooting your electronics.

Printing Supplies

Once you have your printer up and running, you will still need a few tools and supplies around (see Figure 1-19) to help with making good prints and to fix little problems that pop up. The necessity of some of these supplies, like acetone, will depend on the type of plastic you predominately use.

Figure 1-19. *Assorted printing tools and supplies*

Figure 1-19 shows the following tools and supplies:

- 135mm or wider polyimide tape

- 20mm or narrower polyimide tape

- Acetone or nail polish remover

- Oil or silicone lube

- Tweezers

- Spatula or putty knife

- Clean, cloth rags

The necessity of polyimide tape, also known as Kapton tape, depends somewhat on the filament you are using. It is an essential surface for the build platform if printing in ABS, although it also works great for PLA. When covering your printbed, it is easiest to use tape that is as large as your printbed. I usually apply it with some soapy water and a small card or squeegee to spread the tape smoothly over the build surface, as discussed in Appendix A. Smaller polyimide tape can be pretty handy for general attaching and repairing. It is generally a good idea to clean the print surface daily with acetone on a clean rag to remove any dust or grease and ensure the plastic sticks when printing. While printing, tweezers are helpful for removing stray bits of plastic. The spatula or putty knife (preferably rounded and smooth) can help remove the finished print. Finally, it's a good idea to periodically grease your smooth rods with a lightweight oil or grease.

Summary

We covered a lot of ground in our first chapter, but now you should have a fairly good theoretical understanding of how a 3D printer works. You might have a better idea of which type of 3D printer is a perfect fit for your needs if you don't already own one. If you already own a 3D printer, then you have a better picture of where yours fits in the larger spectrum. We also discussed how to begin buying the filament needed to print objects with your 3D printer. And now you know some of the basic tools and supplies that you should have on hand during the build process and while you are printing objects.

Because every 3D printer is completely different to build, we are going to skip the build process for your particular 3D printer. Instead, in our next chapter we will jump into the 3D printer toolchain, as we did with our general survey of 3D printers, specifically looking at some of the more common options for electronics, printer firmware, model slicers, and printer interfaces, and how all of these different parts work together. Because several different printers might use the same electronics, or several different slicers can be used in different interface applications, Chapter 2 helps to focus on the similarities between each printer and provides options for setting up your printer the way that you find most comfortable. So if you haven't already, get the printer building underway as you read through the next chapter.

CHAPTER 2

■ ■ ■

3D Printer Toolchain

We are still a long way from having our personal 3D printers work just like our microwaves, yet there has been a lot of progress made by a group of intrepid developers to not only give you options for how you want to use your 3D printer but to make it more reliable and easier to use. How we interact with our 3D printer is determined by the printer's toolchain: the electronics, firmware, control software, and slicing software that take a 3D model to a 3D object. If you bought your 3D printer as a complete kit or preassembled, then you probably have a set toolchain provided by the kit manufacturer. On the other hand, you might be piecing your 3D printer together from a variety of sources and are choosing parts of the toolchain that best fit your needs. Either way, this chapter is here to help you understand how these different parts of the toolchain work together. This chapter also introduces the idea of the 3D printer workflow as a way to use our printer's toolchain to make 3D prints.

You might later decide to upgrade parts of your toolchain, so this chapter will help give you a place to start. For example, we might want to upgrade our three-year-old MakerBot Cupcake with new electronics running new firmware with advanced features originally designed for a RepRap. We might also want to upgrade our slicer program to make repairing models for printing a little easier. All of this would give us a significant upgrade in an older printer's print quality and performance, breathing new life into it.

This chapter will cover the following:

- The basic ins and outs of the 3D printer workflow and the parts of the toolchain

- How 3D printer electronics work on some of the commonly available models

- The use of model slicers to generate toolpaths for your 3D printer

- An introduction to various host software to print objects on your 3D printer

Before we get down to the nuts and bolts of the printer's toolchain, let's first take a quick overview of how these things work together.

From a 3D Model to a 3D Object

If I want to print a document in my home office, I simply hit the print button in whatever application I'm using and the document is beamed over the radio waves of Wi-Fi, waking up my laser printer that then springs to life to churn out my finished printed piece of paper. Printing 3D objects on your personal 3D printer is not this simple yet. That's not to say that it is all that difficult either; it's just that we need to follow a few steps in order to go from a 3D model that we downloaded or made on our computer screen to holding the actual plastic object in our hands. This process is called the *workflow* and this chapter intends to demystify the whole 3D printing process, including the workflow and the specific components involved. Let's begin with Figure 2-1.

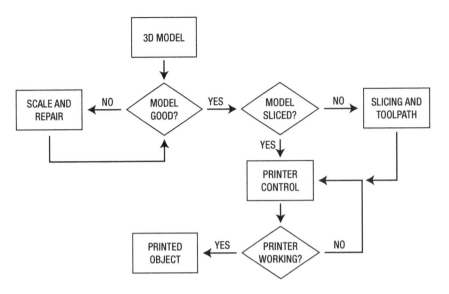

Figure 2-1. *3D printer workflow*

In this image, we have the overall organizational flow that combines to form the entire 3D printing process, from starting with a 3D model that you either downloaded or created, to holding the finished object in your hands. Let's take a look at how this breaks down in much more detail.

3D Models

The whole process begins with a good 3D model. This might be something you download from a resource online or something you've made after working through the projects in this book. Generally, the model we are looking for will be in the STL, or stereo lithography, file format. This model should also be scaled appropriately for the size of our printer and it should be a clean and manifold model—more on this last one in a bit. If the file doesn't fit these basic requirements, it will need to be scaled or repaired using one of several different techniques that we will cover throughout this book.

Slicing and Toolpath

If our model is good, then we are ready to process the model for printing. Because our 3D printers print by laying down successive layers of filament, one layer at a time, we need to slice the model into these layers and generate the toolpath that tells the extruder where to go and when to extrude plastic. This process is called slicing. It will involve one of several applications called slicers that generate a set of commands for the 3D printer to follow, called G-Code. This is an instruction set that's been around for a while and appropriated for use with our 3D printers. We can slice a model by launching the slicing application independently, but we can usually launch this application through our printer control.

Printer Control

The printer control is a host application that fittingly enough controls our printer and will generally form the hub from which everything is operated. From this application, we can launch our slicing application; control the printer's three axes of movement; set and monitor the temperature for our extruder and printbed; and start, pause, and cancel print jobs. Most host applications will provide some visual indication for the model or G-code file to be printed. The most important job for the host software is to process the G-code file and by communicating with the printer's electronics, it will send these commands to the 3D printer to build our objects layer by layer.

So, What's a Toolchain?

This general workflow wouldn't be possible without a series of applications and hardware that we will need to use at each stage of the process. These individual pieces that play such a crucial role in the day-to-day printing process are what make up our 3D printer's toolchain. For the intent of this book, our toolchain begins with our host software and includes the slicing application; the code, or firmware loaded on the electronics; as well as the electronics and the wiring. In a simple sense, this toolchain is represented in Figure 2-2.

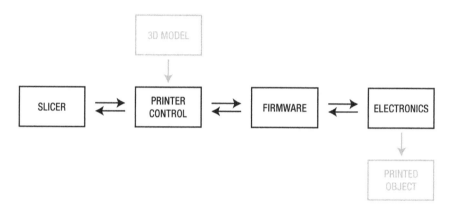

Figure 2-2. *The 3D printer toolchain*

Referring to this simplified illustration, the printer control application will bring in the 3D model and send it to a slicer application, if needed. The printer control then communicates with a specialized set of code called *firmware*, which runs on the electronics platform. The firmware controls the electronics hardware to build our 3D objects according to the instructions received from the printer control and sends data—like temperature, positioning, and other information—back to the control application.

While there are many different toolchains made from different combinations of slicers, printer controls, firmware, and electronics, all of the 3D printers that we looked at in the last chapter share the same basic toolchain structure and can often use different parts of the toolchain interchangeably. For example, it might be possible to use many different electronics platforms with any one printer or to make use of many different printer control applications with any one set of electronics.

Before we get to how to put our toolchain to use, let's look at each of these elements in closer detail to see what options are out there. As with our discussion of 3D printers, this survey will only briefly look at the most common options available, beginning at the bottom of the chain.

Electronics

If we start at the bottom of the chain, we have the electronics platform that controls our 3D printer and communicates through its firmware to the control application. Most of the time you do not have much choice on which electronics come with your printer, so this will likely serve as a summary that gives you an idea of the capabilities of the electronics platform of your printer in relation to the other available options out there. On the other hand, having an understanding of these different platforms will open possibilities for swapping out your printer's electronics to later gain additional functionality.

The electronics of your 3D printer includes many different parts working together to build your 3D prints. These components include a microcontroller, a main board, motor drivers, stepper motors, a hot end, a printbed, and parts like endstop or limit switches and temperature sensors. To help map how these different parts work together, let's look at Figure 2-3.

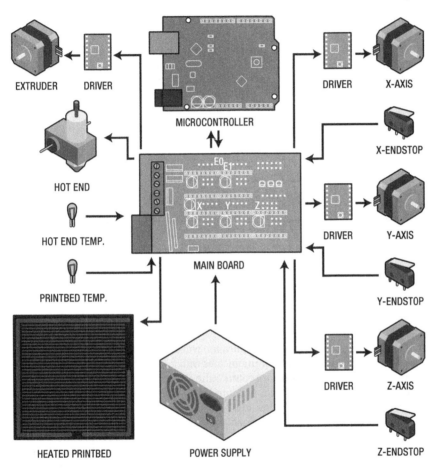

Figure 2-3. 3D printer electronics map

In this 3D printer electronic map, you can see how each of the different parts of the electronics system interconnect, with arrows representing the direction of control from one component to the next. Central to the electronics platform is a controller main board that connects all the different hardware needed by a 3D printer to the microcontroller; it is essentially the brain of the entire system. To switch the high current associated with the printbed and extruder heaters, the main board will have specialized switching hardware rated for the necessary maximum loads. Most electronic main boards have the capability of reading resistive-based temperature sensors called *thermistors*, while others can make more-accurate readings using a type of sensor called a *thermocouple*. The main board also forms the power hub to the whole system, taking in a high current power source and distributing power to the other systems as needed. Finally, the main board will also need to interface with the endstop limit switches on each of the axes to allow the printer to locate its print head prior to a print job.

The microcontroller, found on the main controller or on a separate board entirely, is a small, simple computer that runs specialized code called firmware to allow it to read and interpret sensors like temperature sensors and limit switches, as well as controlling motors using motor drivers and switching high loads using high current transistors called MOSFETs. Most of the electronics packages for personal 3D printers use the Arduino microcontroller. An open-source hardware design, the Arduino ecosystem promotes the use of its hardware in other platforms so that developers can use Arduino's C-based programming language across several different electronics platforms.

To drive the stepper motors that are used with our 3D printers, the control electronics use a separate stepper motor driver for each motor. While dedicated stepper drivers have existed for a while, a little, $12 stepper breakout board, shown in Figure 2-4, is very popular. It is produced by Pololu Electronics (`www.pololu.com/catalog/product/1182`) and is in demand for several of the electronics platforms.

Figure 2-4. *Pololu stepper driver breakout board*

This little board is a simple breakout board for the Allegro A4988 stepper driver chip. It can drive a single stepper motor and is used by a few different controller boards for driving each of the printer's axes. Other controller boards use the same basic hardware found in the Pololu breakout board and either make their own boards or build the separate drivers onto the single control board.

Chances are, if you bought a preassembled 3D printer or an inclusive kit, then your printer probably came with some form of electronics package that includes all of these separate bits and pieces. If instead you are building your own 3D printer from scratch or you're looking to upgrade that three-year old MakerBot Cupcake, then we should look at a few of the more common controller boards—the most significant part of the 3D printers electronics. These three controller boards—RepRap Arduino Mega Pololu Shield, Sanguinololu, and Printrboard—represent only a small selection of the options out there, although they are somewhat common and readily available. Some printers, like the Ultimaker or MakerBot Replicator, ship with controller boards that are specific to those printers. And even though those controllers would work just as well on other printers, they are not currently available for sale separately, so we will stick with the more flexible of the controller boards.

RepRap Arduino Mega Pololu Shield

The RepRap Arduino Mega Pololu Shield, known affectionately as RAMPS, is shown in Figure 2-5.

Figure 2-5. *RepRap Arduino Mega Pololu Shield*

This electronics package has the following features:

- Up to five stepper driver boards using Pololu 4988 or similar

- Three high-power switched loads fused at 5 amps and 11 amps for the extruder and printbed

- Six endstop connections

- Three thermistor connections

- Dual-power input of 12 to 35 volts at up to 16 amps

RAMPS (http://reprap.org/wiki/RAMPS_1.4) is a two-board solution that consists of a separate Arduino Mega microcontroller board and a specially designed shield that plugs on top of the Arduino. The Arduino Mega provides the brains of the platform, while the shield provides the switching hardware for the heater and printbed, along with the option to interface with up to five Pololu stepper driver boards. Four of these boards are shown installed on the shield in Figure 2-3, with a fifth one used for the possibility of adding a second extruder.

Because of its shear capacity for possible future upgrades, RAMPS has become very popular and will most likely be the platform that paves the way for dual extruders on platforms outside of the MakerBot. This platform is in use by many RepRaps, the MakerGear Mosaic, and a distantly related version of the board is used by the Ultimaker. Part of the draw to this platform is that it comes with a stock Arduino Mega microcontroller, making uploading firmware that much easier especially for those new to the Arduino microcontroller.

The RAMPS controller sits in the middle of the road when it comes to overall size and cost, making it a very popular choice among DIYers. RAMPS highlights include the following:

- Uses standard Arduino electronics, making the platform easier to use

- Additional power output for switchable cooling fans

- Future support for dual extruders built right in

- Mid-range cost, sometimes difficult to source

Sanguinololu

The Sanguinololu, shown in Figure 2-6, is a single-board electronics controller solution with a very silly name.

Figure 2-6. *Sanguinololu*

The Sanguinololu has the following features:

- Four stepper-driver boards using Pololu A4988 or similar

- Two high-power switched loads rated at 30 amps for extruder and printbed

- Three endstop connections

- Two thermistor connections

- Single-power input of 7 to 35 volts

- Onboard microcontroller and USB

Being a single-board controller, the Sanguinololu (http://reprap.org/wiki/Sanguinololu) has the microcontroller and the switching hardware and stepper drivers on a single electronics board. This means that the Sanguinololu is smaller, simpler, and cheaper than RAMPS. Its name is a mashup taken from the Sanguino, a derivative Arduino-compatible microcontroller, and the Pololu stepper driver boards. The Sanguinololu only has the option for four stepper drivers and two high-power-switching circuits, so it will only work with a single extruder. It also only works with a single external power supply, so if you have a more elaborate setup for your heated printbed, then this solution will not work.

While the Sanguinololu is in many ways a simpler, more direct solution than the RAMPS, if you choose to build a Sanguinololu yourself, then you will need additional Arduino hardware to upload the Sanguino bootloader (special code needed to make the microcontroller Arduino-compatible) on the board. This means that if you have no previous experience with the Arduino, it is a little more complicated to get up and running. As more developers work with the Sanguinololu, and as additional derivatives get released, such as Teensylu and Melzi, this platform may become much more common.

The following is a summary of the Sanguinololu:

- The smallest single-board electronics controller
- The most inexpensive controller available at about $100 in kit form
- Only supports machines with single extruders
- Can be a little more complicated to set up

Printrboard

The newest single-board electronics solution for personal 3D printers is the Printrboard, shown in Figure 2-7. It was developed by the team working on the Printrbot series of entry-level 3D printers.

Figure 2-7. *Printrboard (courtesy JDS Labs, 2012)*

The features for the Printrboard include the following:

- Four non-replaceable onboard stepper drivers
- Two high-power switched loads rated at 30 amps for the extruder and printbed
- One low-power switched output for the cooling fan
- Three endstop and one emergency stop connection
- Two thermistor connections
- Single power input of 12 to 20 volts
- Onboard microcontroller with integrated USB and onboard MicroSD

The Printrboard (`http://reprap.org/wiki/Printrboard`), a distant relative of the Sanguinololu, is the newest option in the lineup of electronics controllers for personal 3D printers. Unique to the Printrboard is the onboard microcontroller that features integrated USB, allowing the Printrboard to communicate with the host computer at a much faster native speed. This prevents any pauses that might happen during a print whenever the computer sends commands to the controller, a problem that affects print quality. The Printrboard also has a MicroSD card reader built on the board so that you can load sliced files onto an SD card and be able to print models and still disconnect your computer from the printer.

The Printrboard is designed to be manufactured and is not available as a kit, so all Printrboards come prebuilt from the supplier. This makes it even easier for someone new to electronics, although it does mean that all four of the motor drivers are irreplaceable. This is really only a problem if you happen to damage your motor drivers because of a silly mistake; but mistakes happen, which make some people nervous about this board. Either way, this is the most inexpensive preassembled option for printer electronics, and the easiest to get up and running, so there are many reasons why this board makes a lot of sense for your next 3D printer.

The Printrboard can be summarized as follows:

- Inexpensive, preassembled single-board controller

- Integrated USB and onboard MicroSD

- Only supports machines with single extruders

- Onboard motor drivers might be a problem down the road

While there are other electronics platforms for personal 3D printers at various stages of development (and, of course, those like the MakerBot MightyBoard that come included in the MakerBot Replicator), these three platforms represent some of the more common options for those wanting to build their own RepRap or are looking for an upgrade.

Let's move on to talking about the specialized code called firmware that runs our electronics.

Firmware

Every control board needs specialized code called firmware loaded on its microcontroller to make the electronics come to life. The firmware is responsible for interpreting the G-code commands sent to the electronics from the printer control application. How well the firmware does this will determine how well your 3D printer will print objects.

If you bought a 3D printer in a kit—which you did right?—then the electronics in your kit will generally come preinstalled with its own firmware from the manufacturer. This lets you jump straight to printing 3D objects without ever thinking twice about the firmware installed on your electronics. This is a good thing. If, however, you are looking to squeeze out every last possible ounce of print quality in your 3D printer, or if you were one of the adventurous types to source and build their 3D printer from the ground up, then you will want to experiment with using different firmware and adjusting the firmware settings to get your 3D printer just right.

Sometimes just moving to a different version of firmware will bump up your print quality enough to make the upgrade worth it. For example, if buying a Prusa or Mosaic 3D printer kit, the usual default firmware to ship with the included RAMPS electronics is the Sprinter firmware. Sprinter has been around in one form or another for a while and is a stable and reliable printer firmware. Using default firmware is a good choice if you are getting started on these particular platforms because the firmware will work and there is always the knowledgeable community available if something doesn't. With that said, a new firmware called Marlin is picking up steam at the time of this writing. It improves on Sprinter by better supporting arcs and print speed acceleration using a technique called "look-ahead" to more efficiently plot the movement of the extruder, resulting in much cleaner and more precise prints.

While changing the firmware might result in better prints, and in some cases it's needed to properly calibrate your printer, if your printer works out of the box with the default firmware, only venture forth with firmware modification if you are an advanced user and feel confident with your knowledge of your 3D printer.

Sprinter

Sprinter (https://github.com/kliment/Sprinter) is a popular firmware for RepRap, MakerGear, and Ultimaker 3D printers. It is generally the easiest firmware to get up and running and works with the greatest number of machines. Sprinter was based on earlier firmware designs and through this combined development has been in use for quite awhile, so it is often easy to find help online.

Sprinter is designed for electronics controllers such as RAMPS and Sanguinololu, although it has been shown to work on other platforms. It can be easily configured through the `configuration.h` file in the Sprinter package. Features of Sprinter include the following:

- Movement acceleration for fast and controlled prints

- Min and max endstop support

- PID temperature control

- SD card support

Marlin

Marlin (`https://github.com/ErikZalm/Marlin`) is fairly new to the scene, but it has been pretty popular on the RAMPS and Ultimaker platforms, and is seeing a lot of development. It is a mashup between Sprinter and Grbl, an open-source CNC firmware for Arduino microcontrollers.

Like Sprinter, Marlin is designed for some of the more standard platforms like RepRaps and Ultimakers. Marlin, however, features a number of improvements over Sprinter that result in cleaner, smoother prints. This includes a better interpretation of acceleration that uses a look-ahead feature to anticipate the upcoming moves to prevent any unnecessary stopping in midprint. Marlin also supports printing true arcs and information display through an external LCD.

The following is a summary of its features:

- Acceleration with look-ahead to keep speeds fast with arc acceleration planning

- Temperature oversampling for more accurate readings

- PID temperature control with automatic PID tuning

- Early LCD display and SD card support

SJFW

Every other week it seems as though someone new has written an alternate firmware. Most of the time the code doesn't last, but ScribbleJ's firmware (`https://github.com/ScribbleJ/sjfw`), also known as SJFW, is an alternative firmware that works with systems like RAMPS and Sanguinololu, as well as the older MakerBot Generation 4 electronics, making it versatile and a popular choice for a greater range of machines.

SJFW is a bit of a best-of-mix tape, cribbing a lot of code from other firmware. What makes it unique is support for MakerBot electronics, meaning it is possible to give your old MakerBot printer a new life. It supports acceleration and Marlin-style look-ahead, along with SD card support and native display on an LCD. The SJFW can be summarized as follows:

- Acceleration that does not need to slow down between moves

- LCD and SD support

- Supports MakerBot Generation 4 electronics

- Compatible with ReplicatorG

MakerBot

If you have a MakerBot printer, then more than likely you will be using MakerBot's custom firmware. To update the firmware on MakerBot electronics, you need to download ReplicatorG (`http://replicat.org`) and choose the Upload New Firmware... option from the Machine menu.

MakerBot firmware has the single virtue of working out-of-the-box with MakerBot electronics. It's not any more complicated than it needs to be and it handles many of the configuration settings for the different MakerBot printers in a separate XML-format configuration file. Once you get it working, then that's about all there is to it. Highlights include the following:

- Most compatible option for MakerBot printers

- Supports multiboard MakerBot electronics

- Does not support other third-party main boards

Slicers

To generate the path for our printer's extruder, we need to use a separate application called a *slicer* to take our solid 3D model and slice it into layers suitable for 3D printing. This process makes the code that tells the 3D printer where to move the extruder, when to extrude plastic, and how much plastic to extrude. These commands, or G-code, are sent from our printer control software to the firmware on our electronics, which are responsible for interpreting these codes to control the printer's motors and heaters. To get a sense for what this toolpath looks like, we've sliced a bunny—not literally—using the slicer application Skeinforge to see the resulting path and direction of the extruder in Figure 2-8.

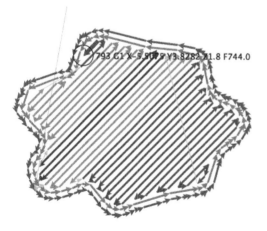

Figure 2-8. One layer of the Stanford bunny

The model shown in Figure 2-8 is the Stanford bunny (`www.thingiverse.com/thing:3731`), a perennial favorite on Thingiverse, the 3D model-sharing web site. The lines show the path the extruder takes when printing this layer of the model; the arrows show the direction the extruder travels. The short, highlighted line at the top of the image is generated from the following line of code:

```
793 G1 X-5.5075 Y3.8282 Z1.8 F744.0
```

In this line, 793 is the particular line of code. G1 tells the firmware to perform a controlled move to the following X, Y, and Z coordinates; for example, X-5.5075 moves the extruder in a negative direction along the x-axis. The last value, F744.0, specifies the federate, or how fast the axes are expected to move in millimeters per minute.

For every line seen in Figure 2-8, there is a line of G-code similar to the one just explained, building the 3D model line by line and layer by layer. When the model is put back together, we end up with a finished sliced object, as shown in Figure 2-9.

Figure 2-9. *Sliced bunny*

In this image, we have the bunny put back together after being sliced into layers. Each alternating band of dark and light gray is about five layers, for a total of 100 layers in the finished print. In order for the slicer to be able to generate these sliced layers, it needs some general information about your printer and filament, such as the filament diameter, extruder nozzle size, and layer height, as well as a few specific print settings for the job, such as the number of outlines to make for each layer (Figure 2-7 has two), the amount to infill each layer (Figure 2-7 is set at 100 percent), and the print speed for different parts of the model.

While not all slicers can be directly integrated with all printer control applications, and in very rare cases, the sliced G-code might not be compatible with a particular firmware, G-code is a reasonably standard code, so you can often use multiple slicers with your toolchain, depending on your circumstances. That way, when the next "greatest thing in slicers" rolls out, you'll be able to take advantage of better quality prints simply by switching to the new slicer.

Let's take a quick look at a couple of the major slicers that are in use today.

Skeinforge

Skeinforge (http://reprap.org/wiki/Skeinforge), shown in Figure 2-10, was the slicer that started it all. It has been in use since the RepRap project first got under way.

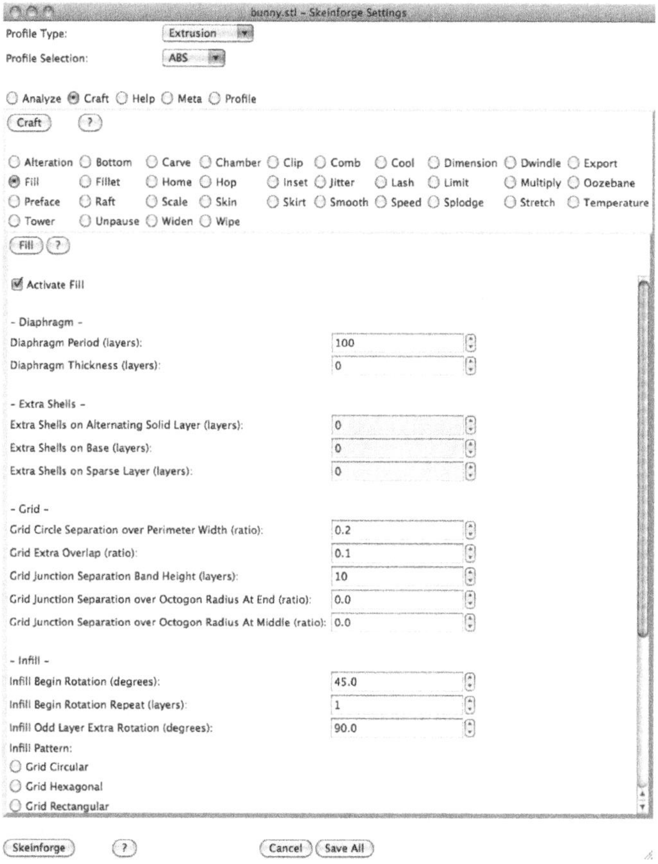

Figure 2-10. *Skeinforge 49*

At the time of writing, we are nearing the fiftieth revision of this collection of Python scripts that create the G-codes needed to print a 3D model. Skeinforge has been put to use by nearly every personal 3D printer out there, offering the greatest level of configurability and customization. This rich feature set comes at the cost of overall complexity, both in the sheer volume of options that can be set and in the cryptic settings themselves. If, however, you are looking for the most options in your slicer, then this is the one for you.

SFACT

Take Skeinforge, put it on a diet, have it make a little more sense, and you end up with SFACT. SFACT (http://reprap.org/wiki/Sfact) caught on in popularity pretty quickly due to its slimmed-down option list and for making the configuration of your printer easier handle with settings that automatically configure themselves. It also helps that SFACT slices a model much quicker than Skeinforge, letting you get back to your printing. Unfortunately, not all control applications support SFACT, so you might still be stuck with Skeinforge unless you use SFACT by itself.

Slic3r

The newest guy on the block, Slic3r (http://slic3r.org), shown in Figure 2-11, is a complete, ground-up revision of what a slicer application can be.

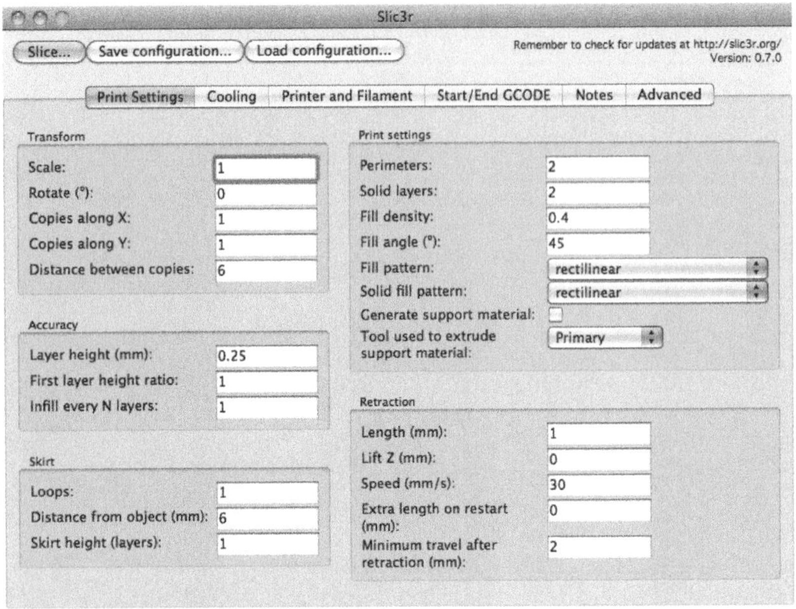

Figure 2-11. Slic3r 0.7.0

Slic3r is quickly becoming one of the more popular slicers because of its ease of use, blistering slicing times, and remarkable print quality. It previously lacked some of the features that the more mature slicers have, but with the addition of cooling and support material, it has addressed many of its faults. Where Skeinforge asks users to make a lot of calculations regarding the filament extrusion, Slic3r calculates all of these values under the hood after inputting only a few parameters about your printer, the filament, and the desired print settings. While I have personally used just about every slicing application out there, Slic3r has become the only one I use to slice 3D models because it is so easy to use and for its consistent high-quality results.

Printer Control

The printer control, also known as the host software or printer interface, is where the entire personal 3D printer toolchain comes together. From this application, we can connect to our printer and talk to its firmware, move the three different axes, read and set the temperature for the hot end and the printbed, launch our slicer application, and print our 3D models. While the printer control application is sometimes provided by your printer's manufacturer you might still be able to use other applications of your choice. For example, if you are building one of the RepRap printers, the world is open to your choice of printer control; however, if you have a MakerBot, then you will most likely use ReplicatorG. Of course, you can always exchange your electronics for something different, so it is possible to run that MakerBot Cupcake with an entirely non-stock printer control and toolchain.

ReplicatorG

Where Skeinforge was the slicing engine that was widely adopted in the early days of the RepRap project, ReplicatorG (http://replicat.org), shown in Figure 2-12, and the popularity of the MakerBot printers made this application synonymous with 3D printing.

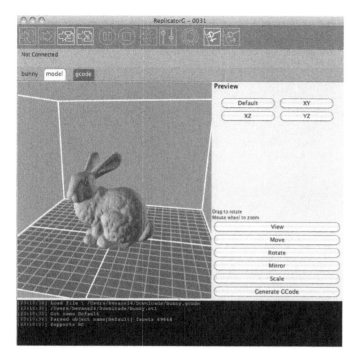

Figure 2-12. *ReplicatorG 0029*

ReplicatorG is a surprisingly versatile tool, far beyond its use as a printer control. This application displays a 3D model inside a bounding box that represents the build volume of your 3D printer. It also provides options to rotate, scale, and move the model. Even though ReplicatorG only directly links to Skeinforge—other slicer applications can be used independently to create G-code files that can later be opened in ReplicatorG—and it is limited to specific version releases only, the team at MakerBot have worked hard to simplify Skeinforge settings with the use of the Print-O-Matic printing option, shown in Figure 2-13.

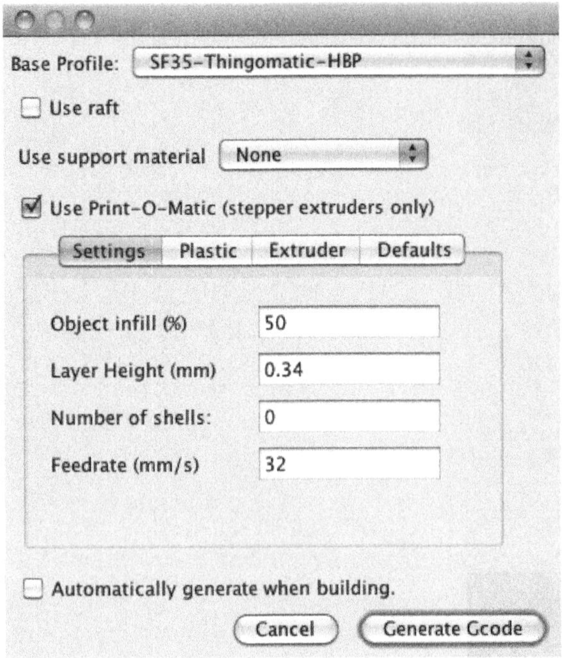

Figure 2-13. *Print-O-Matic*

By specifying details about your printer, filament, and extruder, Print-O-Matic automatically configures Skeinforge using optimized presets to generate G-code that will work for most situations. It is still possible to enter Skeinforge if you want to muck about with parameters for specific prints. After slicing your model from within ReplicatorG, you need to open the separate control panel, shown in Figure 2-14, to control and monitor your printer.

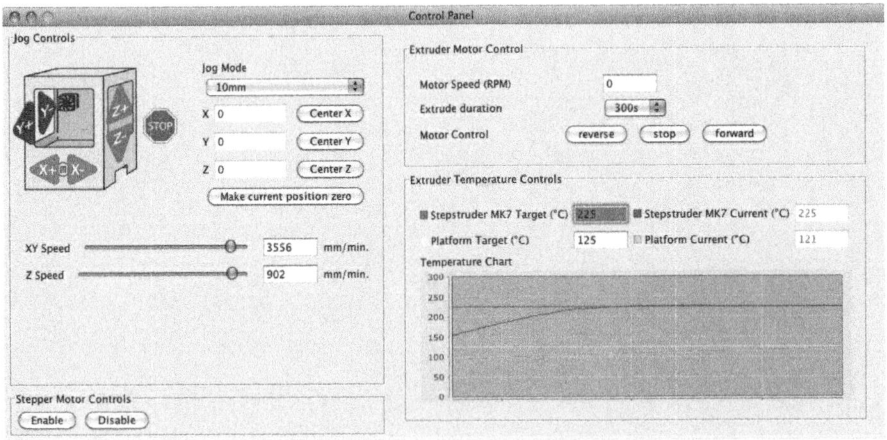

Figure 2-14. *ReplicatorG control panel*

In this window, you can control the three axes of the printer by clicking on the green, red, and blue arrows for the x-, y-, and z-axes respectively; enable or disable the stepper motors; and set and monitor the temperature for the extruder and printbed. To start a print, you need to leave the control panel and, using the icons in the main ReplicatorG toolbar, connect to the printer, and hit the Build Model button.

ReplicatorG uses a machine profile system to interface with different 3D printers; however, support for machines other than MakerBot's and the Ultimaker are limited and generally fairly experimental. With that said, ReplicatorG's support for those two types of printers is unparalleled. It is recommended if you own one of them.

Pronterface

While not as full-featured as ReplicatorG, Pronterface (https://github.com/kliment/Printrun), shown in Figure 2-15, has managed to become the de facto printer control for RepRap machines in a very short time. It works equally well with other printers that use compatible electronics.

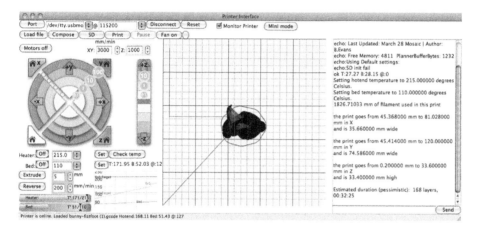

Figure 2-15. *Pronterface*

Pronterface is part of a larger package of applications called Printrun that allows for command line integration and other advanced features. Like ReplicatorG, we use the control panel from Pronterface to connect to our printer, move its axes, set and monitor the temperature, and open and slice models. While not as robust when it comes to seeing and modifying 3D models, Pronterface has the handy feature of visualizing the resulting G-code toolpath layer by layer so that you can quickly see how the print might turn out before hitting the print button.

Because of its more open architecture, Pronterface can be configured to work with any of the slicer applications available today by using the Settings ➤ Options dialog box shown in Figure 2-16.

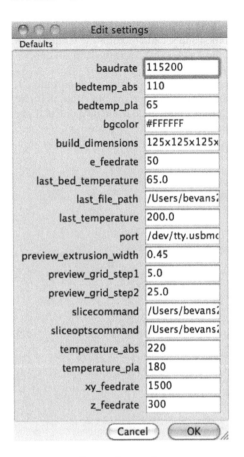

Figure 2-16. Pronterface options

To integrate the slicer of your choice into Pronterface so that you can directly load an STL file to be sliced automatically, you should pay close attention to the options slicecommand and sliceoptscommand. The two boxes provide the path to the slicer application on your computer. Instructions for filling these out can be found on the Pronterface and slicer home pages. In addition to specifying the desired slicer, this window provides options for the printer's build area, default temperature used, and settings for how fast to move each of the motors.

I use Pronterface daily for my MakerGear Mosaic and Prusa Mendel because it is very easy to use and is always reliable. It also works with my favorite slicer application, Slic3r—this duo being particularly compatible.

RepSnapper

RepSnapper (https://github.com/timschmidt/repsnapper), shown in Figure 2-17, is one of the first real alternatives to ReplicatorG.

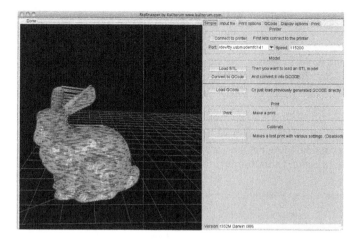

Figure 2-17. *RepSnapper*

RepSnapper has its own integrated slicer to make things simpler and more integrated; however, it might not give you the most feature-filled options for slicing your models. It's also a little difficult to get up and running with the newest versions because there are no readily available precompiled distributions. All that said, the interface is clean and simple and provides a spectacular view of your sliced model, making it a worthy alternative if you have a RepRap machine.

Repetier-Host

The newest member of the printer control applications, Repetier-Host (`http://reprap.org/wiki/Repetier-Host`), shown in Figure 2-18, is chock-full of things to tinker with.

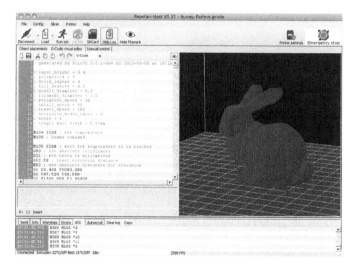

Figure 2-18. *Repetier-Host*

Unique to Repetier-Host is the ability to modify the G-code file and see the alterations in real time in the preview pane. This gives you some unprecedented access to the nuts and bolts of the 3D printing process. This host uses Slic3r as its default slicer application, although Skeinforge and others could be used instead. It is still a fairly new printer control application, so long-term reliability and updates are yet to be seen. It also is a little clunky with its integration for Mac OS X, so it can be a little buggy; the developer promises a solution in a future release.

netfabb Engine

Where Repetier-Host is for the hard-core tinkerer, netfabb Engine (`www.netfabb.com/engines.php`), shown in Figure 2-19, is made for those folks that just want to get on with printing things.

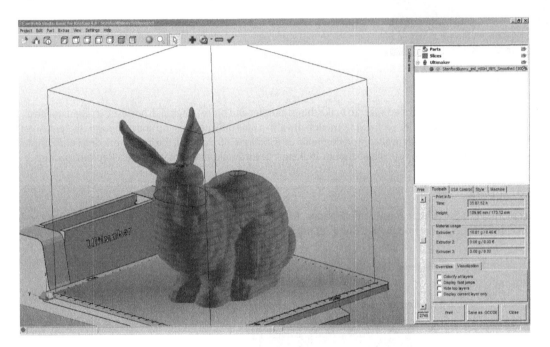

Figure 2-19. netfabb Engine for Ultimaker (courtesy Florian Horsch, 2012)

Where all of the other printer controls are open-source software made by individual developers, netfabb Engine is a commercial printer control made for specific printers by a company known for its outstanding 3D modeling software. Yes, this means you will have to pay for this printer control application, at a cost of around $200. Support for personal 3D printers is currently limited to only the Ultimaker, although MakerBot and RepRap versions are promised.

High cost and limited availability aside, this is the 3D printer control to watch. Not only can the application fix problem 3D models, but it also slices with impressive speeds using its built-in slicer. The prints that Ultimaker users have posted using netfabb Engine are quite simply astonishing. Using this control, it is even possible to get layer resolution reliably and effectively down to 0.02mm or 20 microns in height, making for very smooth finishes, even if they take some time to print.

As commercial manufacturers take notice of the personal 3D printing phenomenon, we will start to see more applications like this one that take all the guesswork out of 3D printing, making it ever closer to the experience that we expect out of our office laser printers.

Summary

And with that, we conclude our summary of the parts of the 3D printer toolchain. If you are building your 3D printer from the ground up, then you will need to spend time trying out the different elements in the toolchain to see what works for you. If you've wisely bought a 3D printer in kit form or already assembled, then you, at least initially, are best off using the applications made for your printer. Keep in mind that new electronics, slicers, and printer controls are being developed all the time, so don't be afraid to try something new to improve the print quality of your 3D printer. Even a three-year-old MakerBot Cupcake can be given a new lease on life by upgrading to a Sanguinololu using Sprinter, Slic3r, and Pronterface.

In the next chapter, we will put our toolchain to use as we prepare the very first prints for our 3D printer. Even if you bought a kit, there will invariably be a little calibration that is needed to get your printer fully functional. (Anecdotally, this is even needed by $30,000 commercial printers.) So we will take a look at how to talk to our printer and get it to move and extrude some plastic. Then we will load up some test prints and see how our printer stacks up. Finally, we might need to change some of the settings on our 3D printer, so we will look at that, as well as tips and tricks for getting really good prints.

CHAPTER 3

■ ■ ■

Calibrating Your Printer

Now that we have a basic theoretical understanding of how the diverse components of our 3D printer work together to build 3D models, it's time to take our new 3D printer and put it to work. Remember though, we are not quite to the point of being able to hit a print button in our software and have the printer build a model. This is especially the case if you have just built your 3D printer from a kit—and even more so if you built the printer from the ground up. Instead, we need to go through a process to verify the operation of the printer to better prepare it to properly and accurately make prints. This process is known as *commissioning* and includes verifying the movement of each axis; testing and homing the endstops, if equipped; heating the extruder; extruding plastic; and testing the heated printbed, if equipped. Then we will need to calibrate our printer, which might include making mechanical adjustments to the printbed or endstops, setting parameters in firmware, and testing print settings like print speed, temperature, and layer height. Even if you already have a working 3D printer, spending some time with it to better calibrate the printer can pay off big with future prints. This chapter walks you through all of the steps, so that you can move from your recently built 3D printer to making your first 3D prints.

In this chapter, we will discuss the following:

- The first steps needed to verify, test, and commission the 3D printer
- How to download and print some useful 3D models to make your prints better
- Calibrating the print settings to find the optimal conditions for printing
- Tweaking the firmware to dial-in the settings for your printer

This is going to be a fun chapter because it's time now to make things move and to print some plastic. Before we jump headlong into making our first prints though, let's take a few baby steps just to make sure our new printer is working according to plan.

The First Steps

There's two schools of thought when it comes to putting your brand new 3D printer into action: go hell for broke, find the craziest thing to print, and see what happens; or take it a little slow and test your printer in stages. While I like the spirit of the former, I am personally more comfortable with the latter. After all, you have made a considerable investment to get to this point; if you take your time now, you will find 3D printing to be much more of a rewarding—rather than frustrating—experience. Even so, our first little steps here can be a lot of fun because we can now start making things move.

Each of the four following steps will be used to test the proper operation of your 3D printer:

1. Test communications.
2. Check axis movement and direction.

3.   Make sure that each axis homes.

4.   Verify extruder and/or printbed heaters.

Even if you have purchased a prebuilt machine, these steps are generally a good idea, just to familiarize yourself with your new machine. If something doesn't work according to plan, then double-check everything and try again. If it's clear something isn't right, then you might need to fix a cable or plug, replace a part, or update your printer's firmware (explained later in this chapter). Let's start with talking to the machine.

Talking to the Machine

First, we need to connect to the electronics on our printer by using the printer control application of choice and verify communications with the printer. Because every printer control application is different from the next, I will assume you've managed to find the printer control of your choice and had it properly installed. With that said, let's begin by selecting the correct serial port—most likely USB—that the printer is connected to. In Pronterface, head for the serial port menu in the top left of the control panel. In ReplicatorG, you need to click on Machine ➤ Connection in the menu bar. On a Mac, chances are the serial port begins with /dev/tty.usbmodem …; while on a PC you need to find the COM number that matches your board. If you're not sure which one to choose then pick one and if it doesn't work, just try again.

Next, depending on your control application, we need to select a communication rate, or baud rate, that corresponds with the speed that the electronics has been set to. If using RAMPS or Sanguinololu electronics, then this will most likely be set to 115200 bps (bits per second); on an Ultimaker the default baud rate is set to 250000 bps; while older MakerBot electronics default to 38400 bps, which is automatically set in ReplicatorG.

Once our serial port and speed have been set, we need to hit the Connect button to establish communications with the electronics. If everything works out, we should have a confirmation of the connection, similar to what is shown in Figure 3-1.

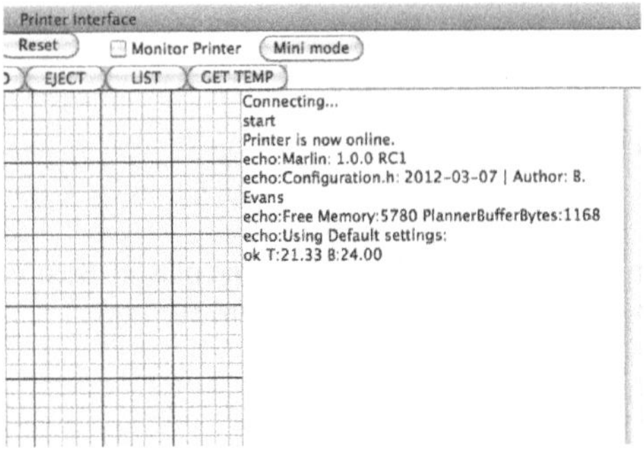

Figure 3-1. Connected to a printer in Pronterface

If the printer doesn't connect on your first try, double-check that your printer has power and that it is connected to your computer, check the serial port and communication rate, and try again. Once connected, we are now ready to go to the next step and start making things move.

Making Things Move

Now for the fun part: with our printer control successfully connected to our printer, it's time to test its movement. At this point, it's a good idea to manually move each of the axes by hand to verify that everything moves smoothly and freely, and then position each axis somewhere in the middle of the print volume. This will keep things from going haywire if the axis runs out of room to move.

All of the printer control applications have a way for moving each of the axes on a 3D printer, including settings for the movement speed (feedrate) and the amount to be moved. The jog controls in Pronterface are shown in Figure 3-2.

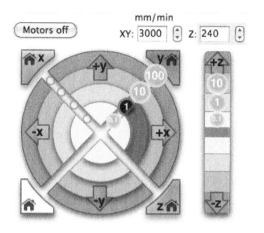

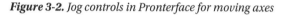

Figure 3-2. Jog controls in Pronterface for moving axes

The jog controls in Pronterface consist of a circular bull's-eye for the x- and y-axes and a vertical bar for the z. For x and y, the circular control is divided in four quadrants, +x, −x, +y, −y, with four rings to move each axis a distance of 0.1 millimeter, 1 millimeter, 10 millimeters, and 100 millimeters in that direction. Start by moving one of the axes a short distance, like 1 millimeter, as highlighted in Figure 3-2. If all is well, then the axis will move in the direction you told it to by the specified distance. In this example, by clicking the ring that highlights the number 1 in the +x direction, turning that segment a darker shade of grey, the x-axis carriage should move to the right by 1 millimeter. Keep in mind that this direction is the direction of the extruder in relation to the printbed. So on a machine like the RepRap Mendel where the printbed moves on the y-axis, moving in the +y direction will cause the printbed to move towards the front of the printer.

There are two things that might go wrong here: the axis might move in the wrong direction or the axis might not move at all. To fix the axis moving in the wrong direction, you need to jump ahead to the Mechanical Settings subsection (under the "Firmware Settings" section) later in this chapter.

If the axis doesn't move at all, you might have one of three possible problems: motor wiring, endstops, and driver current. The first thing to do is check your printer's documentation to verify that the wiring of the motor is properly connected and in the correct orientation and sequence. After that, it's possible that the motor is hitting the endstop or the endstop is incorrectly wired. Try turning the motors off, moving the axis by hand, and checking the endstop connection before trying again with the control panel. Finally, it's possible that the current on the stepper driver board is set too low. Adjust the trimmer potentiometer on the stepper driver board (as shown in Figure 3-3) by only the tiniest amount using a small screwdriver, and try the axis again.

Figure 3-3. *Adjusting current on stepper driver*

Beginning at the far counter-clockwise position, the potentiometer should be adjusted clockwise up to where the axis begins moving and just a hair more. This adjustment will give more current to the motor, helping it to move better. It is possible to overheat your motor, and in extreme situations burn out the stepper driver board so please be careful as you make this adjustment.

Now, check each of the axes in turn, moving them by little amounts in the control panel, verifying that the motors move and are in the correct direction. You might need to make adjustments to the belts or smooth rods, oiling as necessary to ensure that each of the axes move smoothly. Once you are confident that the axes are moving correctly, let's check the endstops and see if the printer will go home.

Going Home

Most personal 3D printers have at least one endstop on each of the printer's axes so that the printer can find the starting point on the printbed before every print. This is helpful for keeping the print on the printbed and to avoid driving one of the axes too far and hitting something. To test the endstops, you should have one hand near the endstop (like the one shown in Figure 3-4) to trigger it if something unexpected happens.

Figure 3-4. RepRap Prusa Mendel y-axis endstop

With the other hand, hit the Home button for one of the axes in the control panel and watch what that axis does. If it moves in the correct direction towards the endstop, you can remove your hand. When the axis reaches its limit, it should tap the endstop, back up slightly, and then slowly hit the endstop again. This jerking motion allows the printer to more precisely locate the limit of that axis. If the axis moves in the wrong direction, tapping the endstop with your hand should stop the axis moving; but if this happens, the firmware will need to be updated before printing. Likewise, if the axis fails to home at all, then the firmware is most likely to blame. This is also covered in Firmware Settings later in this chapter.

Heating Things Up

If our machine is talking to us and moving in the right direction, the last thing to check are the heaters used in the plastic extruder and heated printbed (if equipped). Before we even attempt to fire up these heaters, we should first check that the temperature sensors are reading correctly so that we don't inadvertently set the heaters on a path to self-destruction. Out of pure habit, every time I connect to my 3D printer I check the current temperatures for the extruder and printbed. In Pronterface, the Check Temp button is on the left of the control panel (see Figure 3-5).

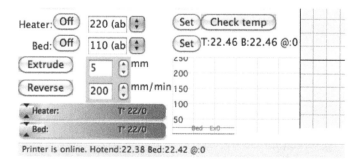

Figure 3-5. Temperature reading in Pronterface

If you are just connecting to the printer after it has been powered down for a while, the temperatures should read somewhere around 22°C to 25°C, which is roughly room temperature. (Of course, if your 3D printer is in the backyard shed in the middle of winter, this reading will be lower; although you might have other problems.) If instead, you have a 0°C reading or some other temperature way outside of the range, then there is a problem with your temperature sensor; it needs to be checked out before continuing. In this case, double-check that the thermistor is connected to the electronics correctly and that the wiring is secure. Worst-case scenario, you might need to rebuild your hotend or printbed to find the problem.

Assuming the temperature readings are at room temperature, you can further test this reading by holding the hotend in your hand for a few seconds and then recheck the temperature. If all is well, then the temperature should have abruptly risen a few degrees from the heat in your hand. Now we are ready to fire the printer up by setting either the hotend or printbed to a temperature appropriate for your plastic material by entering a temperature and hitting the Set button. If you plan to use PLA, then you can start the hotend at 185°C and the printbed at 65°C; or instead, if you are using ABS, then 220°C for the hotend and 110°C for the printbed is a good place to start.

■ **Caution**   While heating, be careful with the printbed and especially the near the hotend. These heaters can become hot enough to cause severe burning if you are not careful.

If your hotend and printbed reach the set temperature points and hover somewhere around the target temperature, maybe ± 5 or 10 degrees, then you are ready to feed filament into your extruder and perform a test extrusion. If the temperature does not climb as you expect, even with the heater on, then you should double-check that the thermistor is properly taped or otherwise secured to the heater core or bed. With the heaters working properly, we can perform a test extrusion by setting the extrusion distance to a sufficient length, as much as 50 millimeters, and with the extruder motor moving, feed the filament into the extruder by hand until the drive gear grabs hold of the filament. Continue to extrude through the control panel in short lengths until hot plastic is extruded from the nozzle.

If everything has worked up to this point, you should have a puddle of filament like the one shown in Figure 3-6, which extruded out of the nozzle.

Figure 3-6. Extruded filament

That little ball of filament let's you know that up to now everything has worked just right and you are ready to start printing things. Congratulations! Before we attempt to throw a model at our printer, let's first overview the printing process and follow that with a discussion of the various print settings.

Printing Overview

You've now successfully tested each of the different aspects of your 3D printer using the printer control application of your choice. Hopefully, this has made you more comfortable with how your 3D printer works and given you confidence that your 3D printer is more or less properly set up. Now we need to find a 3D model to slice and send it to our printer to build a 3D model. To begin, we need to find a model suitable for our first attempt at printing a 3D object, and what better model than the famous Stanford Bunny that made a brief appearance in the last chapter. In Figure 3-7, the Stanford Bunny is shown printed at 45 percent scale.

Figure 3-7. *Stanford Bunny (original model, Stanford Computer Graphics Laboratory, 1993-2012)*

This little ceramic bunny was originally scanned in 1993 at the Stanford Computer Graphics Laboratory. It has since made its way to Thingiverse, the web site to find models for 3D printing, where it has been downloaded more than 3,000 times in one form or another. The model sits right at the edge of what is printable on most machines; its silly ears make it a little more difficult to print right out of the gate, but it's worth a shot anyway.

Other models that might make for a more practical first print include the 20mm box found in Coasterman's The Essential Calibration Set (`www.thingiverse.com/thing:5573`) or the immortal Minimug (`www.thingiverse.com/thing:18357`), which was one of the first objects to be printed on a RepRap. For the purpose of walking through our first prints, we will use the bunny model because it's cute and fun, but feel free to try another model using the same steps and settings.

Before we print the little guy, though, we should first review the overall process of 3D printing and then have a look at the settings used for the printing process.

Downloading a Model

We need to start our printing process with a known good 3D model. Fortunately, a cleaned up version of the Stanford Bunny can be downloaded from Thingiverse at `www.thingiverse.com/thing:3731`. While we will discuss Thingiverse in more depth in the next chapter, for now grab a copy of the bunny model by simply looking for the Downloads section in the left-hand side of the model's page, shown in Figure 3-8.

Figure 3-8. Stanford Bunny file downloads

I recommend the bunny-flatfoot.stl version for its ease of printing. Just click the file name to download the file. With the file in hand, we can then send it to our slicer application.

Slice the Model

Now that we have an STL file suitable for 3D printing, we need to open this file in a slicer utility to slice the model and generate the toolpath for our 3D printer, giving the printer the necessary instructions for how to print the model. We will need to tell the slicer a little information about our printer and filament, such as nozzle size and filament diameter; determine the speed at which the model is to be printed; and then define some parameters for our print that control how the model is built, including how solid the object is and what its surface will look like. This is one of the more complicated parts of 3D printing that takes a little practice to see what works and what doesn't on your particular printer.

To give you a good start, however, we will review all of the print settings that are needed to properly prepare the model for 3D printing.

Print the Model

With the model toolpath generated, we have a new file ending in .GCODE, which can be opened in our control panel application. After that, it's time to warm up the printer's heaters; physically prep the machine to get it ready for printing, including cleaning the print surface, if necessary, and making sure we have enough filament for the print job; and then we can begin the printing process. Now, let's back up and look at those print settings in more detail.

Print Settings

All of the personal 3D printers that we have discussed work by laying down an extruded strand of heated plastic filament to print the shape of our model layer by layer. As we are printing our models, there are numerous print settings that we can alter to make our prints high quality. Some of these settings we will probably set once and forget about them, while others will need to be adjusted for each print. Let's look at the first four layers of the Stanford Bunny (see Figure 3-9) after it has been processed by Slic3r for 3D printing.

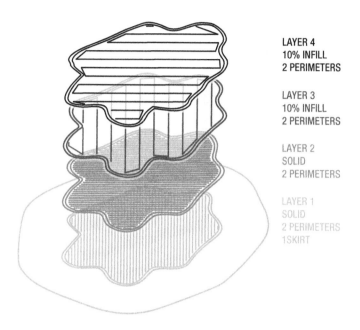

LAYER 4
10% INFILL
2 PERIMETERS

LAYER 3
10% INFILL
2 PERIMETERS

LAYER 2
SOLID
2 PERIMETERS

LAYER 1
SOLID
2 PERIMETERS
1 SKIRT

Figure 3-9. First four layers of the Stanford Bunny

The first four layers have been redrawn to see how they stack up during the printing process, beginning with the first layer at the bottom. In this example, each layer will have two outer perimeters or shells that will print first to outline each layer of the model. Most of the time, the objects that you print will not be solid plastic objects. Instead, for this example, only the first two bottom layers, as well as the top two layers, will be printed to be solid so that each strand of plastic is printed close to the next strand, fusing together to create a solid layer of plastic.

The subsequent layers will be printed at the specified infill density percentage, in this case 10 percent, using one of the specified infill patterns. The infill provides enough of a structure for the model to print well and hold up, while also saving on material and overall print time. For example, this scaled-down model of a bunny printed at 100 percent infill would take 51 minutes to print; while printing the model at 10 percent infill would reduce the time to only 22 minutes. The 10 percent infill version also only uses 1.3 meters of filament as opposed to 4.3 meters with the solid print, saving you a significant amount of plastic.

The last thing to notice here is that the first layer prints with a skirt that is a single strand of plastic, one filament width wide surrounding the rest of the model. This extra little bit of plastic helps to prime the hotend so that the plastic extrudes correctly. And it gives you an opportunity to see if the first layer is printing well and adhering to the printbed. Let's now take a look at each one of these print settings a little closer.

Perimeters

Each layer prints with at least one perimeter or shell to define the outline of that layer. Just like coloring inside the lines in a coloring book, the perimeter helps to make your object as smooth as possible by having the side of the filament form the shell of your model. Depending on the object that you are printing, you might use as little as a single perimeter or as many as five or six. For example, if you are printing a simple geometric shape, a single wall thickness would be more than fine; however, in the case of our bunny, it might make sense to have two or more perimeters. This is shown in Figure 3-10.

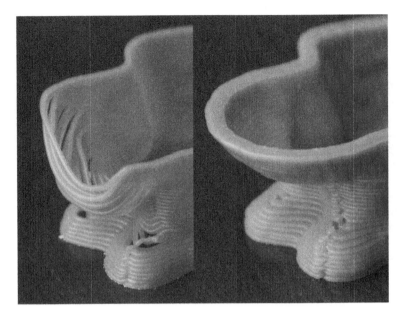

Figure 3-10. *One perimeter on the left vs. three perimeters on the right*

As you can see in Figure 3-10, one perimeter leaves a lot of gaps between each layer and generally doesn't look that swell. That's because this organic model has a lot of variation in shape from one layer to the next; thus, strands of filament are not fully supported by the layer underneath, causing a sagging and drooping print. By adding multiple shells to the model, the filament better fills these gaps, making for a much nicer looking model. If your finished printed model has gaps in the outline or holes in the model, especially around low-sloping sides or gentle overhangs, try increasing the number of perimeters or shells to see how that improves the print.

A good time to use additional perimeters on a geometric model would be when adding rigidity to the outside of the model; for example, when printing mechanical parts for a machine. As a rule of thumb, the more detailed the model or the more the model has angled sides of less than 45 degrees, the greater the chance the perimeters will give a better print. I most often use two perimeters and occasionally more, depending on what I'm printing.

Solid Layers

Just as perimeters define the outer shell of a model, solid layers can be used to define the flat solid surfaces on the top and bottom of a model. Figure 3-11 shows a simple cylinder that is 20 millimeters in diameter and the Stanford Bunny printed with three solid layers and three perimeters.

Figure 3-11. Example of solid layers

Solid layers are not always needed. In fact, hollow forms with no top and bottom can look very striking. For our bunny, however, two or three solid layers better fill the model, creating a more solid look even though the model is not completely solid. In the case of the cylinder, the more solid layers it has, the smoother the top flat surface will be. With only one solid layer and a sparse infill, the top would look more like wavy bacon. Having the additional layers gives the print time to smooth out. Another benefit to this is that, as successive solid layers are printed on top of earlier layers, the fill pattern is rotated by 45 degrees at each layer to strengthen the final print (see Figure 3-9). If the printed model is to be a completely enclosed form, having at least two or three solid layers helps to make for a more solid, durable, and better-looking finished print.

Infill

Where perimeters define the outside of the object being printed, and solid layers determine how many layers on the top and bottom of the model are solid, infill refers to how solidly the interior of the object is printed. We could print objects at 100 percent infill, making a completely solid plastic object, but most people rarely do this because typically a high infill is simply unnecessary. Not only does a solid infill use a lot of material, but it also drastically increases overall print time and sometimes creates cracking in the finished print. Likewise, we can print a hollow object using 0 percent infill; although having at least a little infill in solid models helps to support the sides of the model, creating a better print. Figure 3-12 shows a few examples of different infill patterns, each printed at 10 percent infill.

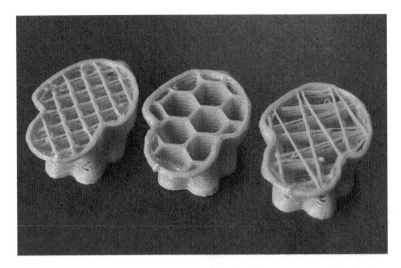

Figure 3-12. Examples of different infill patterns

The strands that make up the infill pattern might not look like much, but they're enough to add strength to the final object and to provide a structure for the upper layers. By default, Slic3r slices models with a rectilinear infill, shown on the left in Figure 3-12. The fill consists of parallel lines angled at 45 degrees and spaced according to the infill percentage.

Most slicers are also capable of producing rather exotic infill patterns, such as the honeycomb, or hexagonal, infill shown in the middle of Figure 3-12. This makes for a striking infill that is surprisingly strong. Finally, on the right of Figure 3-12, we have the simple, line infill pattern that fills with spaced zigzag lines, creating a very quick-to-print infill.

I most often print with either 0 percent infill to make hollow forms or somewhere between 10 percent and 20 percent infill, using the rectilinear pattern infill to add rigidity and extra strength without using too much plastic or taking too long to slice; although I quite like the honeycomb infill.

Layer Height

The height of each extruded layer of plastic directly affects the quality of the appearance of the printed object's surface and, conversely, affects the total print time. So a smaller layer height provides a surface made of much thinner lines, making a smoother appearance, but increases the length of time needed to complete the print. Alternatively, a higher layer height decreases the amount of time to print, but your print will have a more noticeable horizontal banding from each printed layer. Figure 3-13 demonstrates the difference between an object printed at 0.15mm layer height, and the same object printed at 0.3mm layer height.

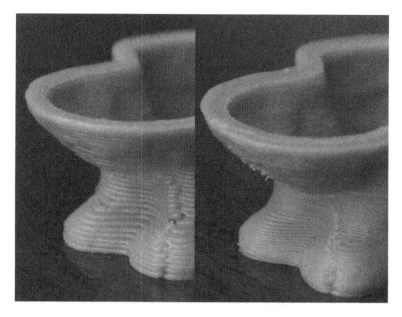

Figure 3-13. *0.3mm layer height (left) vs. 0.15mm (right)*

Theoretically, layer heights as tiny as 0.01 millimeters are possible, which is equal to 10 microns (because microns sounds more awesome), even using larger 0.5mm nozzles. Those microscopic layer heights are awfully difficult to obtain, though, without a very well-tuned machine; and that kind of detail increases your overall print time tremendously. Most of us don't have that kind of patience. Printing at this precision requires that your printer is very precisely calibrated, that the printbed is nearly perfectly level, and that the filament driver is capable of extruding at fairly slow speeds. Even printing at layer heights of about 0.2 millimeters requires a printbed to be accurate by some estimations to ± 0.05 millimeters across the entire surface of the printbed.

The upper limit of possible layer height is determined by your nozzle's diameter and the extrusion diameter of the extruded plastic. The MakerGear Mosaic, for example, comes with a nozzle diameter of 0.35 millimeters, meaning that the extruded plastic, which swells a little bit when it exits the nozzle, will be somewhere between 0.35 and 0.4 millimeters in diameter. To ensure that the layers have enough plastic to fuse together by pushing one layer of filament into the layer below it, the largest reasonable layer height for this nozzle is somewhere around 0.3 millimeters. If we had a nozzle that had a diameter of 0.5 millimeters, then it would be possible to have a maximum layer height somewhere between 0.4 and 0.45 millimeters. Clearly having a 0.5mm nozzle provides the opportunity to decrease print times significantly; however, this comes at the cost of print quality. I generally find printing at 0.25mm layer heights to be an ideal compromise between print quality and overall print time.

Transform

While not used all the time, most slicers have additional options, including the ability to scale or print multiples of a model. The scale setting can come in handy to reduce or enlarge a 3D model. For example, we would enter 0.45 into the Scale option to reduce the bunny to 45 percent of its original size.

The option to print multiples of an object is also available. To print four copies of a model, for example, simply specify two copies along the x-axis and two along the y-axis. The slicer then spaces each object at a set distance and slices all objects simultaneously.

Printer and Filament

While the print settings are the most important settings that we will most likely use on a print-by-print basis, we also need to tell our slicer application a little about our printer and filament. The first item on the agenda is our printer's nozzle size. MakerGear hotends (see Figure 3-14) generally ship with 0.35mm nozzles, while the MakerBot extruders most often use 0.4mm nozzles.

Figure 3-14. *MakerGear hotend with 0.35mm brass nozzle*

The slicer utility uses this information to calculate the die swell of the extruded filament, or the expected diameter of the extruded plastic, as it exits the nozzle. This can then be used to determine the layer width compared to the specified layer height to easily generate exact toolpaths where the strands of extruded filament properly fill the layer shape, fusing to neighboring strands to make a solid infill.

The next part of this puzzle is the diameter of the filament coming into the extruder. Given the amount of material coming in, the slicer can calculate the appropriate feedrate of the extruder to ensure reasonably accurate extrusions. (The recent advances in smarter slicers that make these calculations automatically are greatly appreciated.) To accurately measure the filament diameter, as shown in Figure 3-15, a set of digital calipers is the best tool for the job.

Figure 3-15. *Measuring filament diameter*

To accurately measure filament diameter, set the calipers to millimeters; zero the reading when the calipers are fully closed. Close the calipers with the larger flat sides of its jaws tightly pressed against the sides of the filament. If you use the knife-edge tip of the calipers, the teeth will cut into the filament and give you a false reading. Really good filament is made to a tight tolerance of ± 0.05 millimeters for 1.75mm filament and ± 0.1 millimeters for 3mm filament. As you can see in the Figure 3-15, we are spot-on with our filament diameter. Because filament diameter might change throughout a spool of filament, it's a good idea to take a few measurements along the length of filament and look for an average result. It's also a good idea to measure the filament diameter for any new spool of filament when you load it into your printer.

If when measuring your filament, you notice that the filament diameter changes significantly throughout the spool or that the filament is oval rather than circular, then you should seriously consider ordering new filament from a better supplier. The heartaches that poor-quality filament provide are simply worth no amount of money saved.

With the nozzle and filament diameters worked out, you can enter these measurements into the printer and filament settings along with the print center, if that's an option, to place the center of the print in the center of a the printbed. This should be set to half of the x and y print volume, such as 100 × 100 for the RepRap Mendel, and 63.5 × 63.5 for the MakerGear Mosaic or similar. You will also need to set the temperature for your filament–choose the lowest temperature that gives smooth extrusion during a print. Sometimes it works to print the first layer at a higher temperature (5°C to10°C) than the rest of the model to give the best results and ensure that the first layer properly adheres to the print surface.

Print Speed

With the basic settings in place for our printer, we now need to set the speed at which the printer builds our objects, also called its print speed or feedrate. Whereas we might only change the printer and filament settings when we change the hotend or the filament, print speed depends heavily on the type of model you are attempting to print. Print speed is often a very personal thing, so try a number of settings to see what works for you and your printer. For example, some users have successfully printed at 75 mm/s on a MakerGear Mosaic, but I find the quality of the print and the noise made by the fast-moving printer to be too obnoxious, so I often make prints at half that speed. With that in mind, the following recommendations may be a little on the slow side, depending on your printer; you might have to adjust up or down.

Now, to illustrate some of the different settings, let's look at the bunny again in Figure 3-16.

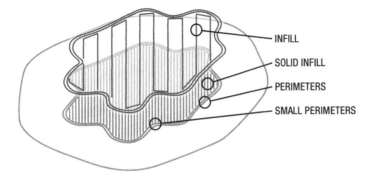

Figure 3-16. *Some of the print speed settings*

Every slicing utility has a different take on the speed settings; for example, there is only one feedrate setting on ReplicatorG's Print-O-Matic, while with Skeinforge, not only can you change the feedrate but also the flowrate, or the speed at which plastic is extruded.

Let's look at some of the more common settings beginning with the perimeters setting, as shown in Figure 3-16. This setting handles the outermost shells that outline each layer of the model. Perimeters can be set at a reasonable midpoint range based on the speed of your printer; this is roughly 30 mm/s on a Mosaic and 50 to 60 mm/s on a Mendel. Small perimeters include the innermost perimeters, or those perimeters that surround small holes like bolt holes, and should be set at the same speed or slightly lower (by 5 to10 mm/s) than the main perimeter's print speed to ensure accurate extrusion.

There are two kinds of infill settings: one to set the solid layer speed and the other for the innermost infill. Solid layer infill can be set faster than the perimeter speed, although you have to be careful of going overboard or the filament will not stick to the printbed. Usually 35 mm/s on the slow side and 55 to 65 mm/s on the fast side should do it. The sparse infill can be set to the same or even slightly faster print speeds than the solid infill because print quality is less of a concern on the interior of a model. An acceptable range would be from 40 to 70 mm/s.

Settings not shown in Figure 3-16 include the bridge print speed for spanning across a gap in midair, which needs to consider not only the print speed but also the temperature and cooling. A faster bridge speed in a range around 60 to 70 mm/s is a good place to start with PLA; and maybe 10 mm/s slower for ABS, with further testing needed.

There is also the travel speed, a maximum speed that the printer can accelerate up to on any of its axes as it moves around the print. This setting has to consider the weight of the moving components on each of the axes, as well as the range of speed capable in the specific motors for each axis. You will undoubtedly want a faster travel speed to help reduce the overall print time of your model, with a range between two and three times the perimeter print speed—easily near the top of you printer's speed range.

One final print speed setting to consider is the bottom layer speed ratio. This is an option to slow down the first layer by a certain percentage to make sure the extruded filament properly adheres to the build surface. I find a factor of 0.25, or 25 percent of the speed settings, provides a nice range for the first layer, making for a quality start to most 3D prints; even slower might be best for tricky prints.

While there are additional print settings available in most slicer utilities, we've looked at the most significant settings that you will need to adjust to make the best prints possible with your machine.

Print the Bunny

Now that you have a grasp on the settings used to generate the toolpath to print a 3D model, we are ready to print something. The following are the basic steps to printing an object:

1. Open the control panel and connect to the printer.

2. Preheat the hotend and printbed to the temperature of your material.

3.   Download the 3D model to be printed.

4.   Set the slicing settings for your print and slice the model.

5.   Load the generated G-code file in the printer control.

6.   Verify the printer is ready to go. Start the print.

First things first, let's get the printer control connected to the printer if it's not already. Then choose a temperature for your hotend and printbed that matches the material you will be using. While the heaters get up to temperature, you can proceed with the rest of the steps; but it's a good idea to start the print once everything has fully warmed up. While preheating, we can slice the bunny model that we downloaded earlier. While your settings are entirely dependent on your printer, my settings for this model are as follows:

```
perimeters = 3
solid_layers = 3
fill_density = 0.15
layer_height = 0.25
scale = 0.45
nozzle_diameter = 0.35
filament_diameter = 1.74
temperature = 175
first_layer_temperature = 185
bed_temperature = 60
first_layer_bed_temperature = 65
perimeter_speed = 30
small_perimeter_speed = 30
infill_speed = 35
solid_infill_speed = 32
bridge_speed = 60
travel_speed = 60
bottom_layer_speed_ratio = 0.25
```

Note that because the bunny model is so large, it would normally take three hours or more to print at its original size. To solve this, I've used the scale function to reduce the finished print size to 45 percent of the original model. This creates a print in about 30 minutes. Now all we need to do is load the file into the printer control, make sure our printer is up to temperature and ready to go, and then we can hit the print button. If all proceeds as planned, your printer will home itself using the endstops on each axis, wait until the temperature stabilizes, and then begin printing. Thirty minutes later, you should have a bunny waiting for you.

Of course, that print may not have worked entirely well. That's okay if it didn't work perfectly the first time. The model is a little small and has several overhangs with its tail, chin, and ears that can droop or catch the hotend during printing. To get a better handle on the conditions of our 3D printer, we need to run a few calibration prints through the machine to dial in certain things like leveling the printbed, setting the print settings, and finding the best print speeds. So before we try that bunny again, let's run through some calibration prints first.

Calibration Prints

While our first 3D print may or may not have been fully successful, we have verified that everything works (mostly) according to plan: the axes move in the correct direction, the endstops work and each axis homes, our temperatures read correctly, the heaters maintain temperature, and our extruder melts plastic. This gives us some hope that the printer will print good models, but the devil is in the details. There might be all sorts of challenges that we need to overcome to get really nice prints. This includes fine-tuning the printer mechanically: adjusting the amount and speed of movement on each axis, adjusting the temperature of our extrusion and printbed, and finding the right print settings for the printer.

The three models we will cover—Build Platform Level Test Pattern, Circle Calibration Set, and the Hollow Calibration Pyramid—provide a reasonable foundation for calibrating and fine-tuning your 3D printer and tell you a lot about its print settings. Each model, available in the STL file format, needs to be downloaded from Thingiverse (`www.thingiverse.com`) and processed through your 3D printer software.

Starting on the Right Foot

One of the more frustrating aspects of making your first prints is starting a new print, only to find the extruded plastic filament tangling up in a cantankerous ball of doom rather than laying down nice and flat on the printbed. There are a couple reasons that this might happen, but they mostly come down to making sure your printbed is properly prepared for the materials you are using—and that it is as level to the printhead as possible. To help get a better foundation for our prints, Ed Nisley's Build Platform Level Test Pattern (`www.thingiverse.com/thing:15709`) is an extremely useful model for testing the quality of your printbed. It is really quick to process and print, something to be appreciated after running through a few dozen of them. The printed test pattern is shown in Figure 3-17.

Figure 3-17. *Build Platform Level Test Pattern*

This test pattern prints a simple, one-layer square with a cross through the middle and shorter lines that indicate the positive direction of the x- and y-axes. The width of the line is set to be two line-widths wide; the height of the model is preset for 0.25mm layer heights. Should you wish to use this test pattern with other layer heights, you will need to venture into OpenSCAD to modify the source file (also provided on Thingiverse) to change the model's parameters to better match your printer. In this example, the standard model was sliced as normal with 2 perimeters, 0 infill, and 0 solid layers.

Once printed, a quick visual inspection should give you a rough idea as to how level your printbed is. Keep in mind, when we say "level," what we mean is that the surface of the printbed is parallel with the movement of the hotend of the extruder. This can be tricky to obtain, however, if the printbed is not level over the extent of its travel; then it becomes especially difficult to create consistently good, quality prints. Now if this print does not adhere to the printbed and instead pulls up from the surface during the print, it could be due to one of the three following situations:

- *The plastic filament does not stick to the printbed because there is a problem with the quality of the build surface.* Use a surface material suitable to your plastic. Polyimide or Kapton tape works well for ABS and PLA. PLA sticks to blue painter's tape and heated bare glass. Make sure that the surface is clean; use a new build surface or clean it with acetone. Finally, make sure the heated bed if available is a suitable temperature, 65°C for PLA and 110°C for ABS.

- *The filament pulls up from the build surface whenever the nozzle is too close to the printbed, causing the extrusion of overly wide layers of filament that drag the filament next to it.* This usually causes a bacon-like appearance in solid infills as the nozzle drags through the hot filament.

- *The filament does not stick to the printbed because there is too much space between the nozzle and build surface.* The nozzle is effectively too far away from the printbed. This causes the loose extrusion to drag across the print surface until it attaches to something else.

Start with a visual inspection of the test pattern, looking for these three conditions. You should try using digital calipers to measure the extruded layer height and compare it to the layer height setting specified in the slicer utility. If these two values don't match, then that is a pretty good clue as to what went wrong. If the layer height is too thin, the printbed needs to be moved further from the extruder to increase the layer height in that part of the printbed, while if the extrusion is too thick, then the printbed needs to be moved closer to the extruder to decrease the layer height. Figure 3-18 shows printbed adjustments being made on a MakerGear Mosaic.

Figure 3-18. *Adjusting printbed leveling*

On the Mosaic, there are three screws on the bottom of the printbed that can be tightened or loosened to adjust the leveling of the printbed. Other printers may have four screws or other mechanisms to alter the printbed height. Adjust in very small increments and retest with each adjustment to see the effect your adjustments are having on the rest of the printbed.

Once you have managed to level the printbed to ideally about ± 0.05 millimeters across the printed test pattern, it's time to test the rest of the print settings.

Circle, Circle, Circle

Say it three times fast while clicking your heels to magically calibrate your printer... or maybe not. At the very least, this Circle Calibration Set by Thingiverse denizen Whosawhatsis (www.thingiverse.com/thing:12259), shown in Figure 3-19, can tell you a lot about your new 3D printer's state of calibration.

Figure 3-19. *Circle calibration set*

With this one calibration set, we can test proper infill settings, thin wall extrusion, and our bridge overhang capabilities, all in one print. It's also useful for checking that the printer is moving nice and true, or else you might end up with ovals instead of circles. To print this set, I like to use 3 solid layers if printing in PLA, 3 perimeters, and 20 percent infill. This print will really test the effect of your print settings, so let's look at a couple of the models in closer detail in Figure 3-20.

Figure 3-20. *Circle calibration set detail*

The first thing to look for with this print is the consistency and smoothness of the layers that form the objects' perimeters. You want to aim for even layers by adjusting the perimeter speed or overall feedrate so that you are printing only as fast as makes for a good print. Next, make sure that the circles are really circles and not ovals. Ovals tell you that you have a problem with backlash on one of the axes, which might be caused by bad or worn-out belts or pulleys, or idler wheels that are not perfectly round or are missing teeth; or you might have a problem with the linear movement caused by a bad bearing or a bent smooth rod. You can also look at the infill of the solid object to determine if there is a problem with filament diameter or if the infill percentage is set too low.

The last thing this set tests is the ability of the 3D printer to render bridges in a print. A bridge is essentially an extreme overhang that should not be technically possible to print because it requires printing over thin air. Bridges will more than often work anyway because a bridge is an area anchored on either side of a gap. If printing in PLA, bridges can be printed at a faster speed and with the help of a cooling fan or if using ABS it might help to slow things down. More often than not, bridges should be printed with a cooling fan aimed at the printed filament set to 100 percent speed. In Figure 3-20, the bridge-test cylinder, shown upside down, has no loose strands of filament and sags downward only a little, making this a successful bridge test.

Pyramid of Power

Now for the real 3D printer torture test. The Hollow Calibration Pyramid model created by Scott Pierce (`www.thingiverse.com/thing:8757`) is nearly impossible to print with 100 percent accuracy, but it is quite useful for dialing in our extrusion temperature, filament retraction, print speed, and cooling. Figure 3-21 shows one of my better prints of this model.

Figure 3-21. Hollow Calibration Pyramid

This model is really good at testing how well you have your temperature and filament retraction speed dialed in. To print this model, I use a very low infill of 5 percent, 2 solid layers, and 5 perimeters to reduce the amount of back and forth the extruder has to do to fill all of the columns of the pyramid. Start towards the upper edge of your filament temperature and reduce it by five degrees with each print until the strands between each of the columns are as minimal as possible. To compensate, it is also a good idea to slightly modify the filament retraction distance or retraction speed.

In the print shown in Figure 3-21, I reduced the extrusion temperature from 200°C to start, down to 185°C for the first layer. I further reduced it to 180°C for all other layers using PLA. Seeing as that is a fairly low temperature for PLA, I decided it was good enough and called it a day. Likewise, the tops of the pyramid almost never come out exactly as they should, mostly due to the debatable state of most slicers' ability to handle layer cooling. Cooling, a new feature for Slic3r, remains a week spot for this slicer utility; it causes the top of the pyramid to come out a little gooey, but close enough.

■ **Note**   Perfection is the enemy of Good Enough. Your 3D printer is still an emerging technology and the quicker we come to terms with that, the faster we can print some cool things.

You might have to print these calibration prints a few times to get your machine dialed in and printing pretty well, but don't despair. Stick with it and you will be rewarded with some really nice prints. You might want to also revisit some of the objects in The Essential Calibration Set (www.thingiverse.com/thing:5573) to further test different aspects of your 3D printer. You could even try that bunny again and see how he does after you've dialed everything in. But for now, let's look at how to adjust your firmware to fix any of the more unusual problems you might have calibrating your printer.

Firmware Settings

Hopefully, you haven't had to worry about firmware up to this point because your machine or kit came with working firmware preloaded on the electronics. If, however, you've built your printer from scratch or find that, after your first test prints, something is clearly not working as well as it should, then it's time to update the firmware. This section is mostly for those with RepRap printers and those printers still clinging to their RepRap roots, like the MakerGear Mosaic. For the MakerBot and Ultimaker printers, uploading new firmware is built into their respective versions of ReplicatorG.

To get started with updating the firmware on a RepRap, you will need the following software:

- Arduino 0023 (http://arduino.cc/hu/Main/Software)

- Sanguino (http://code.google.com/p/sanguino/downloads/list) for Sanguinololu and similar controllers

- Firmware source files, usually Sprinter (https://github.com/kliment/Sprinter) or Marlin (https://github.com/ErikZalm/Marlin)

Even though Arduino has recently released version 1.0 of its popular development environment, the changes made to 1.0 have created problems for the RepRap firmware developers. So instead, we need to use Arduino version 0023, which is the latest release prior to Arduino 1.0. In addition to the Arduino software, we will need the Sanguino extension if we are using a Sanguinololu or similar electronics controller, and, of course, we need the actual firmware source files.

With Arduino 0023 downloaded and installed, you should open your firmware source files and find a window similar to that shown in Figure 3-22.

Figure 3-22. *Arduino 0023 with Sprinter firmware*

Along the top of the window are multiple files associated with the main firmware sketch, named `sprinter.pde`, `marlin.pde`, or some similar name, depending on the version of firmware you are using. While every firmware is a little different in implementation, they are all broadly similar. For the intent of calibrating our firmware, we will use the Marlin/Sprinter firmware as our example.

Initial Settings

If we are starting with a clean copy of the firmware, then we need to set certain initial settings that define our electronics setup within the `configuration.h` file, beginning with the section that defines the motherboard we are using in our printer, as follows:

```
// MEGA/RAMPS up to 1.2 = 3,
// RAMPS 1.3 = 33
// Gen6 = 5,
// Sanguinololu up to 1.1 = 6
// Sanguinololu 1.2 and above = 62
// Gen 7 @ 16MHZ only= 7
// Gen 7 @ 20MHZ only= 71
// Teensylu (at90usb) = 8
// Printrboard Rev. B (ATMEGA90USB1286) = 9
// Gen 3 Plus = 21
// gen 3 Monolithic Electronics = 22
// Gen3 PLUS for TechZone Gen3 Remix Motherboard = 23
#define MOTHERBOARD 3
```

Simply changing the 3 to match the value for your specific motherboard is all that's needed. Next, we need to set the type of temperature sensors in the following section:

```
// 1 is 100k thermistor
// 2 is 200k thermistor
```

```
// 3 is mendel-parts thermistor
// 4 is 10k thermistor
// 5 is ParCan supplied 104GT-2 100K
// 6 is EPCOS 100k
// 7 is 100k Honeywell thermistor 135-104LAG-J01
#define THERMISTORHEATER 1
#define THERMISTORBED 1
```

Unless you know for certain that your hotend and printbed use a specific thermistor, sticking to the first option is generally the safest bet.

Calibrating Axis Movement

Most importantly in terms of calibrating, we need to set the number of steps in firmware needed to move each axis one millimeter. To set these values, we need to look for the following line or one similar to it in the firmware:

```
#define _AXIS_STEP_PER_UNIT {80, 80, 3200/1.25, 700}
```

This single line defines the number of steps it takes for the x-, y-, and z-axes, as well as the extruder, to move one millimeter. As Cartesian robots, our 3D printers rely on relatively exact positioning to correctly make 3D prints. This positioning is dependent on the settings of the stepper drivers, the stepper motors, the types of timing pulleys, and the pitch of the timing belts. It's not as bad as it might sound, but to calibrate these values we have to do a little math.

X and Y Steps

For the x- and y-axes, we would use the following formula to calculate the steps per millimeter:

$$steps = motor\ steps\ per\ revolution \times driver\ microstep \div belt\ pitch \div number\ of\ teeth\ on\ pulley$$

To start filling in these blanks, most motors are of the 1.8 degrees per step variety, meaning that they move 1.8 degrees for each step of the motor; so to complete a full rotation, the motor needs to step 200 times. The stepper drivers on the control electronics are often set to a mode called *microstepping*, allowing the driver to move the stepper motor in increments of a normal step. So for instance, a $1/16^{th}$ microstepping stepper driver is able to move the stepper motor 16 times for each 1.8 degree step. The belt pitch is determined by the distance between the teeth on the timing belt. So a T5 belt has teeth spaced every five millimeters, whereas a GT2 belt is spaced every two millimeters. Finally, we have the number of teeth on the stepper pulley that determines the overall gear ratio of our timing-belt drive. If we were to plug these numbers into the formula for a MakerGear Prusa Mendel, we would have the following equation:

$$steps = 200 \times 16 \div 5 \div 12 = 53.3333$$

Z Steps

For the z-axis, things are a little different because we generally use a lead screw to drive the axis instead of a belt. The formula for figuring out the steps per millimeter on the z-axis looks as follows:

$$steps = motor\ steps\ per\ revolution \times driver\ microstep \div thread\ pitch$$

Instead of the gear ratio between the belt and pulley, we substitute the thread pitch of the lead screw driving the axis. The Prusa Mendel uses standard M8 threaded rod that has a thread pitch of 1.25. Plug this into the formula to get the following:

$$steps = 200 \times 16 \div 1.25 = 2560$$

Extruder Steps

The last bit of math is to calculate the number of steps that our extruder needs to drive 1 millimeter of filament through the extruder. Most extruders use a stepper motor that is geared down to increase torque using either printed drive gears or, in the case of the MakerGear Prusa Mendel, a special stepper motor with an integrated gearbox. This gear ratio along with the diameter of the drive gear—either a manufactured gear or a hobbed bolt—are considered in the following equation:

$$\text{steps} = \text{motor steps per revolution} \times \text{driver microstep} \times \text{big gear} \div \text{small gear} \div \pi \div \text{drive gear diameter}$$

Looking at the MakerGear extruder, the steps per revolution and microstep stay the same. The listed gear ration is 13.6:1, so we can use that as the big gear and small gear values. Finally, with a little digging, the manufactured drive gear for the extruder has a diameter of 10 millimeters. Plug that in for the following result:

$$\text{steps} = 200 \times 16 \times 13.6 \div 1 \div \pi \div 10 = 1385.2846$$

Now if we put all of these values back into that single line of code in the firmware, we have the following properly calibrated result for a MakerGear Prusa Mendel:

```
#define _AXIS_STEP_PER_UNIT {53.3333, 53.3333, 2560, 1385.2846}
```

Mechanical Settings

Having the axial movement properly calibrated should solve any problems with the shape or accuracy of your 3D prints related to the firmware. Now if certain things are not working, like an axis that moves in the wrong direction, then we have some other mechanical settings that are off.

Starting with an axis that moves in the wrong direction, we should start by looking for a section in the code that inverts axis direction, as follows:

```
const bool INVERT_X_DIR = false;
const bool INVERT_Y_DIR = false;
const bool INVERT_Z_DIR = true;
const bool INVERT_E_DIR = false;
```

If for example, sending a command to the printer to move the y-axis +10 millimeters results in the y-axis moving towards the back of the printer as opposed to the front, then you will need to change INVERT_Y_DIR from false to true. Once all the axes are moving in the right direction, you'll need to check the endstops settings in the following block of code:

```
#define X_HOME_DIR -1
#define Y_HOME_DIR -1
#define Z_HOME_DIR -1
```

The firmware, by default, expects endstops to be placed in the minimum positions for each axis. If instead one of your endstops is in the maximum position, then you will need to change the value -1 to 1 for homing to function correctly. The last mechanical configuration to check is the maximum lengths of each axis, defined in the following code:

```
const int X_MAX_LENGTH = 200;
const int Y_MAX_LENGTH = 200;
const int Z_MAX_LENGTH = 100;
```

This firmware assumes that everyone owns a Prusa Mendel with a 200mm² printbed. If you try to upload this setting onto the electronics for a Mosaic with a 127mm² printbed, then the controller can send the axis further than is mechanically possible, creating a horrible noise. Because of the nature of stepper motors, don't worry too much if this happens to you once or twice; chances are slim that something will break, but it is not a good habit to get into. Instead, set these values to something that your printer can comfortably reach within its mechanical restraints.

While there are many, many more settings available in this firmware, these are the settings that are most often in need of calibration—and the most common across different firmware. Let's call it good and move on to uploading the firmware.

Uploading Firmware

With the main settings properly calibrated and updated in our firmware, it's now time to save the file and upload to the electronics board. Before proceeding, make sure that your printer control application has been disconnected from the electronics to free up the serial communications. Next, you need to make sure that you have chosen the correct serial port and board type for your Arduino-based electronics. These settings can be found in the Arduino menu bar under Tools ➤ Serial Port and Tools ➤ Board. With the correct port and board type selected, it's time to upload the file to the board using the Upload button shown in Figure 3-23.

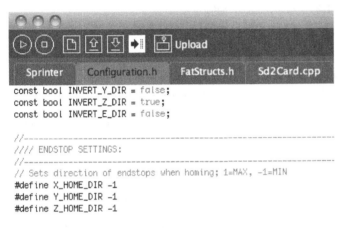

Figure 3-23. Uploading firmware to the electronics

This might take a little while to complete, but if all goes well, you should be greeted with the message "Done uploading." If this doesn't work the first time, try pressing the reset button on the controller board right after you click Upload. Now you are ready to test the movement and temperature settings of your printer, just to make sure we didn't break anything in the process. Then try a few more calibration prints to see if the print quality improves.

Summary

Well, that was surely a lot to take in for a single chapter, but there are a lot of little things that just need to work together in order for your printer to successfully make its first 3D prints. It will get easier because the more time you spend with it, the more it becomes second nature. Once you have your printer properly calibrated, you will most likely need to revisit some of the print settings to find the right combination of factors to print at the highest quality your printer can deliver. A little more fine-tuning here and there, and I'm sure you will have it down.

This chapter is also the last we will see on the mechanical aspects of setting up a 3D printer, at least for a while. Instead, now that we have a working 3D printer, we need to stop fiddling with it and go find some cool models to build.

■ ■ ■

CHAPTER 4

3D Models from the Cloud

Chances are you have had to do some work up to this point to get your new 3D printer up and running. That might not have been all that much fun but now that your robot is all ready to make things, it's time for the rewarding experience of putting that robot to use. If you are lucky enough to have a prebuilt and configured printer, then you have probably skimmed through the previous chapters and are now ready to get your hands dirty. Either way, it's now time to put that shiny new 3D printer to use and see what it can do.

In this chapter, we will do the following:

- Download some models from the cloud to print on our new printer.

- Contribute to the online 3D printer community.

- Use a free online utility to make our models print better.

- Get introduced to some free, web-based 3D modeling applications.

- Make our first project from scratch to stretch our creative muscles.

So, let's fire up our web browser of choice and see what's out there.

Places to Find and Share 3D Models

The quickest way to get started with 3D printing is simply to find models online that others have already created and shared on the internet. The online 3D printing community is growing all the time, so more and more things are being shared every day. Often that means the thing you are looking for might already exist in one form or another; you just need to know the right place to look. Here in this section are two of the most common places to find 3D models from the cloud, including MakerBot Industries' Thingiverse and Google's 3D Warehouse, along with how to set up these files for the best results on your printer. We will also look at what it takes to be a responsible member of the online community and how to give back to it.

Thingiverse

Thingiverse (www.thingiverse.com) shown in Figure 4-1, is my first go-to place for downloading a 3D model. Actually, I check it every day to see what new thing has been posted or to see who's making what, in case I might have missed something cool the last time I checked. We briefly saw Thingiverse in the last chapter when we downloaded our calibration objects, but let's revisit it in more depth.

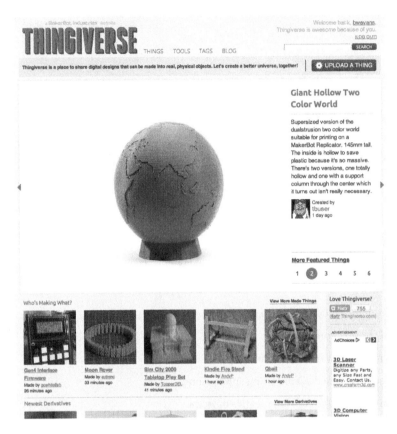

Figure 4-1. Thingiverse homepage

Thingiverse is an active, social community for sharing 3D models. When you create an account, you can bookmark models that you like so that you can easily find them when you are ready to print them. You can also post photos of the things you made, or upload new things to Thingiverse when you design something new, or make changes to existing things and post these designs as derivatives. Let's start with simply making something that we find at Thingiverse.

I Made One

Central to the Thingiverse ecosystem is sharing with the community the awesome things that you make. To begin, we need to find something cool to make, maybe a pirate ship, then we need to download the file, send it to our 3D printer, and post a photo of our finished thing back to Thingiverse. Let's start with MakerBlock's OpenSCAD Pirate Ship, shown in Figure 4-2.

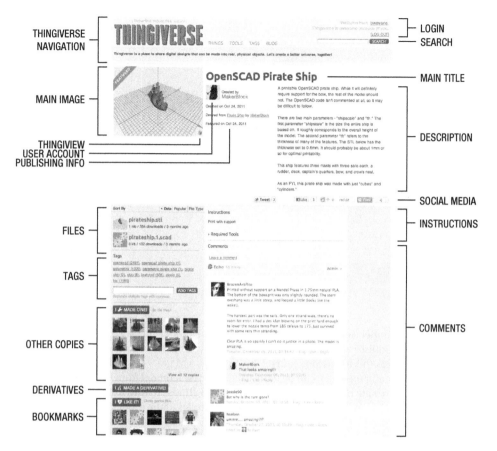

Figure 4-2. *MakerBlock's OpenSCAD Pirate Ship on Thingiverse*

Figure 4-2 illustrates all of the different types of information available on any one thing's page. Here we see all sorts of details regarding the model, including one or more images, the design's title, a brief description, instructions if needed, publishing details, and the files associated with the design. Because Thingiverse is a social community, this page also features comments from the community as well as areas to see copies other people have made, any designs derived from this one, and who has bookmarked this design. To better see a model without downloading it first, Thingiverse has the useful Thingiview feature, shown in Figure 4-3, which can be accessed by clicking the little 3D cube icon in the lower right of the image for each 3D model.

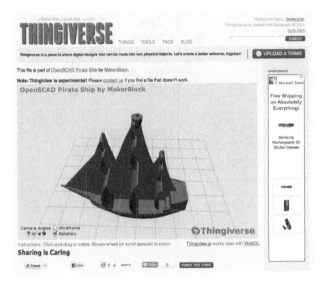

Figure 4-3. *Thingiverse Thingiview*

Thingiview is an in-browser 3D model viewer that allows you to spin the model and see it from all sides before you download it. This viewer requires a WebGL-compatible web browser and even though most modern browsers are compatible, you can check this feature for yourself by heading to `http://get.webgl.org`. While Thingiview does not let you modify or edit the file, it can be fairly useful to view a model from every angle. By default, Thingiview will automatically rotate the model, although you might choose to turn off rotation or to view the model in wireframe, and you can even select predefined camera angles of the model. After having a look at the model, you should download the file from the thing's main page. Often, many designs on Thingiverse will have the source files for the design in whatever native format it was originally created in, however if all you want to do is print the model, you should look for the STL file(s) listed on the left side of the thing's page. Once downloaded, you can open the file in your printer software of choice and process the file as was shown in Chapter 2 with our first calibration prints.

Once you've made a model from Thingiverse, it's a good idea to take a photo of the finished object and post it back to Thingiverse by clicking on the I Made One button on that thing's main page and attaching an image of your finished print, as shown in Figure 4-4.

Figure 4-4. *Thingiverse I Made One*

By posting an image of the thing you made, you contribute back to the community and let others see your version so that they may choose to make one themselves. It also makes the original designer feel good to know that someone else has appreciated his design—something you'll experience yourself before too long.

I Made a Derivative

Because the community at Thingiverse is all about sharing things, designs derived from other's work form an important part of the community-driven design process. The site's I Made a Derivative feature encourages derivatives to be shared. Take DrewPetitclerc's War of The Worlds Playset, shown in Figure 4-5, for example.

Figure 4-5. *A derivative design*

In Thingiverse, derivatives are not a bad thing and, in fact, quite the opposite attitude is encouraged to promote community-driven design through openly improving or modifying original works. For example, the design in Figure 4-5 is a derivative of an earlier War of the Worlds play set designed for fabrication on a laser cutter. The new design has been modified by separating out each of the individual shapes and preparing them to be 3D printable. I took the design one step further and organized each of the separate parts onto two convenient printing plates so that groups of parts could be more easily printed all in one go. This new derivative design is shown in Figure 4-6.

Figure 4-6. *Revised design reposted as a new derivative*

When making a new derivative there are a few files and pieces of information that you should include with it, such as the following:

- Name of the derivative

- An image of the finished model

- STL files for the printable design

- Source files as appropriate

- The thing your design is derived from

- Tags for helping people find your design

- A license appropriate to the original design

When making a derivative of another's work, it is important to keep in mind that any one design is copyrighted by the owner of the design, but it might be shared with different degrees of openness allowed in that thing's usage license. Licenses are an important part of sharing designs on Thingiverse so we will cover this in more detail in a moment.

Upload a Thing

While we are not quite there yet, you will inevitably end up wanting to post new designs entirely of your own creation to Thingiverse for others to use as well. To post a new design, use the Upload a Thing button in the upper-right corner of the Thingiverse main page. From the initial Create a New Thing page, select a file to upload to begin the process that will take you to the Edit Thing page shown in Figure 4-7.

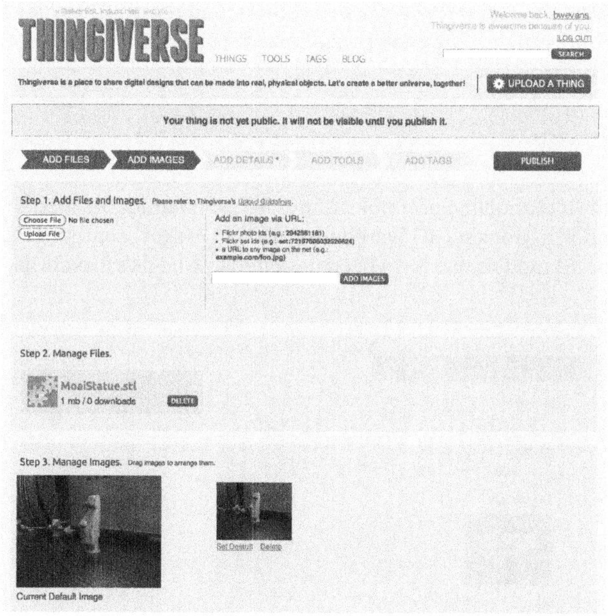

Figure 4-7. *Edit Thing page*

Posting a new design is very similar to posting a derivative with similar types of information needed. In addition, Thingiverse has established a couple loose rules about what kinds of designs can be posted.

- New designs need to represent an actual physical object and should be of your own creation unless the design is open source and properly attributed.

- To keep things family-friendly, designs that are deemed explicit will not be allowed and weapons are generally discouraged.

Central to any new model on Thingiverse is a digital file in a format that is easily accessible. For 3D printing, these models should be STLs along with any source files, if you wish to share them, to allow others to make derivatives. We will revisit posting new things on Thingiverse again a little later, but for now let's look at the issue of licensing in a little more detail.

Open Licensing

When you design something new, that design is automatically protected under various copyright laws for where that design was created. This means that if someone else holds a copyright on a design, then to copy or reproduce that design would be a violation of law. Open-source hardware and software encourages others to make, copy, and improve designs labeled as open source by licensing the use of that design under an open license.

One of the more common licenses at the moment is the Creative Commons Attribution-ShareAlike license (http://creativecommons.org/licenses/by-sa/3.0/), which allows derivatives of a design so long as the design attributes the author of the original and that the new design is shared in a like manner carrying the same license. Other licenses range from the public domain for designs that can be used freely and are no longer protected by copyright law to those that remain fully copyrighted with all rights reserved. Thingiverse has recently moved to a policy that requires all new designs to be posted under an open license in one form or another.

Without an option to reserve all rights, these designs can be shared freely, made by others, and remade into new designs. When making derivatives or using the designs of others, please keep in mind to be respectful of the owner's copyright and follow their posted license accordingly.

Google 3D Warehouse

While Thingiverse is an amazing resource for generally high-quality, printable 3D models, sometimes the model you're looking for is just not available. In that case, I look to Google's 3D Warehouse at `http://sketchup.google.com/3dwarehouse` (see Figure 4-8), a treasure trove for 3D models that have been designed in Google's SketchUp 3D modeling application.

Figure 4-8. Google 3D Warehouse

If you're using SketchUp anyway, then 3D Warehouse is even more useful than it might be for someone just looking for a model for 3D printing. However, since only a small part of the models designed in SketchUp are made for this purpose, not all of the files are suitable for immediate printing. Let's take an example to see how we can get a file from 3D Warehouse into a more usable format.

Downloading a Model

To download a model from 3D Warehouse, all you need to do is find one that you think might work and click the Download Model button. Generally, the available format for the file will be in the SKP format of one variety or another for use in SketchUp. In Figure 4-9, we have Moai Statues from Easter Island created by the user Rebel.

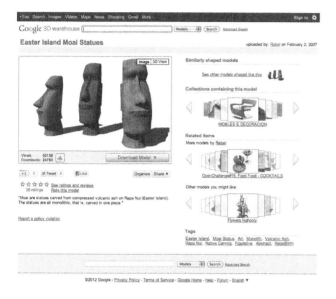

Figure 4-9. *Model from 3D Warehouse*

While many of the SketchUp models rely on image-based texture maps to create detail, this model looks like it might be a potential candidate for 3D printing because of its well-defined form. Because the file is in the SketchUp format, we need to do some processing to the file to get it ready for our 3D printer.

Exporting an STL in SketchUp

The native SketchUp file format is no good to us as is for 3D printing, so we need to convert to a file format that is. For some reason, SketchUp does not support very many file formats natively so we have to turn to a plug-in to do this for us. Fortunately, Nathan Bromham from Guitar-List has written just the plug-in that we need. So in addition to downloading and installing Google SketchUp if you have not already (`http://sketchup.google.com`), you will need to head over to the plug-in's web site at `www.guitar-list.com/download-software/convert-sketchup-skp-files-dxf-or-stl` and download the plug-in for your version of SketchUp, following the installation instructions on that page. Once installed, open the SketchUp file you downloaded. You should find the Export to DXF or STL plug-in listed under the Tools menu, as shown in Figure 4-10.

Figure 4-10. *Export to DXF or STL*

We will return to working with SketchUp later in this book, but for now we are simply using the application to convert the model we downloaded from one file format to another. The Export to DXF or STL plug-in will let you export a part of the model or the entire thing and choose the format to export it in and the units of measure for the final file, with millimeters or centimeters being generally good units for export depending on the size of your file.

Because models in SketchUp are generally made at a very large scale, it might be necessary to further scale the model in a program like ReplicatorG (`http://replicat.org`), introduced in Chapter 2 and shown here in Figure 4-11, or Pleasant3D (`www.pleasantsoftware.com/developer/pleasant3d`), a Mac-only application for viewing and scaling STL files.

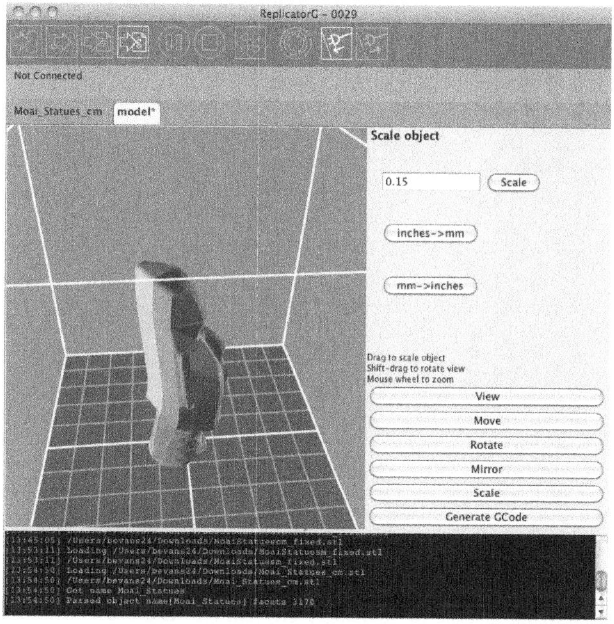

Figure 4-11. Scaling a file in ReplicatorG

To scale a model using ReplicatorG, you simply need to open your STL file, click the Scale button, and enter a value to scale the model by. It might also be a good idea while you are there to click the Move button ➤ Center ➤ Put on Platform. With that done, we are almost ready to print; but we have one more thing to do and that brings us back to the cloud.

Using netfabb to Repair STLs

When exporting a file from SketchUp, you'll often find that there are problems with the file when it is loaded into your printer's software that might prevent it from printing correctly. To proactively fix any of these potential problems, we can use the free, web-based utility called netfabb Cloud Service (http://cloud.netfabb.com), shown in Figure 4-12.

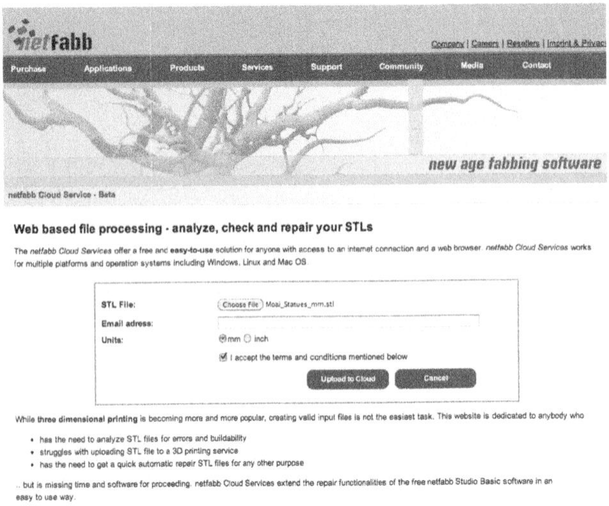

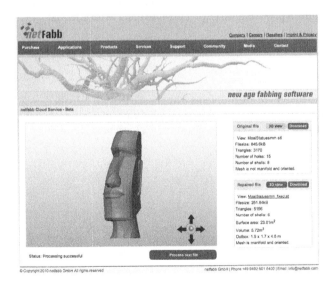

Figure 4-12. netfabb Cloud Service

To use netfabb Cloud Service, you just need to upload an STL file to be processed, enter your e-mail address, choose a unit of measurement (usually millimeters), agree to the terms, and click the Upload to Cloud button. netfabb's custom software will take over from there, cleaning the file, making the file a single-manifold polygon, and repair any holes in the mesh. When everything is done, you can view the repaired 3D model, as shown in Figure 4-13.

Figure 4-13. Processed 3D model

When the file is done, you will be given a summary of the results of the processing. Generally, but not always, the finished file will be smaller in file size, however what you really want to see is the statement "Mesh is manifold and oriented." Once you download the repaired file, you are ready to print!

If everything prints successfully, with the finished object in your hand (as long as it is permitted by licensing), you should take a good photo of it and upload this file to Thingiverse to allow others to easily print this model on their 3D printers (see Figure 4-14).

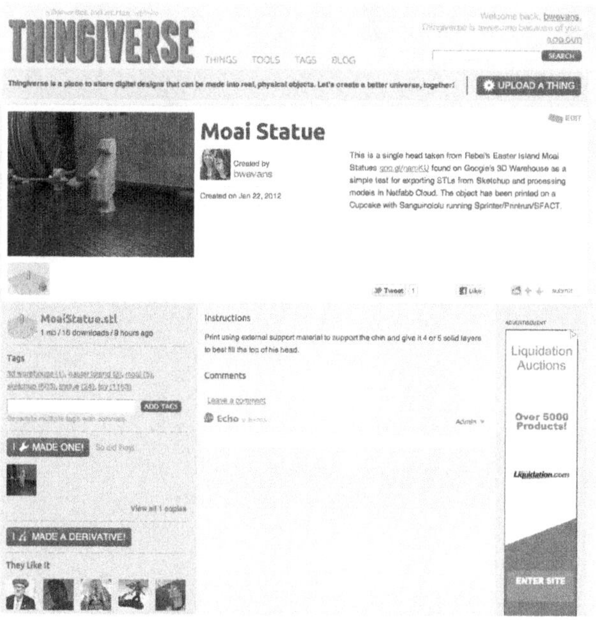

Figure 4-14. Completed thing from SketchUp

After converting a file from the native format of Google SketchUp to an STL suitable for 3D printing, scaling and repairing the finished STL, and then uploading the model design to Thingiverse, we have now successfully posted a new thing. Remember, if you're posting a derivative such as this to Thingiverse and using a file originally obtained from another source, be sure to include the original author and the URL for the original design in the description of your new thing.

From here, let's see how we can use the cloud to make new models—rather than simply finding and sharing them—beginning with some really fun web-based 3D modeling applications, specifically 3DTin and Tinkercad.

Introducing Web-based Solid Modeling

With the advent of WebGL and HTML5, it's now possible to have some fairly powerful 3D modeling applications for creating new designs from scratch that are solely web-based and run entirely in your browser window. In this section of the chapter, we will quickly introduce a couple of applications in this new crop of 3D modeling tools. The first of these applications that we will look at is 3DTin, which has garnered the cornerstone on blocky, 8-bit video game–inspired 3D modeling.

3DTin

Started by Jayesh Salvi, a software engineer based in India in early 2011, 3DTin is first and foremost a voxel, or volumetric-pixel modeling application. This means that you can quickly build an object using simple little blocks, or 3D pixels. All you need to do is fire up the latest version of Google Chrome, Mozilla Firefox, or other WebGL-compatible browser and head to www.3dtin.com. The basic interface for 3DTin is shown in Figure 4-15.

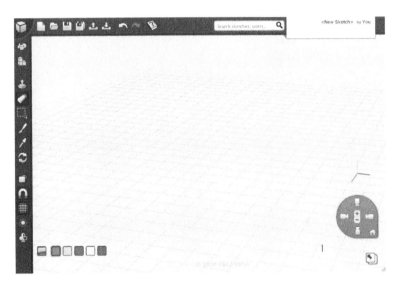

Figure 4-15. 3DTin web-based solid modeling

3DTin's interface is about as minimal as it gets. At the center of the 3DTin window is the workplane, which serves as the place to build your drawing. It has a grid that can be turned on or off using the lower toolbar to the left. In the primary toolbar in the upper-left side of the window, are a collection of tools that we can use for drawing new designs (see Figure 4-16).

ADD GEOMETRIES

ADD CUBES

EXTRUDE

ERASE

SELECT

CHANGE COLOR

PICK COLOR

VIEW ROTATE

Figure 4-16. 3DTin primary toolbar

Moving from the top to the bottom, we have tools for adding limited, predefined geometries—like tubes, pyramids, and cones—to our drawing; the main drawing tool for adding and drawing with cubes; an extrude tool; an eraser; a selection tool; a tool to change the color of an object and one to pick a color; and finally, a tool to pan and rotate the view of the workplane. Along the top edge of the 3DTin window is the file menu, which includes options for starting a new project, opening files, saving, exporting and importing drawings, and the usual undo, redo, and help.

To start drawing with blocks in the modeling space, pick the Add Cubes tool from the left tool palette (the icon of three blocks) and off you go. As you lay down cubes in 3DTin, you need to at least start by stacking blocks on top of one another, beginning with blocks that touch the gridded plane. If for example, you are trying to space blocks over one another with a gap in between, you will need to first build blocks in that area, layer by layer, from the bottom up, and then delete the extra cubes when you have a layer on top, as shown in Figure 4-17.

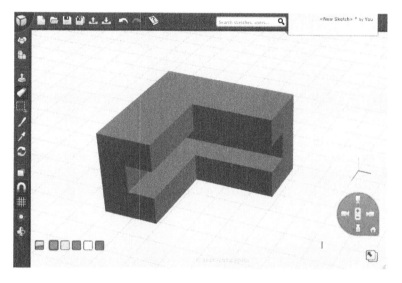

Figure 4-17. *Building forms in 3DTin*

Beyond this, 3DTin is a very simple and intuitive application for creating 3D models. We will further discuss working with 3DTin later in this chapter when we use its blocky aesthetic to build up our first project. For now, let's have another brief introduction to one of the latest web-based modeling applications, Tinkercad.

Tinkercad

Tinkercad is a Finland-based start-up cofounded by programmers and game developers Kai Backman and Mikko Mononen. Even though Tinkercad is another WebGL-based solid modeling application, it differs significantly from 3DTin in its greater diversity of shapes and the ability to add and subtract shapes from one another, allowing for some fairly complex 3D models to be created. Despite the added capabilities, Tinkercad's interface, shown in Figure 4-18, remains fairly simple and straightforward.

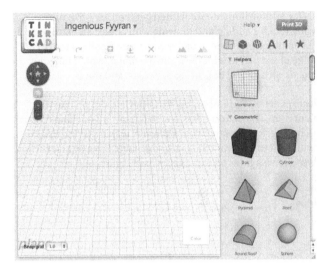

Figure 4-18. Tinkercad web-based solid modeling

In the center pane is the gridded workplane, where 3D models will be drawn. On the right side of the Tinkercad window are a selection of premade geometries or shapes that can be placed into the drawing simply by dragging and dropping the desired shape. Figure 4-19 shows a box being placed into the workplane.

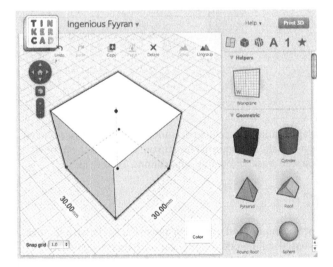

Figure 4-19. Tinkercad box geometry

Unlike 3DTin, where once a geometry has been made it stays that way, once a basic shape has been dropped into the workplane in Tinkercad, it can be adjusted using any of a number of handles that become apparent when the object is selected. By holding down the Shift key while clicking and dragging the handle at the lower-central corner of the box, the shape can be scaled to a desired size while retaining the same dimensions on all sides. To rotate a shape, simply click and drag the arrow-shaped handles that correspond with the axis of rotation, as shown in Figure 4-20.

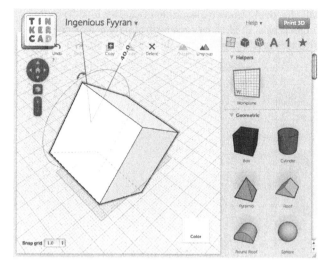

Figure 4-20. *Rotating a shape*

While rotating an object, Tinkercad displays the angle of rotation just as it showed the dimension of the box when enlarging it. Any of the geometries provided can be freely rotated along each of the three axes. While rotating the shape, its outline will be shown on the workplane to allow for precise alignment with other shapes. Working with multiple shapes is where Tinkercad significantly diverges from 3DTin, specifically in the ability to subtract one shape from another, as shown in Figure 4-21.

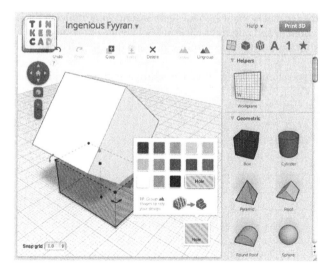

Figure 4-21. *Subtracting one shape from another*

In this example, a second box is used to flatten the corner of the first box that extended below the workplane in our rotation earlier. To perform this operation, place the second box below the workplace and size it appropriately. To subtract it from the first object, select the box to be subtracted, and choose the translucent striped color labeled Hole in the color palette. This will effectively remove the corner of our first box. To see the finished form, however, you will need to select both objects by shift-clicking each form and then clicking the Group icon at the top of the window. It is possible to create some complex forms through these relatively simple operations, as shown in Figure 4-22.

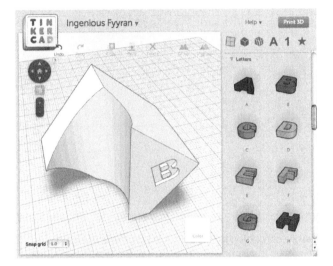

Figure 4-22. Complex forms in Tinkercad

In this example, we have further removed a cylindrical space from another corner of our first box and even subtracted a three-dimensional letter B from its side. This shows some of the additional shapes available to Tinkercad, such as letters, numbers, symbols, and other complex shapes. To navigate around your model in the workplane, use the mouse or track pad and scroll to zoom in and out, right-click and hold while dragging the mouse to rotate the workplane, and finally hold the shift key down while right-clicking and dragging to move the view to a new position.

Once your design is finished to your satisfaction, you should save it. Then it is a simple matter to prepare the file for 3D printing, as shown in Figure 4-23.

Figure 4-23. *Print 3D dialog box*

By clicking the Print 3D button in the top-right corner of the Tinkercad window, the Print 3D dialog box will appear. From this window it is possible to send your design to one of a couple 3D printing service bureaus or, more importantly for the purpose of this book, download the finished model in a format for 3D printing using the Download STL button. Tinkercad has been extremely reliable with the quality of its models, so once you have your STL saved to disk, feel free to send it to your 3D printer and see how it comes out.

So that's a fairly brief introduction to two of the major, web-based, solid modeling applications available for use today. Let's use one of them for a keepsake project to see how we can design something from scratch for our 3D printer.

Project: Alien Invaders

The newest version of Tinkercad is decidedly pretty cool, but there is no denying the simple, 8-bit charm of 3DTin. For this project, let's revisit our first web-based solid modeling application and put it to use at what it does best: making some 8-bit 3D icons. When I think about the 8-bit aesthetic characterized by early video games, I can't help but think of one particular game of alien invaders from the days of the early Atari, made popular recently by a fairly prolific street artist with a similar name.

Let's bring back 3DTin to start drawing up some alien invaders of our own suitable for key chains, pendants, or who knows what else.

Drawing with Cubes

While we can draw with cubes with any of the applications that we use in this book, 3DTin is really good at it. 3DTin allows us to quickly draw something up so that we can spend less time drawing and more time printing. The tool that does this is the Add Cubes tool; it is shown in Figure 4-24 being put to use making the basic shape for our first invader.

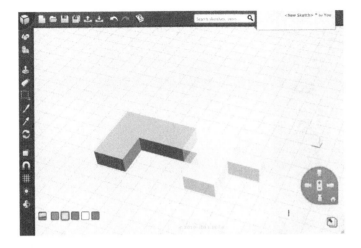

Figure 4-24. Drawing with cubes

With the draw tool, you can place cubes anywhere on the workplane by clicking an empty space, so long as the cube is flat against the workplane or on top of an existing cube. If you click and hold while drawing with the mouse, this will draw one continuous shape made of smaller cubes, as shown in Figure 4-24. While drawing with cubes, the color selected will appear translucent until the mouse button is released, at which time the color becomes solid. As long as Snap to Grid is on, each cube placed on the workplane beside another cube will result in one solid object. This way you don't need to worry that you might be creating a tiny little gap that would create printing problems later. If you accidently draw over a space or need to delete cubes later, you can use the Erase tool (see Figure 4-25).

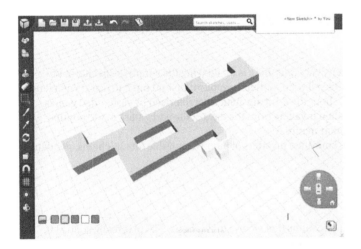

Figure 4-25. Erasing cubes

With the Erase tool selected, when the cursor hovers over any existing cube, that cube will be outlined in red. Clicking this cube will erase it from the drawing, turning it translucent until you release the mouse button, when the cube disappears.

Extruding Shapes

With the basic design drawn out to one layer of thickness, it is possible to extrude the form in one operation to give it more thickness, as shown in Figure 4-26, without needing to manually draw a whole bunch of cubes.

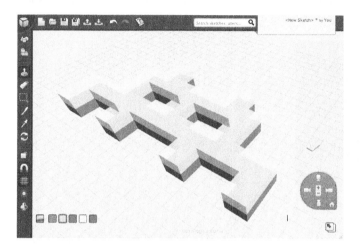

Figure 4-26. Extruding shapes

To extrude our flat drawing, select the Extrude tool from the menu and hover the cursor over the top surface of our design. If you have selected the correct layer, a new layer above it should appear in the same translucent color as when we were drawing with cubes. By clicking the mouse, 3DTin will make this layer solid, effectively doubling the thickness of our drawing. Clicking the surface a few times will give us a reasonable thickness for printing, as shown in Figure 4-27.

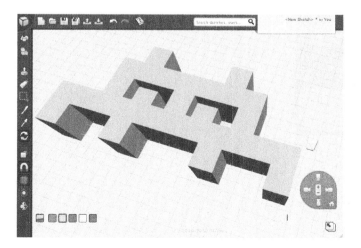

Figure 4-27. Finished alien invader

After making the model a little thicker and adding some eyes at a different layer height just to give it some dimension, we are now finished with our first invader. Now that the design is done, we need to save the design, export the model to a file format that we can print, and send it off to our printer.

Saving and Exporting an STL for Printing

To get our newly created alien invader to our printer and into our hands, we need to export the model to a file format suitable for 3D printing, in this case an STL. First, we need to click the Save button in the top file menu to save the file and either choose a license or save it privately (if you upgraded to the premium version) and add any tags to the file (see Figure 4-28).

Figure 4-28. *Saving the Invader file*

With the file saved, we can then click the Export button in the file menu to bring up the Export dialog box, shown here in Figure 4-29.

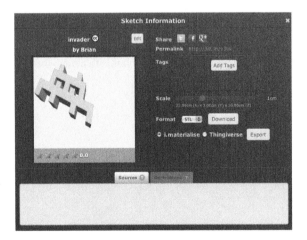

Figure 4-29. *Exporting an STL*

96

In this window we have the option to choose a file format from several options, although we are primarily interested in the 3D format STL. We can then choose a destination for the file, which includes downloading the file to our desktop, to send the file to the 3D printing service bureau i.materialise, or to send the file directly to Thingiverse. Before we upload our new design to Thingiverse, let's test the design first by downloading to our desktop and printing the model. To do this, click the Download button to process the file and when it's ready, hit the button Click to Download. This will download the file and we are ready to wrap things up.

Wrapping It Up

3DTin is the perfect application for that chunky, nostalgic, 8-bit look, and it allows you to quickly design some models for 3D printing. This type of modeling using solid geometries like cubes and cylinders is called *solid modeling* and is something we will use a lot of in this book. After drawing up a few more variations of our model and giving them a go on a 3D printer, we now have some alien invaders to show off, seen here in Figure 4-30.

Figure 4-30. Printed alien invaders

Congratulations, you have now designed some quirky 8-bit alien invaders to hang about the house. For these objects, we printed them one at a time with two perimeters, two solid layers, and a 20 percent infill using neon green ABS. Now that our models printed successfully and we know that our design is viable, we can go ahead and post our designs up on Thingiverse so others can make them or make derivatives from them.

Summary

In this chapter, we started with a working and properly calibrated 3D printer, and quickly moved into printing and sharing objects that we found and contributed to on the object sharing sites Thingiverse and 3D Warehouse. Continuing on with our theme of 3D models from the cloud, we briefly looked at two of the most popular web-based applications for 3D solid modeling: 3DTin and Tinkercad. These applications are great for their super-low learning curve, giving anyone elementary school–age and older access to simple tools for making 3D models. We even put one of these applications through the design process using 3DTin's clunky yet charming 8-bit aesthetic to make our own project from start to finish. We can now place these alien invaders on our bookshelf with pride as we continue onwards with a couple new applications for 3D modeling to expand our 3D printer toolbox.

CHAPTER 5

3D Haiku

When we teach fine art and design students at the college and university level, we often start with drawing or other 2D projects in the first year and then have to transition students to working three-dimensionally in projects that usually incorporate both 2D and 3D elements. In this chapter, we will do that very same thing beginning with one tool for making 2D drawings and bringing that drawing into a 3D solid modeling application to make our flat drawing come to life in three dimensions. For this project, we will start with some 2D drawings that use text that will be extruded and modified to make a 3D haiku, although you could use the same techniques for any vector drawing.

In this chapter, we are going to cover the following:

- Making a 2D image using the free and open-source application Inkscape

- Working with and exporting vector images

- Using the script-based application OpenSCAD for 3D modeling

- Extruding 2D images into a complex 3D model

By the end of this chapter, we will have moved from a simple 2D drawing to holding in our hands a 3D printed, text-based object. Let's get started.

Making a Vector Image

Our 3D haiku starts simply enough with making a 2D vector image. A vector image is an image created using mathematical paths to describe lines, curves, shapes, or polygons as opposed to a raster or bitmap image that is made up of thousands or millions of individual pixels. A vector image can be scaled with no loss of clarity while a raster image looses clarity at significant magnification. Figure 5-1 illustrates the difference between these two types of images under magnification.

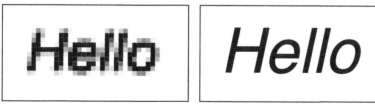

RASTER   VECTOR

Figure 5-1. Raster vs. vector image comparison

While raster images have their uses, for this project we need to work with vector images to create a 2D drawing that can be put to use by our 3D modeling application, OpenSCAD. To make this image, we will use the open-source vector graphics editor, Inkscape.

Working with Inkscape

Inkscape is an open-source vector drawing tool similar to Adobe Illustrator, CorelDraw, and others. It natively supports the Scalable Vector Graphics (SVG) format, and for our purposes can export drawings in Drawing Exchange Format (DXF), which can be used with our computer-aided design (CAD) program. If those are enough three-letter words for you, head over to the Inkscape web page and download the latest version of Inkscape for your computer platform at `http://inkscape.org/download`. Once downloaded and installed, open the Inkscape application, as shown in Figure 5-2.

Figure 5-2. *Inkscape new project*

Inkscape is a massive program that would take a book, if not several, just to discuss every feature. We're not going to do that here. Instead, we will look at just a few of the basic tools shown in Figure 5-3.

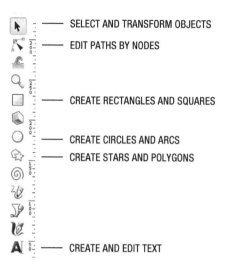

— SELECT AND TRANSFORM OBJECTS

— EDIT PATHS BY NODES

— CREATE RECTANGLES AND SQUARES

— CREATE CIRCLES AND ARCS
— CREATE STARS AND POLYGONS

— CREATE AND EDIT TEXT

Figure 5-3. Some of Inkscape's basic tools

Using just these basic tools, we can create a simple vector drawing that can be turned into a three-dimensional model using the process I will describe in a moment. Before we get to our project drawing though, let's see how these basic tools can be put to work.

Drawing Shapes with Inkscape

Let's start drawing in Inkscape with some basic shapes, as shown in Figure 5-4.

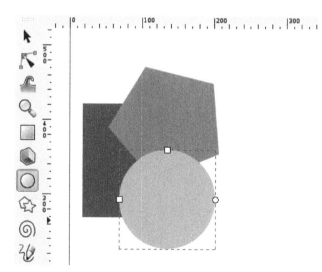

Figure 5-4. Drawing basic shapes in Inkscape

Using one of the several shape tools in the left-side toolbar, you can easily draw rectangles, ellipses, polygons, and spirals. If you hold down the Control key while drawing a rectangle, the shape will stay square with equal length sides; while likewise, an ellipse will become a circle. Shapes can be scaled and rotated by selecting the arrow tool in the toolbar, and then clicking on the shape to toggle the resize or rotate arrows. Simply click and drag the appropriate handle to scale or rotate the shape, as shown in Figures 5-5 and 5-6.

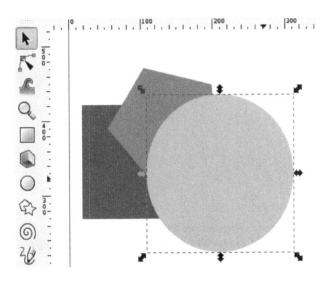

Figure 5-5. *Scaling shapes in Inkscape*

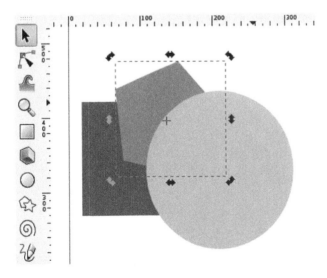

Figure 5-6. *Rotating shapes in Inkscape*

In this example, we actually have three shapes in the native Inkscape format stacked one on top of another. This will not work for our 3D modeling later in this chapter, so it's important to remember when designing a 2D drawing for this purpose that all of the shapes combined need to be one continuous path before proceeding. There are several ways to do this using a few of the built-in path operations.

Inkscape Path Operations

We want to take a drawing composed of multiple shapes stacked on top of each other and get it to work in our 3D modeling application. To make this compound shape workable, we need to perform one of several possible path operations. Path operations include functions to combine several individual paths, subtract shapes from one another, and create shapes from the intersection of two shapes. Specifically in Inkscape, these operations include union, difference, intersection, exclusion, as well as a few others. These tools can be found under the Path menu in the menu bar shown in Figure 5-7.

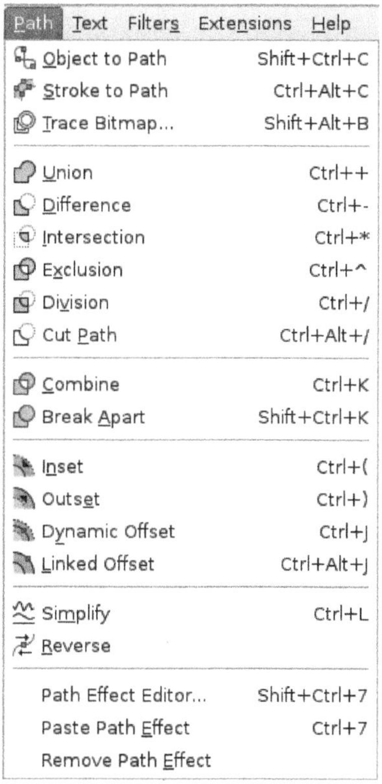

Figure 5-7. *Inkscape Path menu*

   Each of these operations has a particular effect on multiple shapes that have been selected with the selection tool. The shapes can be selected by click-dragging over multiple objects or holding down the shift key while clicking on the objects individually. Let's look at two of these operations, union and difference, just to get a feel for how they work. The union operation joins the paths of multiple shapes to create one continuous new shape, as shown in Figures 5-8 and 5-9.

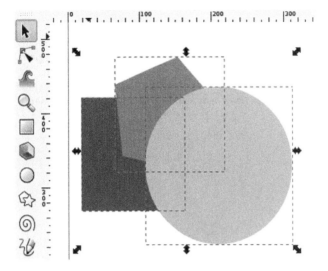

Figure 5-8. *Selecting multiple shapes*

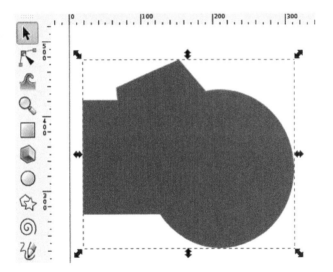

Figure 5-9. *Union of multiple shapes*

After selecting the shapes to be joined, use the Path ➤ Union operation to create one new shape that has the combined outline of all of the shapes selected. After the operation, you should be able to see that there is only one dotted-line box around the final form, rather than three. With a few more modifications, which we will look at later, this is one way for easily creating complex 3D forms in OpenSCAD. Rather than joining multiple shapes together, we can subtract one shape from another using the Path ➤ Difference operation shown in Figure 5-10.

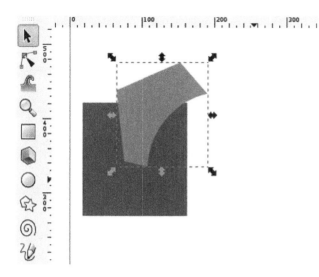

Figure 5-10. *Difference between two shapes*

The difference operation works by subtracting the topmost shape from the bottommost shape when two shapes are selected. In this example, we selected both the circle and the pentagon and, because the circle was on top, the difference operation removed the area where the circle overlapped with the lower pentagon. To raise or lower a shape, we need to select the object to be moved and then choose either Object ➤ Raise or Object ➤ Lower to change the order of the shapes either up or down, respectively.

Union and Difference are just two of the available path operations, and you should definitely play around with the others to see how they work. For now though, let's jump into how we can use text in Inkscape so that we can begin planning for our 3D haiku.

Working with Text

To begin working with text in Inkscape, all you need to do is select the Text tool from the toolbar (the big letter A icon), click any open space in the document, and then start typing. A simple text entry is shown in Figure 5-11.

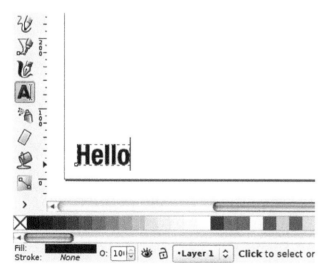

Figure 5-11. *Working with text*

105

Once you've entered your text, it can be modified by highlighting the text and using the text menu bar (see Figure 5-12).

Figure 5-12. *Inkscape text menu bar*

From this menu bar you can specify the font, size, bold, italics, justification, subscript or postscript, the leading (spacing between lines), and the kerning (spacing between characters). As you can see, using text in Inkscape is pretty much the same as any other program, but there are some things we can do with text in this drawing tool that are quite unique. To better explore some of the more advanced vector editing, let's jump into designing our project for this chapter in more depth.

Designing the 3D Haiku

The inspiration for this project came from what seems to be a common desire of those new to 3D printing: making 3D text. When I think of short yet beautiful sources for text, I think of haiku. There are some tricks and many different ways to incorporate text into a 3D model, but we are going to use a simple method involving a 2D image from Inkscape. For this project I wanted to use the following American-style haiku from the author and poet Jack Kerouac:

> *A bird hanging*
>
> *on the wire*
>
> *At dawn*

This short haiku was written some time between 1960 and 1966. I think it would be a lot of fun to give these few words a physical presence in 3D. Let's start by entering this haiku using the text tool in Inkscape (see Figure 5-13).

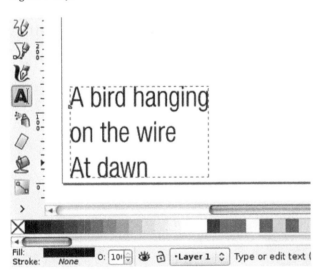

Figure 5-13. *Typing the haiku*

That's a start, but in order to give this project the best chance of printing, we need to give our text a little more presence through character weight and bring the spacing in a little tighter. After adjusting the font, kerning, and leading using the toolbar shown earlier in Figure 5-12 we end up with the finished text in Figure 5-14.

Figure 5-14. *Finished haiku text*

For this project, I'm using the font Helvetica Neue, although most of the sans serif fonts will more or less work just as well, including Helvetica, Arial, and Inkscape's Sans. For the rest of this project to work with the given values, your finished text block should fit to an area approximately 4¼ inches wide × 1¾ inches tall; or using Inkscape's default units of pixels, about 400 pixels wide × 175 pixels tall. Just remember that when we get to extruding the vector image later in OpenSCAD, you might need to adjust some of the values accordingly.

Now you might notice that I've placed the text in the lower left-hand corner of the document roughly at position 0,0. This will help us later on when we import this text into our CAD program. For now though, we've done all of these edits while the text remains editable text; but what we will want to do is actually convert our text into shapes. It's probably a good idea to hold off on that for as long as you can because once the text is converted, it becomes quite a bit harder to edit it. Now we are ready to prepare our file for 3D modeling.

Preparing the Vector Image

To prepare our drawing for 3D modeling, we will need to complete a few steps to use our vector image in our 3D modeling application. In this section, these steps break down into the following:

1. Convert shape objects and text to paths

2. Select all nodes of all paths

3. Insert new nodes into selected segments

4. Make selected segments lines

That might seem like a lot, but it's not too bad once you get the hang of it. Let's get started.

Converting to Paths and Working with Nodes

Our export of the 2D drawing will not work so well if we have text or the default Inkscape shapes still in the file. Instead, we need to select the text or shapes, if our drawing had them, and choose from the menu bar Path ➤ Object to Path. Now that won't be that impressive because it doesn't look like anything happened; however, if we zoom up on the letters, select the node selection tool from the toolbar, and then click one of the letters, we should see little gray boxes or nodes surrounding the perimeter of our letter (see Figure 5-15).

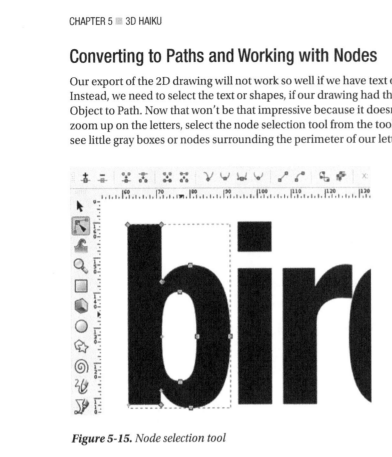

Figure 5-15. *Node selection tool*

These gray boxes show that our letter is now a path. If we then select all of the nodes by click-dragging a box around them with the shape still selected, we should see the gray boxes sprout little handles, as we see in Figure 5-16.

Figure 5-16. *Curved segments*

These little handles tell us that the shape is made from curves. If you wanted, you could grab the handles and change the curve of the shape. Unfortunately, the file type we need to place our drawing into does not support curved segments in a shape, and we will need to do something about that.

Converting Curves to Lines

To force our drawing to use straight lines instead of curves, we need to convert these curves into straight lines. To do this, we will be using two functions of the Nodes toolbar shown in Figure 5-17.

INSERT NEW NODES   MAKE SELECTED SEGMENTS LINES

Figure 5-17. Nodes toolbar

We could first try (with the nodes still selected) clicking the Make Selected Segments Lines tool in the menu bar shown in Figure 5-18.

Figure 5-18. Make selected segments lines first attempt

Well, that didn't exactly work as expected. Part of the problem is that curves are generally more efficient at describing a curvy shape like our letter b, so it needs only a few points. By converting our segments to straight lines, we actually need more nodes to make it look right. That way, with a lot more straight lines we can at least approximate a somewhat curved line. So, let's undo that last step and, with the nodes still selected, click the tool in the menu bar labeled Insert New Nodes Into Selected Segments (see Figure 5-19).

Figure 5-19. *Insert new nodes into selected segment*

You will actually need to click this button a few times to add enough nodes to make for a modestly round-ish shape. Don't go too crazy though because too many nodes will make things a little difficult later on. With the extra nodes in place, we can go back to make the selected segments lines (see Figure 5-20).

Figure 5-20. *Make selected segments lines second attempt*

Now that's pretty close to a rounded shape, but if you look closely, you'll see that the outline is just a collection of straight lines. Now we need to repeat that for each of the letters in our drawing. The quickest way to do that is with the node selection tool. Shift-click each of the rest of the letters to highlight all of the nodes, then click-drag to select all of the nodes in one big group to show the curved path. Then add nodes to the selected path and follow up with making those segments lines. With all of text convert to straight line–based shapes, it's now time to export our drawing as a DXF.

Preparing the File

After converting our text to straight-lined shapes, we should have a drawing that looks like Figure 5-21. We are now ready to export our drawing into a format that our 3D modeling application can use.

Figure 5-21. *Finished 2D drawing*

Setting Up Layers

To give us a little flexibility later on in this process, we need to move each line of the haiku to its own layer inside Inkscape. To do this we can start with the Layers palette (see Figure 5-22) by choosing Layer ➤ Layers... from the menu bar or hitting Shift+Ctrl+L.

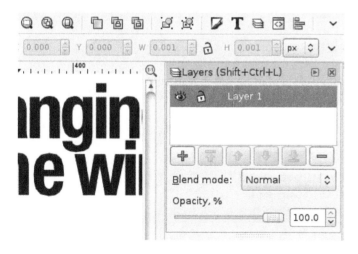

Figure 5-22. *Inkscape Layers palette*

To set up the three layers that we need for each line, we can start with renaming the first layer, Layer 1, to something like line1 by clicking the name of the layer and typing in a new name. Then we hit the + button in the Layers palette to open the Add Layer dialog box shown in Figure 5-23.

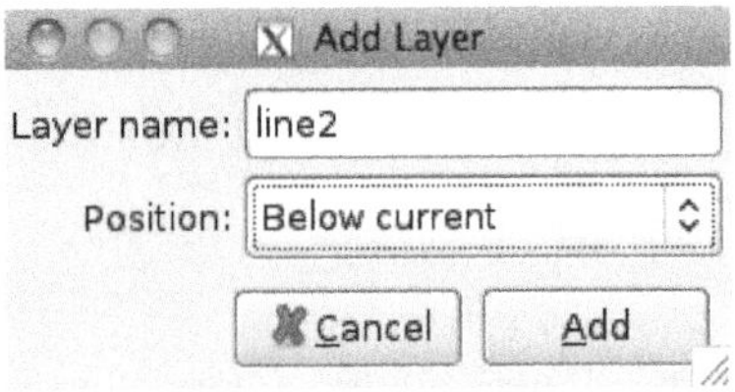

Figure 5-23. *Add Layer dialog box*

Choose line2 for the layer name and Below Current for the position. After repeating these steps for the next line3 layer, your finished layers should look like Figure 5-24.

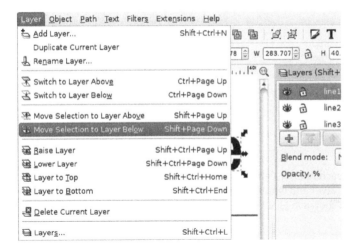

Figure 5-24. *Final three layers*

Now we need to move the second and third lines of our drawing to their respective layers. Select all of the shapes in the second line and then choose Layer ➤ Move Selection to Layer Below from the menu bar, as shown in Figure 5-25.

Figure 5-25. *Moving selection to layer below*

This step will need to be repeated again to move the third line all the way to the third layer, but when everything is set, we should have each line of text in its own layer. We are now ready to save the file.

Saving the File

The format for the finished file will be DXF, which is a format often used by CAD programs to layout 2D drawing files. You might even find designs on Thingiverse in DXF format designed for laser cutters or CNCs that through using the process in the rest of this chapter, you could convert to 3D printable objects. Before proceeding though, be sure to save the original drawing in Inkscape's native SVG format. This will allow you to go back and make edits later.

To save our drawing as a DXF, choose File ➤ Save As... from the menu bar, give the file a name (such as haiku.dxf), and then choose Desktop Cutting Plotter (R13) (*.dxf) under the file type drop-down menu. The Select File to Save To dialog box is shown in Figure 5-26.

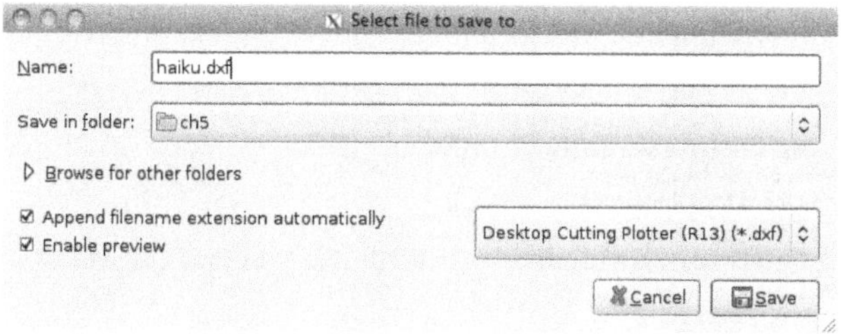

Figure 5-26. Inkscape's Save As... dialog box

With each line of text given its own layer and our drawing saved as a DXF file, we are now ready to fire up our 3D modeling application and make a 3D model.

Extruding a Vector Image

Up to this point, we have been working with the vector drawing application Inkscape to create a flat two-dimensional drawing that we could use as a basis for making a three-dimensional model. To do this, we've had to be careful about how we made our drawing and to save the drawing in a file format that we will be able to use. Now we are ready to have a look at our computer-aided design application, OpenSCAD, to create our final 3D model.

Working with OpenSCAD

OpenSCAD is a bit different from other solid modeling applications in that the visual tools and interactive modeling have been replaced with a script-like language that the application renders the 3D models from. With this powerful application, you design 3D models by writing simple scripts that allows the designer to create very accurate 3D models and even parametric designs that can be easily adjusted by simply changing certain parameters. OpenSCAD is a lot like C—although only in appearance—but it is so easy to pick up, even beginners can put it to use. It's also free and open source. The latest precompiled version can be downloaded from www.openscad.org. When installed and run for the first time, you should be presented with the minimalist interface shown in Figure 5-27.

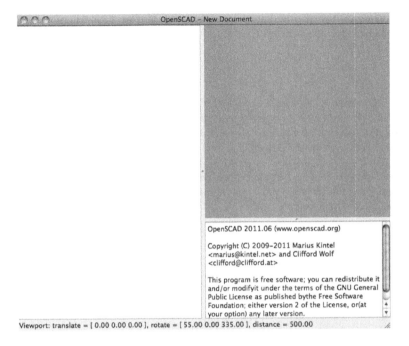

OpenSCAD 2011.06 (www.openscad.org)

Copyright (C) 2009–2011 Marius Kintel <marius@kintel.net> and Clifford Wolf <clifford@clifford.at>

This program is free software; you can redistribute it and/or modifyit under the terms of the GNU General Public License as published bythe Free Software Foundation; either version 2 of the License, or(at your option) any later version.

Viewport: translate = [0.00 0.00 0.00], rotate = [55.00 0.00 335.00], distance = 500.00

Figure 5-27. OpenSCAD new document window

Okay, there's not much there, but don't worry. Whereas other applications hit you with a wall of buttons and options, OpenSCAD's interface gives you an empty editing pane on the left, where you will write the script that becomes a model, a viewing area, and a terminal window. On the upper right is the viewing area where models are rendered. This area can be navigated with your mouse or trackpad, zooming in and out using the scroll wheel, click-dragging the model to spin it, and right-clicking and dragging to move the viewing position. The terminal window in the bottom right is used by the application to report errors, provide information about the model, or to display information that you build into the model script. With a few simple commands that you'll learn in this and the next couple of chapters, we will fill up that empty window with some fantastic 3D models.

Like Tinkercad from the last chapter, OpenSCAD is a solid modeling application that works with simple geometric primitives like cubes and cylinders. The objects can then be combined to or subtracted from each other to generate some fairly complex shapes. If you ever get stuck with something not explained in this book, or you are looking for more information, be sure to check out the OpenSCAD Manual at http://en.wikibooks.org/wiki/OpenSCAD_User_Manual. To start, let's look at how to make a few of the basic objects in OpenSCAD and some of the operations that we can perform on these objects.

Making Objects in OpenSCAD

Let's say that we want to make a simple cube that measures 10 millimeters on all sides. For this we will need to use the cube() module and type the following line of code in the editing pane:

```
cube(size=[10,10,10]);
```

To make a cube object with this module, we need to only specify the size of the cube in the three dimensions (x, y, and z) in millimeters. At the end of each call to a module like cube(), we need to place a semicolon to let the compiler know when that line has finished. Once our line of code has been entered, all we need to do is select Design ➤ Compile from the menu bar or hit F5 on the keyboard to see the finished object shown in Figure 5-28.

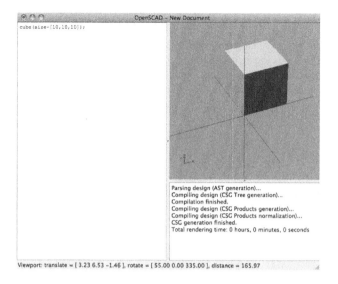

Figure 5-28. *A 10 mm cube in OpenSCAD*

And that's all there is to making a simple object in OpenSCAD. As you can see, the cube is drawn from the lower corner of the cube starting at 0,0,0. Let's now try a different module to make a cylinder 10 millimeters in diameter and 10 millimeters tall using this line of code:

```
cylinder(h=10, r=5);
```

With this module, we need to specify the height and the radius of the cylinder. And with that information entered into the editing pane in place of our earlier cube, and then compiled, we should end up with the shape shown in Figure 5-29.

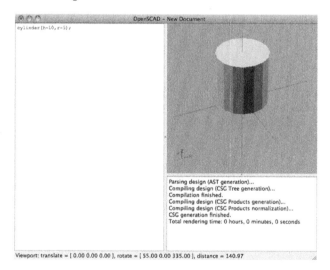

Figure 5-29. *A 10 mm cylinder in OpenSCAD*

As you can see, the cylinder is placed with the center of the circular face of the cylinder at position 0,0,0. With two simple shapes now under our belt, let's very quickly look at what happens when we add or subtract these shapes from one another.

Add and Subtract Objects

Most designs—even complex ones—that are made in OpenSCAD are generally made from the combination of many simple shapes like our cube and cylinder. Where this intrinsic capability comes from is in the use of Boolean operations to add or subtract objects using modules such as union() and difference(). Let's take a quick look at how these work, starting with adding two objects to make a new object we would use the union() function, like in the following example:

```
union() {
      cube(size=[10,10,10]);
      cylinder(h=10,r=5);
}
```

The union() module combines all of the objects inside its matching curly braces into one solid object, as shown in Figure 5-30.

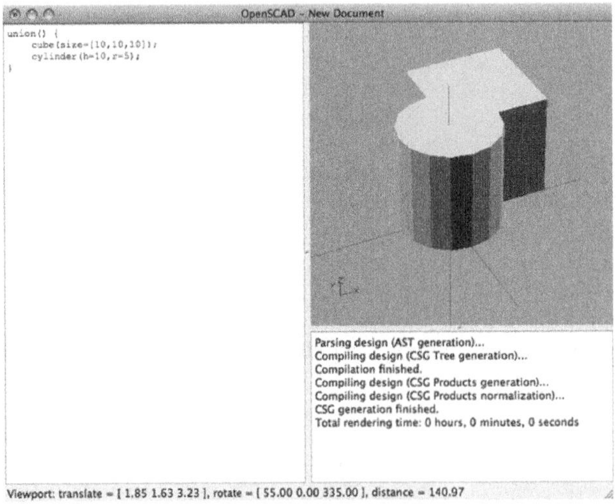

Figure 5-30. Adding a cylinder and a cube

The opposite module, difference(), subtracts all of the subsequent objects from the first object in the curly braces. In this case, we are removing the area of the cylinder object that overlaps with the cube from the cube to create a new object. Here's what the code looks like:

```
difference() {
      cube(size=[10,10,10]);
      cylinder(h=10,r=5);
}
```

The result of this operation will look like Figure 5-31.

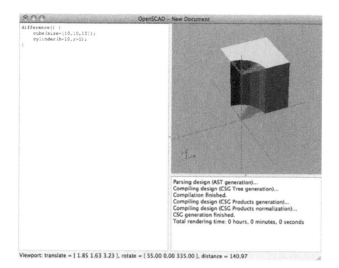

Figure 5-31. *Subtracting a cylinder from a cube*

It is important when using both of these modules and others like them to remember the opening and closing curly braces surrounding all of the objects to be included in the operation.

Move and Rotate Objects

So far in the few examples that we have looked at, we have simply left the objects right where OpenSCAD renders them. Invariably, you will need to move and rotate objects if you are going to model anything more substantial. To move our 10 mm cube 5 millimeters along the x- and y-axes, we would use the `translate()` module and specify the distance to be moved along any of the axes as follows:

```
translate(v=[5,5,0])
    cube(size=[10,10,10]);
```

All we need to do is tell the `translate()` module how far we want to move the following object in which vector along either the x-, y-, or z-axes by giving it a value in the order of x, y, z. In this case, we moved the cube 5 millimeters in the x and y direction and 0 in the z direction. You'll notice there is not a semicolon after the `translate()` module because the compiler needs to know which object to move. When this example is compiled, we end up with what is shown in Figure 5-32.

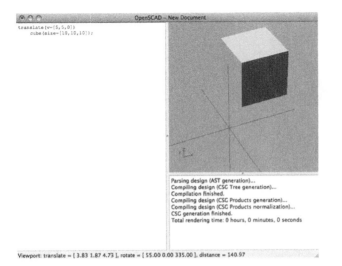

Figure 5-32. *Moving a cube with translate()*

Building on this, if in addition to moving the cube, we also wanted to rotate the cube 45 degrees along the y-axis, we could use the `rotate()` module, which works in a very similar manner. Take the following example:

```
translate(v=[5,5,0])
    rotate(a=[0,45,0])
        cube(size=[10,10,10]);
```

This example leaves us with a tilted cube, as shown in Figure 5-33.

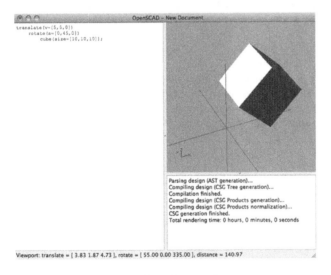

Figure 5-33. *Rotating a cube with rotate()*

All we need to do is specify the amount to rotate in degrees and along which axis to rotate. Like `translate()`, this line does not explicitly need a semicolon and it is possible to rotate in any direction along as many axes at once. With that said, it is possible to nest each of these functions inside matching curly braces—a useful trick for performing the same operation on multiple objects. For example, we could take our last object and rewrite it as follows:

```
translate(v=[5,5,0]) {
    rotate(a=[0,45,0]) {
            cube(size=[10,10,10]);
    }
}
```

Adding the curly braces like this will usually make your code easier for others to read and will often save some headaches when things don't work out right along the line. You will see several ways to write the syntax for 3D models when we get into OpenSCAD in much greater depth later on in this book, but for now we are going to bring things back to our 3D haiku project and look at how to transform our 2D drawing into a 3D model. As we continue our discussion of OpenSCAD, we will provide the code in a separate section and only show a screen capture of the actual model when something changes.

2D to 3D

The module we will be using to turn our 2D drawing into 3D is called `linear_extrude()`. Start a new OpenSCAD document and save it to the same folder where your DXF drawing was saved to earlier. Now enter the following code in the editing pane and compile to test things out.

```
linear_extrude(height=6, convexity=30) import(file="haiku.dxf", layer="line1");
```

You should end up with something like Figure 5-34.

Figure 5-34. Extruding the first line of our drawing

So what happened? In this example, we used the `linear_extrude()` module and specified the height in millimeters and the level of complexity of the model specified in terms of the convexity of the curved shapes. Next, we need to specify the 2D file to be extruded immediately following this module using the `import()` module. This will bring in the 2D file by specifying the file name of the DXF file, and the layer name to be extruded. When the line of code was compiled, OpenSCAD located our DXF drawing that we prepared earlier and extruded it to a height of 6 millimeters. Pretty cool, right? Now let's add the other two lines of our drawing and see what that does. The following is what the finished code should look like:

```
linear_extrude(height=6, convexity=30) import(file="haiku.dxf", layer="line1");
linear_extrude(height=6, convexity=30) import(file="haiku.dxf", layer="line2");
linear_extrude(height=6, convexity=30) import(file="haiku.dxf", layer="line3");
```

And when that is rendered, it should look like Figure 5-35.

Figure 5-35. *Extruded drawing*

And just like that, we have a finished 2D drawing that has been extruded into 3D, and all it took were three simple lines of code. The neat thing here is that because we kept each line of text in the right location when we moved them to their own layers, when we bring them into OpenSCAD they stay in the same position. Now, we could just call it a day there and try to give it a print, but I'd like to make things a little more interesting and in the process maybe increase our chances of successfully printing this model by making a few additions.

Making Things Interesting

If we were to run this design on our 3D printer right now, it would probably work but you might experience problems getting that many individual pieces to all stick to the platform and not move around during the printing. Likewise, each of the letters would be a separate piece, including the dots in the lowercase i's, which might make it difficult to do anything with this object when it's done printing. I think it would be a good idea to give it a little structure that links all the letters together in a way befitting our haiku. While we are at it, we might as well play with each line of the text to make the most use of designing an object in three dimensions. So, let's start by seeing what we can do if we experiment with extrusion heights and move the lines around a bit.

Moving and Rotating the Haiku

To start making things interesting, let's try tilting the lines of text at odd angles and give them some various heights. Changing the height of each line is pretty easy: all we need to do is change the 6 from the earlier code example to something different. To tilt each line though, we need to add a rotate() module to each line of code. Let's change the last example code to look like the following:

```
rotate(a=[-12,0,-4])
    linear_extrude(height=12, convexity=30) import(file="haiku.dxf", layer="line1");
rotate(a=[8,0,1])
    linear_extrude(height=8, convexity=30) import(file="haiku.dxf", layer="line2");
rotate(a=[10,0,6])
    linear_extrude(height=20, convexity=30) import(file="haiku.dxf", layer="line3");
```

To start with, we changed the heights of each line from 6 to 12, 8, and 20 for the first, second, and third lines respectively. Feel free to make these as tall or short as you wish. Next, we added a rotate() module before each of the lines that we started with, choosing some random values to spin each line of text around the x- and z-axes. Again, these values and axes were chosen simply at random to make something look neat—you should feel free to adjust at whim. One thing to keep in mind is that generally our DIY 3D printers don't handle massive overhangs very well, so it's a good idea to keep the rotation angles to less than 30 degrees. When this code is compiled, your model will look like that in Figure 5-36.

Figure 5-36. Rotated text

And with that, we've already made things a little more interesting by giving a bit of a lilting look suitable for a bird on a wire. If you spin the model around and look at the bottom side of our text, you'll see that unlike when we started, where each of the lines of text sat on the same horizontal plane, now all of the lines are floating in space. Clearly this is not 3D printable because we need a good, solid, flat surface to begin with. We will need to do several things to make this all work in the end, but for now we could begin with moving each of the lines of text, in part to make sure that they all stick below the horizontal plane (we will flatten this off later) and to make the text read better. Let's modify our code from before to include a translate() module for each line:

```
rotate(a=[-12,0,-4])
        translate(v=[-2,0,6])
            linear_extrude(height=12, convexity=30)
                import(file="haiku.dxf", layer="line1");
rotate(a=[8,0,1])
        translate(v=[-2,-1,-4])
            linear_extrude(height=8, convexity=30)
                import(file="haiku.dxf", layer="line2");
rotate(a=[10,0,6])
        translate(v=[-2,0,-5])
            linear_extrude(height=20, convexity=30)
                import(file="haiku.dxf", layer="line3");
```

Again, with just some random numbers to position each line so that they all extend below the horizontal plane and generally look good. We've also had to break up the lines a little bit just to try and make this code a little easier to read. This is not a problem, as OpenSCAD will simply ignore any white space or tabs. Now, compile the updated code; you should see that the lines are a lot closer at the bottom and make good contact with one another. This will help printing later. For now, you should have something similar to Figure 5-37.

Figure 5-37. *Moved text*

With our text now in a place that we are happy with, we will need to add a few things to help in printing the finished design.

Adding to Our Design

The first thing we need to do is to add something to our design that will make all of the individual letters one solid piece. This will help make printing the piece easier and it will make displaying it on our bookshelf that much easier too. Remember that for this design I am using the font Helvetica Neue with a finished vector drawing of roughly 4¼ inches wide × 1¾ inches tall. You might need to adjust these numbers as we add complexity to better fit your original drawing.

To make our design more printable, we could possibly add a simple, flat plaque that the text can sit on top of; but in the spirit of our haiku, it might be neat to add some 3D lines suggestive of wires in the background. I'm thinking a 4 mm × 4 mm box, as long as or a little longer than the text, should be enough to easily print and connect all the letters together. Maybe we could even add two of them at different angles crisscrossing through our haiku. After some playing around, we can add the following additional lines to our existing script:

```
rotate(a=[0,0,15])
    translate(v=[0,2,0])
        cube(size=[115,4,4]);

rotate(a=[0,0,-10])
    translate(v=[-6,40,0])
        cube(size=[110,4,4]);
```

With these 3D lines, I wanted to keep them flat against the horizontal plane but spin them about at somewhat random angles on the z-axis so that the lines link each of the letters together while still looking like a pair of power lines. When these lines of code are added to our existing sketch and recompiled, we should end up with Figure 5-38.

Figure 5-38. Added wires to our 3D haiku

Now, spinning our model around and having a closer look at things, you might notice that the dots in the top two lowercase i's are hanging out there as loose shapes. It might be nice if we could connect these somehow while still keeping the look of the letter. I'm thinking two small cubes that are the same thickness of the lowercase i's and tilted at the same angle and positioned just right so that they link at the base of the i but don't extend all the way to the top to keep it looking right. Let's add a few more lines of code to our model:

```
rotate(a=[-12,0,-4])
    translate(v=[24.625,38,+8])
        cube(size=[2.75,6,8]);
rotate(a=[-12,0,-4])
    translate(v=[82.75,39,+8])
        cube(size=[2.75,6,8]);
```

So these cubes are only 2.75mm wide—determined by tinkering with the model until it looked right—and each of them moved into position so that everything lines up. Now if we look at the model closely (see Figure 5-39), you'll see how we fixed this problem.

Figure 5-39. *Connecting the letter i with cubes*

We are almost there with our finished model. All that's left to do is to clean up the bottom of the model so that it is flat and printable. To do that we might need to restructure our code a little bit, so let's jump in.

Make Ready for Printing

To make this model suitable for 3D printing, we need to make sure the model has a flat bottom to print from. The most direct way I can think of to take care of this is to subtract the shape of a cube from the bottom of the model to make for a flat surface. In order to do this, we need to add all of the objects that we have made so far to create one solid object out of them using the union() module. With a little reshuffling of our spacing, our code should now look as follows:

```
union() {
      rotate(a=[-12,0,-4])
            translate(v=[-2,0,6])
                  linear_extrude(height=12, convexity=30)
                        import(file="haiku.dxf", layer="Line1");

      rotate(a=[8,0,1])
            translate(v=[-2,-1,-4])
                  linear_extrude(height=8, convexity=30)
                        import(file="haiku.dxf", layer="Line2");

      rotate(a=[10,0,6])
            translate(v=[-2,0,-5])
                  linear_extrude(height=20, convexity=30)
                        import(file="haiku.dxf", layer="Line3");

      rotate(a=[0,0,15])
            translate(v=[0,2,0])
                  cube(size=[115,4,4]);

      rotate(a=[0,0,-10])
            translate(v=[-6,40,0])
                  cube(size=[110,4,4]);

      rotate(a=[-12,0,-4])
            translate(v=[24.625,38,+8])
                  cube(size=[2.75,6,8]);
```

```
        rotate(a=[-12,0,-4])
            translate(v=[82.75,39,+8])
                cube(size=[2.75,6,8]);
}
```

Okay, nothing changed... yet. All the same, joining all of the objects together will let us now put the `difference()` module to use to make for a flat bottom. It might take some experimentation to find out the size of the cube we will need to use to do this and we will need to restructure our code a little more to place the `difference()` keyword at the top and to put the bottom of our model at the bottom of the code. Clear as mud, right? No worries. Let me show you the finished code in Listing 5-1.

Listing 5-1. Finished 3D Haiku Code

```
difference() {
    union() {
        // extrude inkscape vector drawing
        rotate(a=[-12,0,-4])
            translate(v=[-2,0,6])
                linear_extrude(height=12, convexity=30)
                    import(file="haiku.dxf", layer="Line1");

        rotate(a=[8,0,1])
            translate(v=[-2,-1,-4])
                linear_extrude(height=8, convexity=30)
                    import(file="haiku.dxf", layer="Line2");

        rotate(a=[10,0,6])
            translate(v=[-2,0,-5])
                linear_extrude(height=20, convexity=30)
                    import(file="haiku.dxf", layer="Line3");

        // add the lines across text
        rotate(a=[0,0,15])
            translate(v=[0,2,0])
                cube(size=[115,4,4]);
        rotate(a=[0,0,-10])
            translate(v=[-6,40,0])
                cube(size=[110,4,4]);

        // connect the dots in the i's
        rotate(a=[-12,0,-4])
            translate(v=[24.625,38,+8])
                cube(size=[2.75,6,8]);
        rotate(a=[-12,0,-4])
            translate(v=[82.75,39,+8])
                cube(size=[2.75,6,8]);
    }

    // make a smooth bottom surface to print from
    translate(v=[50,50,-50])
        cube(size=[200,200,100], center=true);
}
```

There we have it: the finished code for our 3D haiku model. Writing code to make a 3D model might look a little intimidating here, and it can be a little hard to get used to at first, but just remember that we built this model up object by object to accomplish the finished design. The cube that we added in the final code is found at the end of this listing to make a smooth surface to print from. It needed to be as big as the entire model area and be positioned below the horizontal plane. To accomplish this, we started the cube at 50 millimeters in the x, 50 millimeters in the y, and –50 millimeters in the z to position the cube somewhere in the middle and below the design. Then we made a cube 200 mm square and 100 mm tall and set center=true to draw the cube from the center of the shape. This way, any part of our model that extended below the horizontal line was removed creating a nice, flat surface to work from.

In addition to spacing things out a little, we also used line comments to identify what each section of our code does. Line comments begin with a double forward slash like so:

```
// This is a line comment
```

Anything after the // is ignored by the compiler for the remainder of that one line. This let's us place all sorts of important information into our code so that others can see why we did what we did, which includes our future selves. The nice thing about comments are that the do not affect our model at all—they exist in the code purely as commentary.

So far, when we compile our script, we only get a very simple, but quick preview of the finished model in the preview pane. At some point when our model is done, or to get a better rendering of it in progress, what we actually need to do is fully render the model using the option in the menu under Design ➤ Compile and Render or F6 on your keyboard. This takes a little longer to complete, which is why I don't often use it unless I absolutely need to, but it is essential for a better view of the finished model. It is used in the next step to prepare the file for 3D printing. For now, when you hit Compile and Render, your finished model should look like Figure 5-40.

Figure 5-40. *Finished 3D haiku model*

Okay, one last thing. We need to prepare our model for 3D printing. After we have compiled and rendered our model, all we need to do is head to the menu and choose Design ➤ Export as STL..., then name your file and location, and save the file. That's it! Open the finished STL in your printer software, slice the model, and get printing.

Wrapping It Up

I know that OpenSCAD can be intimidating at first, but it is really not all that bad and look what we made with it. When printing our model, it is important to check that you have a really flat and level print bed because the model is so large, being off even a little bit will affect the printed object. The finished printed model is shown in Figure 5-41.

Figure 5-41. *Finished 3D haiku print*

This level of complexity might give your 3D printer some difficulty with getting into the really fine detail stuff, but try a few settings first to see what works best. DIY 3D printers have come a long way and you'll see on modern printer designs that challenges like stringy prints and inaccurate positioning start to go away. For this print, I printed the model with two solid layers on the top and bottom, one perimeter, and 20 percent infill using silver-gray PLA plastic. It might also be helpful to print designs of this complexity at a slightly slower speed to increase accuracy.

Summary

Now we've really got the ball rolling with doing something on our 3D printer. In this chapter, we started with a simple 2D vector drawing that we made in Inkscape and turned it into a 3D model in our second project, jumping headlong into designing a new object using OpenSCAD, the script-based solid modeling computer-aided design application. This technique can be really helpful for creating tricky or intricate models that would start to get tedious if made with just cubes and cylinders alone. In this way, you can draw the basic outline of a complex shape and simply extrude it to the dimensions needed. Hang on, though, because we're not done with OpenSCAD yet. For our next project, we are going to get pretty ambitious and make a nice big multipart Victorian steampunk warship. I mean, really, we all need our own warship!

CHAPTER 6

■ ■ ■

Steampunk Warship

In the last chapter, we got a little taste for solid modeling using geometric primitives in the open-source computer-aided design package OpenSCAD, a surprisingly versatile tool for 3D modeling. I am aware that working only with geometric primitives might sound, well, primitive, however, with these simple forms we can build up some rather complex 3D models. In this chapter, I hope to convince you of the utility of script-based modeling with geometric primitives as we pick up a few more OpenSCAD techniques while making a fully parametric design. And what better way than to make a model of a steampunk warship—specifically the *HMS Thunder Child* from H. G. Wells' *The War of the Worlds*.

In this chapter, we will accomplish the following:

- Learn several intermediate techniques for working with OpenSCAD

- Make a new design that is fully configurable with a few key parameters

- Develop a complex model through the use of simple geometric primitives

- Prepare the model, then print and assemble a finished project using multiple parts

To get started, let's open OpenSCAD once again and quickly look at a few of the intermediate techniques that we will use in this chapter.

Intermediate OpenSCAD Techniques

The last time we used OpenSCAD, we looked at some of the basic forms that can be made using it. We also discussed how to simply modify these forms by moving, rotating, adding, and subtracting them. Before we get to modeling our steampunk warship, let's looks at a few more OpenSCAD techniques, beginning with how variables are used.

Variables

There are a lot of similarities between the style of OpenSCAD's language and the C computer programming language. For the most part, these are only cosmetic similarities. For example, variables are often used in C to store data that may change during the course of the codes operation. Variables in OpenSCAD are a little different, specifically because they are processed when the code is compiled, as opposed to during runtime.

In fact, variables in OpenSCAD are more like convenient labels that help us humans understand what is going on in any one model. The following example shows how variables are declared:

```
filament_dia = 1.7;
```

In this example, taken from our upcoming project, we have declared a variable named filament_dia and assigned this variable the numerical value 1.7. Now, whenever we use this variable name in our code, the value assigned to the variable will be substituted when the model is compiled. Variables can also be used for a tricky mathematical expression. Take the following example:

```
printbed_max = sqrt(pow(printbed_w,2)+pow(printbed_d,2));
```

In this case, I wanted to figure out the maximum diaganol length across my printer's build platform. I knew the width and depth of the platform, and I also knew that the product of two sides of a triangle equals the square root of the hypotenuse. So using the equation of a2 + b2 = c2, I could figure out the diagonal of the platform. By using OpenSCAD's sqrt() and pow() functions to calculate the square root and product of an integer to a power, respectively, I can use the variable printbed_max to perform a one-time calculation that I can also use elsewhere in my model.

Using variables in our script for common values that we often need to use helps make the script more readable, troubleshooting our model easier, and gives others an idea as to what our code does.

Special Variables

Special variables represent a few features that can be reconfigured in OpenSCAD relating to the way that circles and arcs are rendered. There are three special variables that we will use in our model; each begin with the symbol $.

$fn

$fn is a special variable to set the number of facets used in a circle or cylinder. For the most part, we will leave this set at 0; however, it can be quite useful for creating other polygons, like hexagons. For example, if we were to make a cylinder with $fn set to 6, like so:

```
cylinder(h=10,r=5,$fn=6);
```

This line will generate a hexagon that is 10mm high with a radius of 5 millimeters, as shown in Figure 6-1.

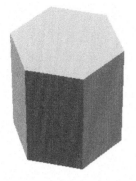

Figure 6-1. *Using cylinder() to make a hexagon*

■ **Tip**   To make a space for a captive nut in your design, divide the width of the nut by the square root of three, using a cylinder with six facets. For example, an M3 nut is 2.4mm thick and 5.5 millimeters across its flats, so we would use the line `cylinder(h=2.4,r=5.5/sqrt(3),$fn=6);` to make a hexagon the same size as an M3 nut.

$fa

The special variable $fa is not as useful as the other two. It determines the minimum angle used to render any fragment. We will keep this to the minimum value of 0.01.

$fs

To set the minimum size of a facet, we can use the $fs special variable. This is especially useful in setting the number of facets (or the smoothness of all curves) globally by disabling $fn and $fa at the beginning of our code. To do this, I generally use the following block of code in all of my designs:

```
// disable $fn and $fa, do not change these
$fn=0;
$fa=0.01;
// use $fs to control the number of facets globally
// fine ~ 0.1 coarse ~ 1.0
$fs=0.3;
```

In this way I can set the quality of all of the curves in my model by adjusting the value for $fs, with 0.1 for fine and 1.0 for coarse. Even though $fn is set to 0 globally, any time I change the number of facets in a module, that module will override the global value.

■ **Note**   While it might work on some platforms, it's standard practice to always use leading zeros with decimal values as in 0.1 instead of .1.

The following two images demonstrate the difference this can have on curved objects. $fs is set to 0.1 in Figure 6-2 and it is set to 1.0 in Figure 6-3.

Figure 6-2. *$fs set to 0.1*

Figure 6-3. *$fs set to 1.0*

While it might be tempting to set $fs to 0.1 all the time, this will slow down rendering your model and make your object print slower. The trick is to find a suitable balance between your printing resolution and computer horsepower, or otherwise set this value high until you are ready to export the finished model and lower it at that time.

Strings

Every now and then, it might be helpful to receive feedback from the compiler about certain operations or other details about your model. To do this, we can use the echo() and str() functions.

echo()

This function can be used to send data back through the information window for debugging our code using both strings of text enclosed by double quotes and/or variables or values. Multiple items can even be used in one instance of the echo() function as long as they are separated by commas. For example, take the following:

```
echo("Hull length = ", shipscale,"mm");
```

This line will provide the following information:

```
ECHO: "Hull length = ", 121.421, "mm"
```

str()

To clean up our last example a little, we can use the str() function to first convert the echo() data into a string before displaying it; for example

```
echo(str("Hull length = ", shipscale,"mm"));
```

Will now give us the following:

```
ECHO: "Hull length = 121.421mm"
```

A simple addition, but it makes our feedback a little easier to read.

Modifiers

Modifiers are frequently used during the construction of a module to affect how an object or group of objects is displayed or treated. There are four modifier characters, each with their own specific purpose, of which we will begin with the background modifier.

Background Modifier

The background modifier, or % symbol, is placed before an object or group of objects to ignore that object in normal rendering and instead display that object in transparent gray when compiled. This can be especially useful for displaying objects that should be otherwise ignored because they are not expressly part of the model, like connecting parts, or for general troubleshooting. I often use this to display construction guides like the build envelope of the printer I'm designing an object for.

Let's look at the following script:

```
cylinder(h=10,r=5,center=true);
% rotate([0,90,0]) cylinder(h=10,r=5,center=true);
```

This creates two cylinders at right angles to one another. The first is the root object of the model with the second cylinder changed to transparent gray using the background modifier. The result is shown in Figure 6-4.

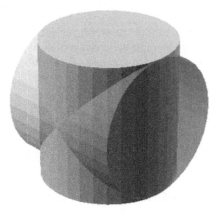

Figure 6-4. *Background modifier applied to secondary object*

Debug Modifier

Most commonly used with the difference() module, the debug modifier, or # symbol, displays an object in transparent pink. This object is included in the normal rendering process, which is quite useful for seeing negative shapes that you are attempting to subtract from another shape. Take the following example:

```
difference() {
        cylinder(h = 10,r = 5,center = true);
        # rotate([0,90,0]) cylinder(h = 10,r = 5,center = true);
}
```

This sample uses the difference() module to subtract the second cylinder from the first. In order to still see the full extent of the negative shape, use the debug modifier to see what is in Figure 6-5.

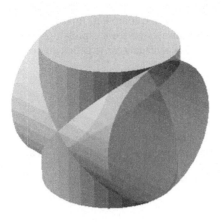

Figure 6-5. *Debug modifier applied to secondary object*

Root Modifier

The root modifier, or ! symbol, is used during troubleshooting to ignore everything but the object this modifier is placed in front of. This then makes the modified object the root object and displays only that one object. Let's take the following, for example:

```
difference() {
        cylinder(h = 10,r = 5,center = true);
        ! rotate([0,90,0]) cylinder(h = 10,r = 5,center = true);
}
```

By placing the root modifier in front of the secondary cylinder, the first cylinder is ignored and only the secondary cylinder is displayed. This can be helpful to better see an object you are working with before committing to certain changes.

Disable Modifier

Another useful modifier for troubleshooting, the disable modifier, or * symbol, ignores the following object and any transformations associated with it. Let's revisit our last example.

```
difference() {
        cylinder(h = 10,r = 5,center = true);
        * rotate([0,90,0]) cylinder(h = 10,r = 5,center = true);
}
```

By changing the root modifier to a disable modifier, we have reversed the end result and now only the primary cylinder will be displayed. This let's you disable a problem that an object and its transformations might extend across several lines.

Modules

Somewhat similar to functions in C, modules provide much of the flexibility and benefit of designing models through this script-based method. Essentially, modules can contain convenient and reusable chunks of code that can be used throughout your script. Modules are declared with the module keyword followed by a unique name, optional parameters to pass to the module, and a matching pair of curly braces. Take the following, for example, if we wanted to make a 10mm cube into a module to be repeated elsewhere:

```
module box() {
        cube([10,10,10]);
}
```

To use this module elsewhere in the code, we simply need to call it like other modules we have already used, as follows:

```
box();
```

While this example works, there might be times when we need a 20mm box instead. If we changed our module just a little, we could use a parameter to pass a value to the module. In the following example, we've added the parameter size:

```
module box(size) {
        cube([size,size,size]);
}
```

Obviously, in this example there are no preset values in the module. This way, when we call the module, all we need to do is give it the size that we want for our box, as follows:

```
box(20);
```

Now there is one last thing we can do with modules: pass a module multiple parameters, each separated by commas. For example, if we wanted to set the width, depth, and height of our box, we might do the following:

```
module box(w,d,h) {
        cube([w,d,h]);
}
```

So that when this module is called, we pass it three parameters instead of just one, like so:

```
box(10,20,15);
```

Now this is a fairly silly example because obviously, we already have the cube() module that does exactly this. But it does give you a sense for how to send specific values to a module to be reused. It is something we will use when we get to more of our project, which is right about now.

Designing the Steampunk Warship

For this chapter, it was important to have a project that gets us right into the thick of things with OpenSCAD in order to show how complex models can be made using simple geometric primitives. This project needed to be a multipart design to both use OpenSCAD's modules and to design something with interlocking parts. The design also needed to be parametric, meaning that the design could be easily adapted by changing a few key parameters, such as the build volume of your printer or the size of your printer's filament. So whether a reader wanted to make a steampunk warship or an obscenely practical part for an obscure vacuum cleaner, this chapter presents many useful tools for making a model of this complexity. I simply chose to go with the steampunk warship.

Not just any warship would do, though. I took as inspiration for this project a tiny passage in H. G. Wells' *The War of the Worlds* that describes a valiant warship that charged headlong into the invading Martian war machines to protect a civilian steamship. This ship was named the *HMS Thunder Child* and plays a brief, yet heroic part in the book.

> Big iron upperworks rose out of this headlong structure, and from that twin funnels projected and spat a smoking blast shot with fire. It was the torpedo ram, Thunder Child, steaming headlong, coming to the rescue of the threatened shipping.

Seeming like an appropriate challenge, I started my research for this project by looking at not only the few illustrations of this warship challenging the alien war machines, but I also looked at similar ships of the late nineteenth century, specifically the British torpedo ships. These ships were relatively small and sat low to the water. They were designed to sneak up on the enemy in the quiet of the night, and if things didn't go as planned with their short-ranged torpedoes, they would simply ram the opposing ship. These compact ironclad ships bristled with cannons of every caliber, and rising from their backs are two iconic smokestacks.

With our design settled on, it's time to start modeling it.

File Setup

To make the design parametric, we need to rely on variables and modules to make for a scalable project. For example, rather than trying to print little gun barrels, I decided to use short lengths of the same filament I print with as the barrels and masts of the ship. The challenge with that is that if you choose to print the design a little larger or smaller, it might throw off this critical measurement in our design. Instead, we can set up the file to determine the maximum print volume for us and scale our warship appropriately—keeping the size of the barrels the same diameter no matter the outside dimensions of the model.

As mentioned earlier, we start this project by setting the number of facets in our design globally at the beginning of our script.

```
// disable $fn and $fa, do not change these
$fn = 0;
$fa = 0.01;
// use $fs to control the number of facets globally
// fine ~ 0.1 coarse ~ 1.0
$fs = 0.3;
```

I've chosen 0.3 for the facet size special variable, $fs, as a reasonable compromise in detail and rendering speed. Next, we need to set the variables that we will use in the rest of our model.

```
filament_dia = 1.7; // used for cannon barrels
printbed_w = 100; // set to the width of your printbed
printbed_d = 100; // set to the depth of your printbed
printbed_max = sqrt(pow(printbed_w,2)+pow(printbed_d,2)); // calculates diagonal
shipscale = printbed_max-20; // shipscale should not exceed build platform size
```

We begin with a variable to set the filament diameter that we use with our printer. It's okay to round up, but don't make this value too large or your barrels won't fit in later. The variables printbed_w and printbed_d are the size of our printbed in millimeters. This is used in the next line to calculate the length of the diagonal across our printbed to set the maximum size of our model. Finally, the variable shipscale is used to make sure that our model comfortably fits within the print area of our printer and is used throughout our code.

We can use the echo() function to let us know the result of the calculations for ship length and ship width, as follows:

```
echo(str("Hull length = ",shipscale,"mm"));
echo(str("Hull width = ",shipscale/4,"mm"));
```

Now each time our script is compiled, we are given the following helpful reminder:

```
ECHO: "Hull length = 121.421mm"
ECHO: "Hull width = 30.3553mm"
```

Of course, the precise numbers depends on the actual values entered for the printbed, but this gives you an idea as to whether or not your design will fit the available print area. I sometimes get lost creating a ridiculous level of detail that has no hope of working on my printer; so I find this a much-needed reality check.

Setting Print Area

Another useful trick when designing a model is to give yourself some indication of the available print area. To do this, I often make a very thin cube the size of the print area and position it out of the way of my model. I place this after all of the variables and debugging statements are out of the way. For this model, I used the following line:

```
% translate([0,0,-5]) cube([printbed_w,printbed_d,0.5], center = true); // printbed
```

In this case, I simply set the cube to the width and depth of the printbed and chose 0.5 millimeters for the height. I also like to use the background (%) modifier to make this area a transparent gray. Finally, if this starts to annoy me, I use the disable (*) modifier to make this object go away while I'm working on something else.

Creating Modules

Now we are ready to call the root object of our model, which we will use for displaying each of the separate parts of our design. This module is simply named `warship()` and is called in our code, like so:

```
rotate([0,0,45])
warship();
```

The `rotate()` module is used just to make sure our warship fits on our build platform, although this only works for square printbeds. For a printer like the MakerBot Replicator with a 225 × 145 printbed, this module will need to be rotated 30 degrees instead of 45 degrees. We could, of course, rotate our model in our printer interface software, but this way it's built right into the design. To display the various parts of the warship, we need to create the basic structure for this module, as follows:

```
module warship(size = shipscale) {

}
```

For this module, we pass it the variable size, which is equal to the value of shipscale that we established earlier. This will be sent to each of the modules in turn later. Now as we add a module to our design, we can place it within the curly braces of the `warship()` module as we go along. Now that our model is all set up, let's look at the first of our shapes: the ship's hull.

Ship's Hull

For the ship's hull, I've decided to focus on the part of the hull that would be visible above water. The general shape was taken from several source photographs that show the aft of the ship mirroring the ship's bow. To make this shape, we can take the intersection of two large circles and stretch this shape a little to get our approximate dimensions. Let's start with the basic structure of the module and the first `union()` that we will need to join the shapes together.

```
module main_deck(hl) {
        union() {

        }
}
```

With this in place, we now have the structure that we will use as we construct the ship's hull. We will use the shipscale value in the variable named hl for hull length, which we can use to generate all of the sizes that we need. For example, if shipscale was equal to the value of 100, then hl / 2 would equal 50. We will need to modify the structure of this module as we develop it, but it works as a place to start. Now, let's look at the following `intersection()` module that we will use to start building the ship's hull:

```
module main_deck(hl) {
        union() {
                intersection() {
                        translate([0,hl*0.375,hl/100]) cylinder(h=hl/16,r=hl/2,center=true);
                        translate([0,-hl*0.375,hl/100]) cylinder(h=hl/16,r=hl/2,center=true);
                }
        }
}
```

The `intersection()` module keeps the central object formed by the common area of two overlapping shapes. This gives us the basic shape shown in Figure 6-6.

Figure 6-6. *Basic ship's hull form*

This gets us close to the basic shape of our ship's hull, but it would be better if we could stretch it out a little. To do that, we can add the `scale()` module in front of the `intersection()` code, like this:

```
scale([1.5,1,1])
intersection() {
        translate([0,hl*0.375,hl/100]) cylinder(h=hl/16,r=hl/2,center=true);
        translate([0,-hl*0.375,hl/100]) cylinder(h=hl/16,r=hl/2,center=true);
}
```

This will scale the x-axis by 150 percent and keep the y- and z axes at 100 percent so that when compiled with this little addition, we end up with a shape that looks more like a ship, as seen in Figure 6-7.

Figure 6-7. *Scaled intersection*

Hull Sides

When researching Victorian warships, a common feature of these vessels were side sponson turrets, which extended into projections on the sides of the ship's hull. To add these features, we can use the `cylinder()` module to create a cone and then stretch the cone a little, making it more suitable for a sleek warship. Our first sponson will be written as follows:

```
translate([hl/6.5,hl/12,hl/100]) rotate([0,0,-10]) scale([1.5,1,1])
cylinder(h=hl/16,r1=hl/38,r2=hl/18,center=true);
```

Here we are using `translate()` to move the cylinder so that the top surfaces align, and rotating it a little to make it better line up with the ship's hull. To make the cone, we simply need to add two different radiuses, labeled r1 and r2, to the `cylinder()` module. We have also added the parameter center = true to place our cylinder not at the center of the bottom surface, but instead at the middle of the cylinder. Again, all of the values that we are using here, as well in the rest of the model, are all based to one extent or another on the overall hull length established in the variable shipscale. Adding four of these cones will result in the following code:

```
module main_deck(hl) {
        union() {
                scale([1.5,1,1])
                intersection() {
                        translate([0,hl*0.375,hl/100])cylinder(h=hl/16,r=hl/2,center=true);
                        translate([0,-hl*0.375,hl/100])cylinder(h=hl/16,r=hl/2,center=true);
                }
                translate([hl/6.5,hl/12,hl/100]) rotate([0,0,-10]) scale([1.5,1,1])
                        cylinder(h=hl/16,r1=hl/38,r2=hl/18,center=true);
                translate([-hl/6.5,hl/12,hl/100]) rotate([0,0,10]) scale([1.5,1,1])
                        cylinder(h=hl/16,r1=hl/38,r2=hl/18,center=true);
                translate([hl/6.5,-hl/12,hl/100]) rotate([0,0,10]) scale([1.5,1,1])
                        cylinder(h=hl/16,r1=hl/38,r2=hl/18,center=true);
                translate([-hl/6.5,-hl/12,hl/100]) rotate([0,0,-10]) scale([1.5,1,1])
                        cylinder(h=hl/16,r1=hl/38,r2=hl/18,center=true);
        }
}
```

When this code is compiled, we should have a better idea about the shape of our model, as shown in Figure 6-8. While the code starts to add up in overall length, don't let that intimidate you—just remember to take this design process one module at a time.

Figure 6-8. *Completed sponsons*

Main Deck

With the basic shape of our hull roughed in, it's time to give it a little detail. If you look at most ships, they have a rail or side that extends up from the deck's surface. To make this in our model, we will need to subtract from the entire shape that we just made a second, smaller version of the same shape. To make this happen, we need to adjust the scale of the copied original shape and use the difference() module to subtract one from the other. We end up with the following modified script:

```
module main_deck(hl) {
        difference() {
                union() {
                        scale([1.5,1,1])
                        intersection() {
                                translate([0,hl*0.375,hl/100])
                                        cylinder(h=hl/16,r=hl/2,center=true);
                                translate([0,-hl*0.375,hl/100])
                                        cylinder(h=hl/16,r=hl/2,center=true);
                        }
                        translate([hl/6.5,hl/12,hl/100]) rotate([0,0,-10]) scale([1.5,1,1])
                                cylinder(h=hl/16,r1=hl/38,r2=hl/18,center=true);
                        translate([-hl/6.5,hl/12,hl/100]) rotate([0,0,10]) scale([1.5,1,1])
                                cylinder(h=hl/16,r1=hl/38,r2=hl/18,center=true);
                        translate([hl/6.5,-hl/12,hl/100]) rotate([0,0,10]) scale([1.5,1,1])
                                cylinder(h=hl/16,r1=hl/38,r2=hl/18,center=true);
                        translate([-hl/6.5,-hl/12,hl/100]) rotate([0,0,-10]) scale([1.5,1,1])
                                cylinder(h=hl/16,r1=hl/38,r2=hl/18,center=true);
                }
                union() {
                        scale([1.425,0.925,1])
                        intersection() {
                                translate([0,hl/2-hl/8,hl/14])
                                        cylinder(h=hl/12,r=hl/2,center=true);
                                translate([0,-(hl/2-hl/8),hl/14])
                                        cylinder(h=hl/12,r=hl/2,center=true);
}
```

```
        translate([hl/6.5,hl/12,hl/14]) rotate([0,0,-10]) scale([1.3,0.8,1])
                cylinder(h=hl/12,r=hl/18,center=true);
        translate([-hl/6.5,hl/12,hl/14]) rotate([0,0,10]) scale([1.3,0.8,1])
                cylinder(h=hl/12,r=hl/18,center=true);
        translate([hl/6.5,-hl/12,hl/14]) rotate([0,0,10]) scale([1.3,0.8,1])
                cylinder(h=hl/12,r=hl/18,center=true);
        translate([-hl/6.5,-hl/12,hl/14]) rotate([0,0,-10]) scale([1.3,0.8,1])
                cylinder(h=hl/12,r=hl/18,center=true);
            }
        }
}
```

In effect, we are subtracting (using the difference() module), two different complex shapes from one another, which were each added together using the union() module. And with that, we are almost done with the ship's hull; but we have a few more simple shapes to add. For reasons that become clear later, I want to place some holes in our ship's hull, which will be used to pin our turrets and midship together using 1.75mm filament. When we add these four extra lines into the code shown in Listing 6-1, we end up with our completed main_deck() module.

Listing 6-1. Completed main_deck() Module

```
module main_deck(hl) {
        difference() {
                union() {
                        // main deck basic form
                        scale([1.5,1,1])
                        intersection() {
                                translate([0,hl*0.375,hl/100])
                                        cylinder(h=hl/16,r=hl/2,center=true);
                                translate([0,-hl*0.375,hl/100])
                                        cylinder(h=hl/16,r=hl/2,center=true);
                        }
                        // side sponsons
                        translate([hl/6.5,hl/12,hl/100]) rotate([0,0,-10]) scale([1.5,1,1])
                                cylinder(h=hl/16,r1=hl/38,r2=hl/18,center=true);
                        translate([-hl/6.5,hl/12,hl/100]) rotate([0,0,10]) scale([1.5,1,1])
                                cylinder(h=hl/16,r1=hl/38,r2=hl/18,center=true);
                        translate([hl/6.5,-hl/12,hl/100]) rotate([0,0,10]) scale([1.5,1,1])
                                cylinder(h=hl/16,r1=hl/38,r2=hl/18,center=true);
                        translate([-hl/6.5,-hl/12,hl/100]) rotate([0,0,-10]) scale([1.5,1,1])
                                cylinder(h=hl/16,r1=hl/38,r2=hl/18,center=true);
                }
                union() {
                        // upper deck indention for side rail
                        scale([1.425,0.925,1])
                        intersection() {
                                translate([0,hl/2-hl/8,hl/14])
                                        cylinder(h=hl/12,r=hl/2,center=true);
                                translate([0,-(hl/2-hl/8),hl/14])
                                        cylinder(h=hl/12,r=hl/2,center=true);
                        }
```

```
            // indention for side sponsons
            translate([hl/6.5,hl/12,hl/14]) rotate([0,0,-10]) scale([1.3,0.8,1])
                    cylinder(h=hl/12,r=hl/18,center=true);
            translate([-hl/6.5,hl/12,hl/14]) rotate([0,0,10]) scale([1.3,0.8,1])
                    cylinder(h=hl/12,r=hl/18,center=true);
            translate([hl/6.5,-hl/12,hl/14]) rotate([0,0,10]) scale([1.3,0.8,1])
                    cylinder(h=hl/12,r=hl/18,center=true);
            translate([-hl/6.5,-hl/12,hl/14]) rotate([0,0,-10]) scale([1.3,0.8,1])
                    cylinder(h=hl/12,r=hl/18,center=true);
        }
        // filament pins
        translate([hl/3.5,0,0]) cylinder(h=hl/2,r=filament_dia*0.55);
        translate([-hl/3.5,0,0]) cylinder(h=hl/2,r=filament_dia*0.55);
        translate([hl/8,0,0]) cylinder(h=hl/3.5,r=filament_dia*0.55);
        translate([-hl/8,0,0]) cylinder(h=hl/3.5,r=filament_dia*0.55);
    }
}
```

When this module is compiled, we should end up with a pretty neat-looking foundation for our warship, as shown in Figure 6-9.

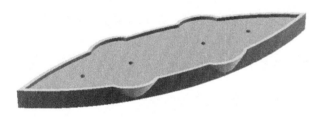

Figure 6-9. *Completed main_deck() model*

Now let's keep going by working on the midship() module next.

Midship

The midship forms the backbone of our warship and is the part of the model that connects the sponsons, towers, and bridge, as well as the smokestacks and vents. On many of these old warships, there were multiple smaller guns bristling over the sides of the ship. For this section, I want to put grooves in the side of the midship, which cannons can be mounted to, looking like seaborne pillboxes.

Sponsons

The sponsons are an easy enough place to start. These forms are simple cylinders, each with a horizontal groove across the face that the gun barrel extends from. Beginning with the module name and first object, we have the following chunk of code:

```
module side_sponson(ss) {
        cylinder(h=ss/1.25,r=ss/2);
}
```

Here we are passing the length of the ship that we are using as our ship scale to the variable ss to set the sponson size. This will result in a simple cylinder, so we need to add the slot for the barrel to give us the finished module in Listing 6-2.

Listing 6-2. side_sponson() Module

```
module side_sponson(ss) {
        difference() {
                // sponson
                cylinder(h=ss/1.25,r=ss/2);
                // gun slot
                translate([0,0,ss/2.75]) cube([ss/2,ss/2,filament_dia]);
        }
}
```

All we have done here is take the difference of a small cube that is as wide as the cylinder's radius and as tall as the filament diameter declared at the beginning of our code. This way, our filament barrels can be slotted into these groves and held in place. Figure 6-10 shows the result of the compiled code.

Figure 6-10. *Completed sponson*

To give us a little control on the finished size and location of this sponson, inside our warship() module we need to make multiple instances of the sponson, and then move and rotate them into position. Using the location of the sponsons on the hull as an approximate guide, the warship() module now looks like the following:

```
module warship(size=shipscale) {
        main_deck(size);
        translate([size/6.5,size/14,size/38]) rotate([0,0,0]) side_sponson(size/16);
        translate([-size/6.5,size/14,size/38]) rotate([0,0,90]) side_sponson(size/16);
        translate([size/6.5,-size/14,size/38]) rotate([0,0,-90]) side_sponson(size/16);
        translate([-size/6.5,-size/14,size/38]) rotate([0,0,180]) side_sponson(size/16);
}
```

This allows us to use the same sponson four times, move these sponsons to each of the four corners of the midship, and orient them to face the correct directions. We have also taken the size variable and divided it by 16 to make the sponsons a more appropriate size. When compiled (see Figure 6-11), we should have the beginning of our midship.

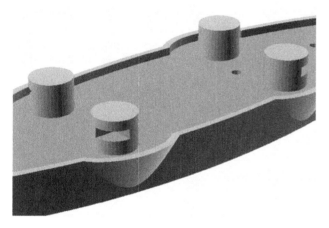

Figure 6-11. *All four sponsons added to our warship*

Midship Cabin

Now we need to connect the sponsons to the main part of the midship. We should probably start by adding the line mid_ship(size); to our warship() module and create a new module with one big cube that spans to each of the sponsons we added earlier. The following is what that should look like:

```
module mid_ship(ms) {
        translate([-ms/6.5,-ms/14,ms/38]) cube([ms/3.25,ms/7,ms/22]);
}
```

Since OpenSCAD draws cubes beginning at the corner and drawing outward, we needed to locate the corner of this cube at the center of the negative-most sponson, located at -size/6.5, -size/14, size/38. With a little math, it was possible to figure out how wide and deep this box should be. To add some visual interest, the height was chosen to be a little shorter than the sponsons. We should now have something that looks like Figure 6-12.

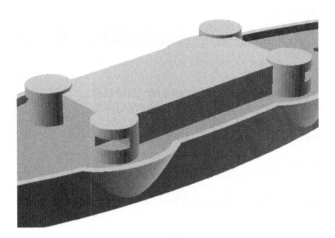

Figure 6-12. *Basic midship form*

Now what we need are more guns! By adding three slots that are the height of our filament along both sides of the midship, we should be able to insert more filament barrels to our ship when we assemble it. We might also add the same holes for the ship's masts, which we added to the hull earlier. When we do this, we end up with the finished module in Listing 6-3.

Listing 6-3. mid_ship() Module

```
module mid_ship(ms) {
        difference() {
                translate([-ms/6.5,-ms/14,ms/38]) cube([ms/3.25,ms/7,ms/22]);
                // gun slits for 1.75mm filament barrels
                translate([-ms/14,-ms/14,ms/18.5])
                        cube([ms/24,ms/20,filament_dia],center=true);
                translate([0,-ms/14,ms/18.5])
                        cube([ms/24,ms/20,filament_dia],center=true);
                translate([ms/14,-ms/14,ms/18.5])
                        cube([ms/24,ms/20,filament_dia],center=true);
                translate([-ms/14,ms/14,ms/18.5])
                        cube([ms/24,ms/20,filament_dia],center=true);
                translate([0,ms/14,ms/18.5])
                        cube([ms/24,ms/20,filament_dia],center=true);
                translate([ms/14,ms/14,ms/18.5])
                        cube([ms/24,ms/20,filament_dia],center=true);
                // mast mounting
                translate([ms/8,0,0]) cylinder(h=ms/3.5,r=filament_dia*0.55);
                translate([-ms/8,0,0]) cylinder(h=ms/3.5,r=filament_dia*0.55);
        }
}
```

The locations for each of the gun slots were spaced evenly along the side of the midship. Vertically, we had to make sure the slots were not too close to the top of the cube to ensure at least a couple layers of plastic would be laid down for a smooth top. When this is compiled, we end up with Figure 6-13.

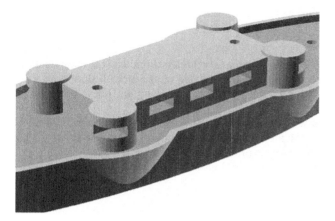

Figure 6-13. *Completed midship() module*

Generally fused filament fabrication 3D printers perform very poorly with areas of designs called overhangs—where there is no support beneath uppermost layers. Our gun slots sort of violate this rule, but this is one exception that we can often get away with. It does this by stretching the plastic across the open area and it generally works fairly well in this case, so long as your printer is fairly well tuned.

Designing the Details

With our basic ship form in place, let's start adding the details that will complete our model. This includes modeling the iconic smokestacks and adding vents; and a warship just wouldn't be a warship without main gun turrets.

Smokestacks

Every Victorian warship needs smokestacks and since a smokestack is nothing more than a simple tube, a pair of these shouldn't be too hard to add to our model. These stacks, at their most basic, can be designed by subtracting a cylinder from a larger one to make a tube. I noticed that on many of the ships I looked at, there was a nice thick ring around the base of the stack; this seemed like a good idea to make our model more interesting.

Listing 6-4 contains the finished stack() module.

Listing 6-4. Completed stack() Module

```
module stack(ss) {
      difference() {
            union() {
                  // main stack
                  translate([0,0,ss/14]) cylinder(h=ss/7.5,r=ss/32);
                  // base
                  translate([0,0,ss/14]) cylinder(h=ss/64,r=ss/24);
                  // rings
                  translate([0,0,ss/5.325]) cylinder(h=ss/100,r=ss/29);
                  translate([0,0,ss/6.75]) cylinder(h=ss/100,r=ss/29);
            }
```

```
                    // inside
                    translate([0,0,ss/14]) cylinder(h=ss/7,r=ss/60);
         }
}
```

As you can see in this script, this module is simply an arrangement of cylinders. By adding the main stack to the rings and base, and then subtracting the interior space, we have a completed smokestack. The inner space is made a little taller than the outside cylinder to ensure that the space is subtracted cleanly and doesn't give us any future problems.

When designing the rings at the top of the stacks, we need to remember the overhang rule and not make the rings so large that they would droop during printing. If they are made just big enough, say one width of the extruded filament, then it's possible for this slightly raised ring to print reasonably fine.

All we need to do is to add the following two lines to our warship() module, positioning the stacks so that they are a little front of center.

```
translate([size/14,0,0]) stack(size);
translate([-size/32,0,0]) stack(size);
```

The finished stacks are shown in Figure 6-14.

Figure 6-14. *Completed stack() modules*

Vents

In addition to smokestacks, the next iconic design detail we need to add are some vents along the midship. These vents were a little tricky to design because even though we can make some complex shapes with OpenSCAD, making curvy ones is quite a bit harder. Before we talk about how to go about making these vents, let's look at one of the vents, shown in Figure 6-15.

Figure 6-15. *Completed vent() module*

To describe this shape, you might call it a short cylinder with one-quarter of a donut shape mounted on top. One possibility for making this shape was to use a built-in module called rotate_extrude() to extrude the donut shape from a circle; but there was no easy way to subtract a block from the finished object. That meant we had to kludge together our own solution instead. Listing 6-5 is the completed vent() module.

Listing 6-5. Completed vent() Module

```
module vent(vs) {
        scale([1.1,1.1,1.1])
        difference() {
                union() {
                        cylinder(h=vs/40,r=vs/80);
                        translate([0,0,vs/55.75]) tube_slice();
                        translate([-vs/530,0,vs/40.1]) rotate([0,30,0]) tube_slice();
                        translate([0,0,vs/31.325]) rotate([0,60,0]) tube_slice();
                        translate([vs/195,0,vs/27]) rotate([0,90,0]) tube_slice();
                }
        translate([vs/200,0,vs/27]) rotate([0,90,0]) cylinder(h=vs/60,r=vs/150);
        }
}
```

The idea here was to start with a short cylinder and then add four wedge-like shapes, rotating and moving each one to stack up nicely, making the 90-degree curve. To make this code easier, we used a second module called tube_slice(), shown in Listing 6-6.

Listing 6-6. Completed tube_slice() Module

```
module tube_slice(vs=shipscale) {
        difference() {
                cylinder(h=vs/60,r=vs/80);
                translate([0,0,-vs/360]) rotate([0,-15,0]) cube([vs/30,vs/30,vs/80],center=true);
                translate([0,0,vs/60]) rotate([0,15,0]) cube([vs/30,vs/30,vs/80],center=true);
        }
}
```

Essentially, this creates a short cylindrical section that has had a cube subtracted from the top and bottom to make a wedge. If we were to look at this module just by itself and use the debug modifier to highlight these cubes, you would have what is shown in Figure 6-16.

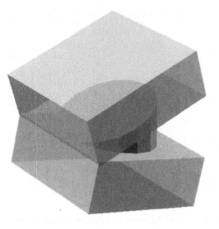

Figure 6-16. *The wedge-shaped tube slice used to make the vents*

While I'm sure there is an appropriately mathematical method for determining the exact location of each slice of the tube, I simply took the direct route of trial and error until I found what looked good to me. We have to be careful about keeping a manifold design as much as possible, meaning that any slice needs to fully contact another slice and not float up in the air—this will either confuse our 3D printer or make some horrible prints. When we have the vent completed, we can then find a suitable place on the ship to put them. For this design, I placed six of them on either side of the midship and rotated each one a little to get them to face out at a diagonal, using the following six lines of code in our warship() module:

```
translate([size/28,size/22,size/14]) rotate([0,0,30]) vent(size);
translate([-size/15,size/22,size/14]) rotate([0,0,30]) vent(size);
translate([-size/9,size/22,size/14]) rotate([0,0,30]) vent(size);
translate([size/28,-size/22,size/14]) rotate([0,0,-30]) vent(size);
translate([-size/15,-size/22,size/14]) rotate([0,0,-30]) vent(size);
translate([-size/9,-size/22,size/14]) rotate([0,0,-30]) vent(size);
```

When these are added to our design-in-progress, we end up with what is shown in Figure 6-17.

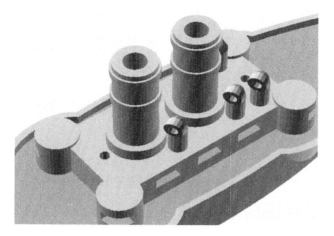

Figure 6-17. *All vents placed on model*

With details like these, the ship really starts to come together. Let's have a look at the last of our modules, beginning with the main turrets.

Main Turrets

This tiny warship has enough room to have two main turrets: one fore and one aft. I wanted these to be both a little clunky and a little sleek. As the basis for this module, we will use an eight-sided cone, as follows:

```
translate([0,0,mt/30]) rotate([0,0,22.5])
        cylinder(h=mt/22,r1=mt/19,r2=mt/24,$fn=8);
```

This cone is rotated 22.5 degrees around the z-axis to get the flat side of the octagon facing forward. We used the facet number special variable in the parameter $fn = 8 to force our cone into an octagon. To make the turret a little sleeker looking, a slope was created on the front of the turret by subtracting a tilted cube. A round base was added for detail. To finish things off, two slots for filament barrels and a hole for a filament pin to attach the turret to the hull were added. The finished module is shown in Listing 6-7.

Listing 6-7. Completed main_turret() Module

```
module main_turret(mt) {
        difference() {
                union() {
                        // round base
                        translate([0,0,mt/38])
                                cylinder(h=mt/86,r=mt/18);
                        difference() {
                                // main turret body
                                translate([0,0,mt/30]) rotate([0,0,22.5])
                                        cylinder(h=mt/22,r1=mt/19,r2=mt/24,$fn=8);
                                // sloped front
                                translate([mt/14,0,mt/22]) rotate([0,60,0])
                                        cube([mt/9,mt/9,mt/20],center=true);
```

```
                            // cannon slots 1.75mm filament cannons
                            translate([mt/38,mt/70,mt/12])
                                      cube([mt/32,filament_dia,mt/16],center=true);
                            translate([mt/38,-mt/70,mt/12])
                                      cube([mt/32,filament_dia,mt/16],center=true);
                 }
        }
        // filament axle
        cylinder(h=mt/18,r=filament_dia*0.55);
    }
}
```

Now we just need to add the following two lines to our warship() module to place the turrets on the ship and have them facing in the right directions:

```
translate([size/3.5,0,0]) rotate([0,0,0]) main_turret(size);
translate([-size/3.5,0,0]) rotate([0,0,180]) main_turret(size);
```

When the code is compiled, we should end up with what's shown in Figure 6-18.

Figure 6-18. *Completed main_turret() modules*

All that is left to finish up our design is to add some towers to our main deck and build a captain's bridge at the front of the ship.

Finishing Up the Model

For these modules, I decided to make something like an elongated octagon by stacking two eight-sided cylinders next to each other. Then, much like what we did with the ship's hull, we had to subtract a scaled-down version of the tower from the larger form to create the suggestion of railings on the different levels. For the bridge, we even cheated a little by making a four-sided cylinder to get it to line up with its basic octagon form. When we put it all together, we end up with the finished model in Figure 6-19.

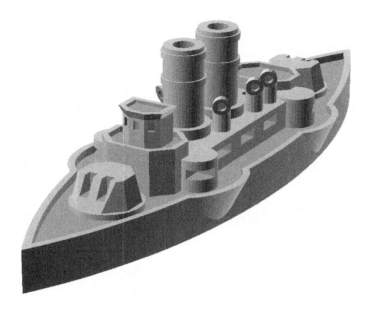

Figure 6-19. *Completed steampunk warship design*

And the code that made this happen is in Listing 6-8.

Listing 6-8. Steampunk Warship Model

```
// disable $fn and $fa, do not change these
$fn=0;
$fa=0.01;

// use $fs to control the number of facets globally
// fine ~ 0.1 coarse ~ 1.0
$fs=0.3;

filament_dia = 1.7; // used for cannon barrels

printbed_w = 100; // set to the width of your printbed
printbed_d = 100; // set to the depth of your printbed

printbed_max = sqrt(pow(printbed_w,2)+pow(printbed_d,2)); // calculates diagonal

shipscale=printbed_max-20; // shipscale should not exceed build platform size

echo(str("Hull length = ",shipscale,"mm"));
echo(str("Hull width = ",shipscale/4,"mm"));

* % translate([0,0,-5]) cube([printbed_w,printbed_d,0.5], center=true); // printbed

rotate([0,0,45])
warship();

module warship(size=shipscale) {
        main_deck(size);
        mid_ship(size);
        translate([size/5.5,0,0]) lower_tower(size);
```

```
        translate([-size/5.5,0,size/38*0.1]) lower_tower(size*0.9);
        translate([size/5.5,0,size/14]) bridge(size*0.6);
        translate([size/6.5,size/14,size/38]) rotate([0,0,0]) side_sponson(size/16);
        translate([-size/6.5,size/14,size/38]) rotate([0,0,90]) side_sponson(size/16);
        translate([size/6.5,-size/14,size/38]) rotate([0,0,-90]) side_sponson(size/16);
        translate([-size/6.5,-size/14,size/38]) rotate([0,0,180]) side_sponson(size/16);
        translate([size/3.5,0,0]) rotate([0,0,0]) main_turret(size);
        translate([-size/3.5,0,0]) rotate([0,0,180]) main_turret(size);
        translate([size/14,0,0]) stack(size);
        translate([-size/32,0,0]) stack(size);
        translate([size/28,size/22,size/14]) rotate([0,0,30]) vent(size);
        translate([-size/15,size/22,size/14]) rotate([0,0,30]) vent(size);
        translate([-size/9,size/22,size/14]) rotate([0,0,30]) vent(size);
        translate([size/28,-size/22,size/14]) rotate([0,0,-30]) vent(size);
        translate([-size/15,-size/22,size/14]) rotate([0,0,-30]) vent(size);
        translate([-size/9,-size/22,size/14]) rotate([0,0,-30]) vent(size);
}


module main_deck(hl) {
        difference() {
                union() {
                        // main deck basic form
                        scale([1.5,1,1])
                        intersection() {
                                translate([0,hl*0.375,hl/100])
                                        cylinder(h=hl/16,r=hl/2,center=true);
                                translate([0,-hl*0.375,hl/100])
                                        cylinder(h=hl/16,r=hl/2,center=true);
                        }
                        // side sponsons
                        translate([hl/6.5,hl/12,hl/100]) rotate([0,0,-10]) scale([1.5,1,1])
                                cylinder(h=hl/16,r1=hl/38,r2=hl/18,center=true);
                        translate([-hl/6.5,hl/12,hl/100]) rotate([0,0,10]) scale([1.5,1,1])
                                cylinder(h=hl/16,r1=hl/38,r2=hl/18,center=true);
                        translate([hl/6.5,-hl/12,hl/100]) rotate([0,0,10]) scale([1.5,1,1])
                                cylinder(h=hl/16,r1=hl/38,r2=hl/18,center=true);
                        translate([-hl/6.5,-hl/12,hl/100]) rotate([0,0,-10]) scale([1.5,1,1])
                                cylinder(h=hl/16,r1=hl/38,r2=hl/18,center=true);
                }
                union() {
                        // upper deck indention for side rail
                        scale([1.425,0.925,1])
                        intersection() {
                                translate([0,hl/2-hl/8,hl/14])
                                        cylinder(h=hl/12,r=hl/2,center=true);
                                translate([0,-(hl/2-hl/8),hl/14])
                                        cylinder(h=hl/12,r=hl/2,center=true);
                        }
                        // indention for side sponsons
                        translate([hl/6.5,hl/12,hl/14]) rotate([0,0,-10]) scale([1.3,0.8,1])
                                cylinder(h=hl/12,r=hl/18,center=true);
                        translate([-hl/6.5,hl/12,hl/14]) rotate([0,0,10]) scale([1.3,0.8,1])
                                cylinder(h=hl/12,r=hl/18,center=true);
```

```
                    translate([hl/6.5,-hl/12,hl/14]) rotate([0,0,10]) scale([1.3,0.8,1])
                            cylinder(h=hl/12,r=hl/18,center=true);
                    translate([-hl/6.5,-hl/12,hl/14]) rotate([0,0,-10]) scale([1.3,0.8,1])
                            cylinder(h=hl/12,r=hl/18,center=true);
            }
            // filament pins
            translate([hl/3.5,0,0]) cylinder(h=hl/2,r=filament_dia*0.55);
            translate([-hl/3.5,0,0]) cylinder(h=hl/2,r=filament_dia*0.55);
            translate([hl/8,0,0]) cylinder(h=hl/3.5,r=filament_dia*0.55);
            translate([-hl/8,0,0]) cylinder(h=hl/3.5,r=filament_dia*0.55);
        }
}
module mid_ship(ms) {
        difference() {
                translate([-ms/6.5,-ms/14,ms/38]) cube([ms/3.25,ms/7,ms/22]);
                // gun slits for 1.75mm filament barrels
                translate([-ms/14,-ms/14,ms/18.5])
                        cube([ms/24,ms/20,filament_dia],center=true);
                translate([0,-ms/14,ms/18.5])
                        cube([ms/24,ms/20,filament_dia],center=true);
                translate([ms/14,-ms/14,ms/18.5])
                        cube([ms/24,ms/20,filament_dia],center=true);
                translate([-ms/14,ms/14,ms/18.5])
                        cube([ms/24,ms/20,filament_dia],center=true);
                translate([0,ms/14,ms/18.5])
                        cube([ms/24,ms/20,filament_dia],center=true);
                translate([ms/14,ms/14,ms/18.5])
                        cube([ms/24,ms/20,filament_dia],center=true);
                // mast mounting
                translate([ms/8,0,0]) cylinder(h=ms/3.5,r=filament_dia*0.55);
                translate([-ms/8,0,0]) cylinder(h=ms/3.5,r=filament_dia*0.55);
        }
}

module lower_tower(lt) {
        difference() {
                union() {
                        translate([0,-lt/60,lt/38]) rotate([0,0,22.5])
                                cylinder(h=lt/14,r=lt/20,$fn=8);
                        translate([0,lt/60,lt/38]) rotate([0,0,22.5])
                                cylinder(h=lt/14,r=lt/20,$fn=8);
                }
                scale([0.85,0.85,0.5]) translate([0,0,lt/6.5])
                union() {
                        translate([0,-lt/60,lt/38]) rotate([0,0,22.5])
                                cylinder(h=lt/14,r=lt/20,$fn=8);
                        translate([0,lt/60,lt/38]) rotate([0,0,22.5])
                                cylinder(h=lt/14,r=lt/20,$fn=8);
                }
        }
}
```

```
module bridge(bs) {
        difference() {
                union() {
                        // bridge form
                        scale([1.25,1.75,1]) translate([bs/120,0,0])
                        union() {
                                translate([-bs/120,0,bs/32.5]) rotate([0,0,22.5])
                                        cylinder(h=bs/12,r=bs/30,$fn=8);
                                translate([-bs/53,0,bs/32.5]) scale([1,1.325,1])
                                        rotate([0,0,45])
                                        cylinder(h=bs/12,r=bs/30.325,$fn=4);
                        }
                        // roof ridge
                        scale([1.25,1.75,1]) translate([bs/120,0,bs/14])
                        union() {
                                translate([-bs/120,0,bs/32.5]) rotate([0,0,22.5])
                                        cylinder(h=bs/60,r1=bs/30,r2=bs/26,$fn=8);
                                translate([-bs/53,0,bs/32.5]) scale([1,1.325,1])
                                        rotate([0,0,45])
                                        cylinder(h=bs/60,r1=bs/30.325,r2=bs/26,$fn=4);
                        }
                }
                // roof platform
                scale([1,1.5,1]) translate([bs/120,0,bs/12.5])
                        union() {
                                translate([-bs/120,0,bs/32.5]) rotate([0,0,22.5])
                                        cylinder(h=bs/12,r=bs/30,$fn=8);
                                translate([-bs/53,0,bs/32.5]) scale([1,1.325,1])
                                        rotate([0,0,45])
                                        cylinder(h=bs/12,r=bs/30.325,$fn=4);
                        }
                // bridge windows
                translate([bs/26.5,0,bs/12]) cube([bs/60,bs/60,filament_dia],center=true);
                translate([bs/36,bs/28,bs/12]) rotate([0,0,36])
                        cube([bs/60,bs/60,filament_dia],center=true);
                translate([bs/36,-bs/28,bs/12]) rotate([0,0,-36])
                        cube([bs/60,bs/60,filament_dia],center=true);
        }
}
module side_sponson(ss) {
        difference() {
                // sponson
                cylinder(h=ss/1.25,r=ss/2);
                // gun slot
                translate([0,0,ss/2.75]) cube([ss/2,ss/2,filament_dia]);
        }
}
module main_turret(mt) {
        difference() {
                union() {
```

```
                        // round base
                        translate([0,0,mt/38])
                                cylinder(h=mt/86,r=mt/18);
                        difference() {
                                // main turret body
                                translate([0,0,mt/30]) rotate([0,0,22.5])
                                        cylinder(h=mt/22,r1=mt/19,r2=mt/24,$fn=8);
                                // sloped front
                                translate([mt/14,0,mt/22]) rotate([0,60,0])
                                        cube([mt/9,mt/9,mt/20],center=true);
                                // cannon slots 1.75mm filament cannons
                                translate([mt/38,mt/70,mt/12])
                                        cube([mt/32,filament_dia,mt/16],center=true);
                                translate([mt/38,-mt/70,mt/12])
                                        cube([mt/32,filament_dia,mt/16],center=true);
                        }
                }
                // filament axle
                cylinder(h=mt/18,r=filament_dia*0.55);
        }
}
module stack(ss) {
        difference() {
                union() {
                        // main stack
                        translate([0,0,ss/14]) cylinder(h=ss/7.5,r=ss/32);
                        // base
                        translate([0,0,ss/14]) cylinder(h=ss/64,r=ss/24);
                        // rings
                        translate([0,0,ss/5.325]) cylinder(h=ss/100,r=ss/29);
                        translate([0,0,ss/6.75]) cylinder(h=ss/100,r=ss/29);
                }
                // inside
                translate([0,0,ss/14]) cylinder(h=ss/7,r=ss/60);
        }
}
module vent(vs) {
        scale([1.1,1.1,1.1])
        difference() {
                union() {
                        cylinder(h=vs/40,r=vs/80);
                        translate([0,0,vs/55.75]) tube_slice();
                        translate([-vs/530,0,vs/40.1]) rotate([0,30,0]) tube_slice();
                        translate([0,0,vs/31.325]) rotate([0,60,0]) tube_slice();
                        translate([vs/195,0,vs/27]) rotate([0,90,0]) tube_slice();
                }
        translate([vs/200,0,vs/27]) rotate([0,90,0]) cylinder(h=vs/60,r=vs/150);
        }
}
```

```
module tube_slice(vs = shipscale) {
        difference() {
                cylinder(h = vs/60,r = vs/80);
                translate([0,0,-vs/360]) rotate([0,-15,0])
cube([vs/30,vs/30,vs/80],center = true);
                translate([0,0,vs/60]) rotate([0,15,0])
cube([vs/30,vs/30,vs/80],center = true);
        }
}
```

Admittedly, seeing all that code laid out like that can be quite intimidating. Just remember, we built this model one chunk of code at a time to make such a complex shape more manageable. Now, let's look at how we are going to bring this model into the real world.

Make Ready for Printing

With our model finished, we need to get it ready for printing. The way this model has been designed, there are two options: export it and print it all in one go, or divide it into two, make two separate prints (they could even be in two colors), and assemble the parts when complete. This later option is what I have opted for here. We will need to first compile and render the hull alone and export this as an STL. To do this, we add the ! symbol, or root modifier, to the beginning of the first line in the warship() module and rotate the main_deck() module to position the hull diagonally across the platform. The finished line will look like the following:

```
! rotate([0,0,45]) main_deck(size);
```

This will ignore everything in our sketch not relating to this one line in the finished object shown in Figure 6-9. After that, we need to hide the ship's hull and render everything else by simply adding the * symbol (the disable modifier) to the beginning of this very same line, as follows:

```
* ! rotate([0,0,45]) main_deck(size);
```

When this is rendered, we have a model that only includes everything above the upper deck, as shown in Figure 6-20.

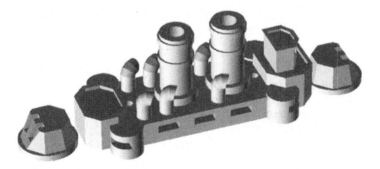

Figure 6-20. *Warship upper deck*

Export both of those models as STLs and process through your printer's software to print as normal.

Wrapping It Up

So if everything worked as planned, you now have a total of four pieces of your warship from two different prints. With these parts, along with a few extra things needed to assemble the model (see Figure 6-21), we are ready to build our finished warship model.

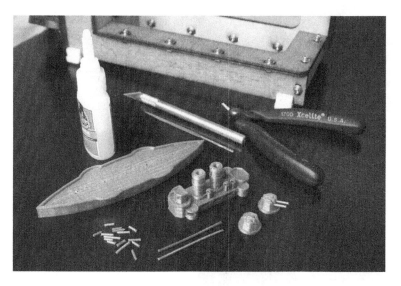

Figure 6-21. *Final printed parts, supplies, and tools*

After cleaning things up, you need to cut some lengths of 1.75mm filament—assuming you printed the ship at about the same size that I did—in the following dimensions:

- Two 28mm pieces for the ship's masts

- Four 10mm pieces for the main turrets

- Four 8mm pieces for the side sponsons

- Six 6mm pieces for the midship guns

- Two 4mm pieces for pinning the turrets to the hull

Test-fit the pieces of filament with the mounting holes on your model. You might need to clean up the model with a hobby knife or drill out the holes with a small hand drill to get these to fit correctly. Once fitted, place a small drop of super glue on the end of the filament and place the barrel into the slot on the main turret, repeating for all of the gun barrels, as shown in Figure 6-22.

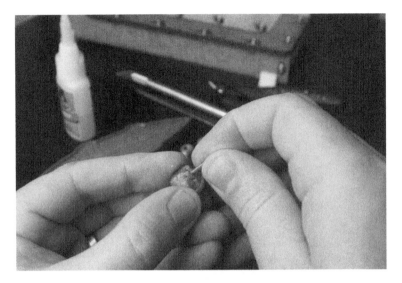

Figure 6-22. *Assembling the model*

To attach the upper deck to the main hull, insert the longer pieces of filament for the ship's masts through the upper deck so that a short length protrudes from the bottom. Using these pins, attach the upper deck to the main hull with the two innermost holes in the hull, as shown in Figure 6-23.

Figure 6-23. *Attaching upper deck to main hull*

Similarly, the main turrets attach to the ship's hull by placing the short length of filament into the upper deck and then sitting the turret on top of this pin. The fit should be loose and allow the turret to spin freely—do not glue this part. Once assembled, step back and admire all of your hard work. You should now have a fighting steampunk warship. Mine is shown in Figure 6-24.

Figure 6-24. *Finished steampunk warship model*

Now all we need are some Martians to attack.

Summary

It's projects like these that really capture my imagination and give me warm, fuzzy feelings when thinking about what 3D printing can do. In this chapter, we looked at how to build a fairly complex multipart model inspired by a classic piece of fiction and using a parametric and modular design approach. This meant we had to pick up a few more design techniques with OpenSCAD along the way to accomplish our design goals. In the end, we made a pretty neat model worthy of a place on the bookshelf. Keep in mind, however, that this was only one example of how to approach a composite design. I'm sure there is something out there that is infinitely more practical waiting to be drawn up.

In the next chapter, we continue with a bit more OpenSCAD and introduce MeshMixer, an experimental 3D modeling application, to make a series of equally unpractical model mashups.

■ ■ ■

CHAPTER 7

Action Hero Mashups

In the last chapter, we really earned our OpenSCAD chops with a very complex project. OpenSCAD is one of those extremely versatile tools that, if you gain even a basic proficiency, you'll be able to quickly accomplish many different kinds of tasks. I think that is a big part of why OpenSCAD has become so popular in the designs posted to Thingiverse. Since we can't dwell too long on OpenSCAD in this book, it's time to investigate a few more applications that are equally useful to designing a wide range of 3D models. We will cover a couple more little projects using OpenSCAD before checking out the still experimental, mesh-bending application, MeshMixer, and wrap things up by putting these two tools together. Our design consideration for this chapter is the action hero mashup. It's an opportunity to design the toys, models, and action figures that your kids—and you—have always wanted, including gangstas, creatures, idols, and a rabbit overlord.

In this chapter, we will create the following:

- Compound forms in OpenSCAD using and importing multiple STL files

- Blended meshes and distorted 3D models in the quirky MeshMixer

- Multipart 3D hybrid models using a printing plate to organize our parts

- An entire army of action hero mashups built from everything we've learned so far

It should be a lot of fun to make our ridiculous army using these applications. Let's get started by talking about just exactly what a mashup is anyway.

A Mashup?

A 3D mashup comes from the tradition of the *Internet memes*—existing images that have been remixed and redistributed through various online communities. With 3D models, it's much the same: borrow a model or part of a model and combine it with another whole or partial model in a new and interesting way, then print and publish it for the world to see and enjoy. The nature of the source material makes these mashups fun, weird, sarcastic, bizarre, flattering, and unflattering. In Figure 7-1, let's look at what goes into a mashup.

Figure 7-1. *The making of a mashup*

Here we have a George. George is made of four separate models downloaded from Thingiverse, which have been modified and recombined to create a truly unnatural, chimera-like creature. The actual models are as follows:

- Allan Ecker's Pony Creation Kit (www.thingiverse.com/thing:6123)

- Hillary Brosnihan's Creatures of Thingiverse (www.thingiverse.com/thing:12652)

- Michael Curry's Turtle Shell Racers (www.thingiverse.com/thing:10526)

- Pomalin's Hipsta (www.thingiverse.com/thing:13468)

This finished mashup was created primarily using OpenSCAD, although the basic concept of mashing together multiple models can be done in many different applications. We will look at a couple of these applications and techniques, beginning where we left off in the last chapter.

Basic OpenSCAD Mashups

We've covered a lot of the features built into OpenSCAD so far in this book, but we have missed an important one: the ability to import and manipulate STL files from directly within OpenSCAD. This can be fairly handy, even if you are using other applications to build your models because OpenSCAD allows you to perform actions on STLs, such as subtracting an STL from a cube to make the impression (negative shape) of that STL. Let's start with simply importing STLs.

Importing STLs

Importing an STL file in OpenSCAD is fairly straightforward, but there are a few things to keep in mind. The first thing to do is to find and save an STL file to your computer; then, start a new project in OpenSCAD and save this file to the same directory. While our OpenSCAD file does not necessarily need to be in the same folder as the STL, it makes creating the file path easier to enter into our model.

To import an STL, we will use the `import()` module with the following syntax:

```
import(file="filename.stl", convexity=30);
```

`filename.stl` is the name and/or path to the STL file to be imported, while `convexity` is an optional parameter that helps in rendering the file in the preview window. To put this to use, we are going to start with Yvo Waldmeier's renowned Gangsta (`www.thingiverse.com/thing:5367`), a model synonymous with the mashup on Thingiverse. After downloading the STL and saving the OpenSCAD file in the same directory, we will use the following line of code:

```
import(file="gangsta.stl");
```

When the file is rendered, we should see the Gangsta (shown in Figure 7-2) pop up in the preview window.

Figure 7-2. *Imported Gangsta model*

Before we get to mashing together more STLs in OpenSCAD, let's first look at some of the operations we can do with our imported STL.

Operations on STLs

After spinning the model around, you'll notice that the bottom of the Gangsta's feet are not very flat. A very practical operation would provide a level surface for it to stand on, making the printing of this model a little easier.

To do this, we will need to subtract a cube from the STL model using the difference() module. By adding to our previous single line of code, we end up with the following:

```
difference() {
        import(file="gangsta.stl");
        #translate([-25,-25,-5]) cube([50,50,5]);
}
```

When rendered, this will result in something along the lines of what you see in Figure 7-3.

Figure 7-3. *Using difference() to remove a cube from an STL*

If we flip the model over, as shown in Figure 7-4, then we get a better idea of what its feet look like.

Figure 7-4. *The results of the operation*

Now that's a simple operation performed on an imported STL, and it helped a little, but that's not nearly enough of a flat foot for it to print very well. To fix this, we need to rotate and move the STL so that it sits flatter. Through some experimentation and trial and error, we end up with the following code:

```
difference() {
        translate([0,0,-1]) rotate([-2,-1,0]) import(file = "gangsta.stl");
        #translate([-25,-25,-5]) cube([50,50,5]);
}
```

This gives us far better feet for the model to stand on, as shown in Figure 7-5.

Figure 7-5. *Improved operation on model*

Just as we can subtract a shape from the STL, we can also subtract the STL from another shape. This could be useful if, for example, Easter is just around the corner and chocolate bunnies seem rather "last year," so instead, you want to make chocolate Gangstas. Using the following code:

```
difference() {
        translate([-20,-20,-5]) rotate([0,0,-45]) cube([15,55,115]);
        import(file = "gangsta.stl");
}
```

We can generate the model shown in Figure 7-6, which, again, might be used for making a mold to cast in chocolate or other materials.

Figure 7-6. *The negative shape of an imported STL*

These few examples show that just about anything you can do with basic primitive shapes in OpenSCAD can be applied to imported STLs just as easily. Let's put this together in a simple OpenSCAD mashup.

Putting Together a Simple Mashup

While during one of my daily perusals of what's new on Thingiverse, I found a walnut. Siderit's Walnut (`www.thingiverse.com/thing:17235`) might seem random, because, well, it is; but it just needed to be made into a mashup. So, by combining the Gangsta and the Walnut we have, of course, the Walnutsta. The following is the code for this model:

```
union() {
        difference() {
                translate([0,0,-1]) rotate([-2,-1,0]) import(file="gangsta.stl");
                #translate([-25,-25,-5]) cube([50,50,5]);
        }
        scale([5,5,5]) translate([-0.5,0.5,20]) rotate([0,-2,-60])
        import(file="walnut.stl");
}
```

Building from the code to give the Gangsta flat feet, we've added this model to the imported STL of the walnut using the union() module, making one solid form. To make a suitable head to replace the Gangsta's, the walnut needed to be scaled, moved, and rotated to perch on the shoulders with dignity. When this model is compiled and rendered, we have the new model, shown in Figure 7-7.

Figure 7-7. *Walnutsta mashup*

Creating mashups can truly be that easy. It takes a little experimenting and playing around to get the models positioned just right, but if you can make a model using basic shapes in OpenSCAD, importing STLs is not that much more difficult. With that said there are a few things to keep in mind.

- The OpenSCAD file needs to be saved in the same folder as the STL file; else, you need to have the correct path included in the file name when you import the STL.

- After you import one or two STLs, the preview window might not display the model correctly when the code is compiled. Set the convexity to a higher value or else chose Compile and Render under the Design menu.

- Some models downloaded from online sources may not import properly into OpenSCAD and are ignored when rendered. If this happens, you will need to run the model through http://cloud.netfabb.com or one of the other 3D model utilities to clean the model before trying again.

With these things in mind, let's have a look at a slightly more complex mashup: George, the Quadspike Hippocorn.

Complex OpenSCAD Mashups

Okay, so the complex mashup is not all that more complex than the simple one. For this mashup, we are using modules to create each of the various parts of the final model, and then moving or duplicating these modules as needed. We've also thrown in a couple of cylinders to act as support material, making the prints turn out better in the end. To start, let's look at each of the modules.

Starting the Mashup in OpenSCAD

The first model is a pony, which will be the base for the mashup. It comes from Allan Ecker's Pony Creation Kit (www.thingiverse.com/thing:6123). Sadly, the pony had to have its head chopped off and its feet flattened. Sounds horrible. The following is the code for the first module and the line that calls it:

```
translate([0,0,28.5]) pony();

module pony() {
        difference() {
                scale([1.5,1.5,1.5]) {
                        import(file="ponybase.stl",covexity=30);
                }
                translate([-10,-25,1.5]) rotate ([16,0,0]) cube([20,40,30]);
                translate([-20,-50,-30.5]) cube([40,100,2]);
        }
}
```

Essentially, we are simply importing the file ponybase.stl and then rotating and positioning one cube to remove its head and another to flatten its feet. When rendered, we have the model shown in Figure 7-8.

Figure 7-8. *Pony model base*

With the body of the mashup in place, we search for its head.

Using MeshLab

As this mashup is the spawn of some really bizarre nightmares, it needed to have the head of a hippopotamus. Seeing as Pomalin had already made a mashup of the Gangsta with a hippo's head (www.thingiverse.com/thing:13468), that's a good place to start. This model needs a little work because in the file hipsta-head.stl, the shoulders of the Gangsta model are included with the hippo's head, so we need to remove that part of the model before adding it to the pony body. To do this, we will use the 3D mesh-editing application, MeshLab (http://meshlab.sourceforge.net).

Removing Parts of the Model

To clean up the model before adding it to our mashup, open the file `hipsta-head.stl` in MeshLab and look for the selection tools in the top of the menu bar, as shown in Figure 7-9.

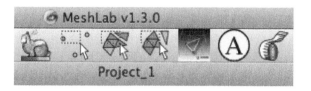

Figure 7-9. *MeshLab selection tools*

Using the Select Faces tool, located in the middle of the toolbar, click and drag around the hippo's shoulder area, as shown in Figure 7-10.

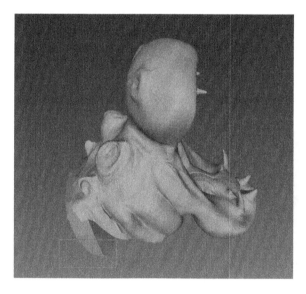

Figure 7-10. *Making a selection in MeshLab*

To alter the selection, press Command on the Mac or Alt on the PC while selecting faces to add to an existing selection. Press the Shift key to deselect faces. MeshLab is a little weird in its selection process in that you need to click the Selection tool to turn it off before you can freely move the model around to select other faces. Once all of the shoulder area has been selected, it should look like what you see in Figure 7-11.

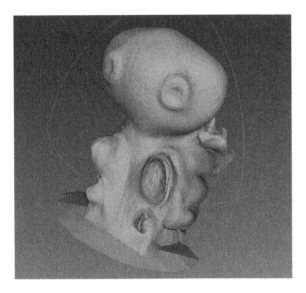

Figure 7-11. *Shoulder area fully selected*

With the area that we want to remove from the model selected, we need to choose Filters ➤ Selection ➤ Delete Selected Faces to delete this part of the model. After a little cleaning up, our modified model is shown in Figure 7-12.

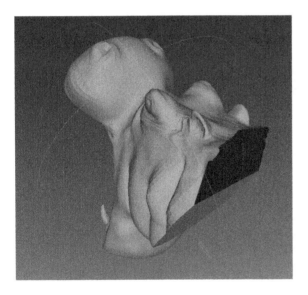

Figure 7-12. *Model after removing selected faces*

The back of the hippo's head is now a big hole that will cause problems for us because the model is not manifold. Before we address this, however, let's perform one more operation in MeshLab to reduce the overall size of the file.

Reducing Faces

This step is not always necessary, but looking at the head, we see that there is a lot of detail—more so than we need for our 3D printer. We can reduce the file size by reducing the number of polygons that make up the faces of the model without reducing the physical dimensions of the model. To do this, we choose Filters ➤ Remeshing, Simplification and Reconstruction ➤ Quadratic Edge Collapse Decimation. This will bring up a dialog box, shown in Figure 7-13.

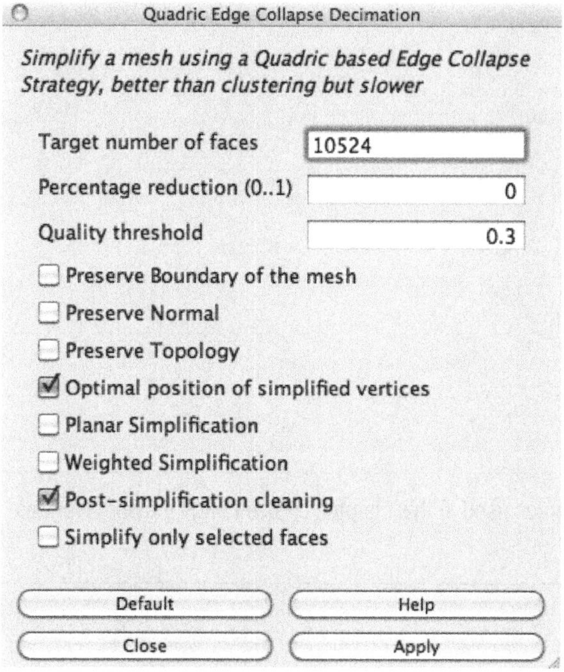

Figure 7-13. *Reducing the number of faces in MeshLab*

This box will give you the total number of faces that make up your model; for the hippo, this was about 30,000 faces. Choose a significantly smaller number, let's say 10,000 in this example, to reduce the detail in the model to a more manageable level, and hit the Apply button. This is a compromise between the total file size and the amount of detail that you want for the model. Find a workable middle ground, and then we are ready to save the file and clean up the hole that we created. Select File ➤ Export Mesh As…, choose the STL file format, and save the file. Next, upload the model to http://cloud.netfabb.com and process the file as we have done before.

Bringing It Back to OpenSCAD

With the hippo head file cleaned up, we can import the finished and processed file back into OpenSCAD, using the following code to add to our pony:

```
translate([-0.25,-7.25,30.25]) rotate([26,0,0]) hippo();
module hippo() {
        scale([0.59,0.55,0.57])
        rotate([0,0,-32]) import(file="hipstahead.stl",convexity=3);
}
```

When rendered, this gives our pony a brand-new hippo head, as shown in Figure 7-14.

Figure 7-14. *Imported hippo head on model*

___

■ **Tip** Be sure that your STL file names match the file names used in this chapter, or else things may not work as you expect.

___

Finishing the Mashup in OpenSCAD

The rest of the mashup is fairly straightforward. George gets a tail thanks to Hillary Brosnihan's Creatures of Thingiverse (www.thingiverse.com/thing:12652). We can use the tail2.stl file, rotated and positioned so that it serves its purpose. If we position the tail so that it touches both hind legs, we can be fairly sure it will print correctly. Figure 7-15 illustrates this point.

Figure 7-15. *A brand-new tail*

Finally, our emerging Hippocorn needs spikes. The spikes in Michael Curry's video game–inspired Turtle Shell Racers (www.thingiverse.com/thing:10526) seemed to fit the bill. In the end, however, it is simpler to make a cone in OpenSCAD rather than modify the original source file. To do this, we use the cylinder() module and specify two separate radiuses, r1 for the base and r2 for the tip of the cone. The following is the resulting spike:

```
module spike() {
        cylinder(h = 10,r1 = 4,r2 = 0);
}
```

Put this all together, and the finished code for our mashup is shown in Listing 7-1.

Listing 7-1. George the Quadspike Hippocorn Mashup

```
translate([0,0,28.5]) pony();
translate([-0.25,-7.25,30.25]) rotate([26,0,0]) hippo();
translate([25,-2,34]) tail();

translate([-3,-2,31.5]) rotate([10,-30,0]) spike();
translate([-3,5,31.5]) rotate([-10,-30,0]) spike();
translate([3,-2,31.5]) rotate([10,30,0]) spike();
translate([3,5,31.5]) rotate([-10,30,0]) spike();

module pony() {
        difference() {
                scale([1.5,1.5,1.5]) {
                        import(file = "ponybase.stl",covexity = 30);
                }
                translate([-10,-25,1.5]) rotate ([16,0,0]) cube([20,40,30]);
                translate([-20,-50,-30.5]) cube([40,100,2]);
        }
}
module spike() {
        cylinder(h = 10,r1 = 4,r2 = 0);
}
```

```
module hippo() {
        scale([0.59,0.55,0.57])
        rotate([0,0,-32]) import(file="hipstahead.stl",convexity=30);
}
module tail() {
        scale([1,1,0.8])
        rotate([180,5,180]) import(file="tail2.stl",convexity=30);
}
```

Render and compile this model to achieve the finished mashup shown in Figure 7-16.

Figure 7-16. *Finished complex mashup*

Adding Support

One last thing: you might find that this model is a little hard to print because the model's body is not supported in the middle and the lower jaw hangs in the air, causing the print to sag or otherwise not print correctly. If your slicer utility has the ability to print with support material, then it is a good option for printing this model. If not, we can create support structures using OpenSCAD to make a more printable model. Take the following three lines:

```
/////// support
translate([0,-19,0]) cylinder(h=24.75,r1=5,r2=4);
translate([0,-1.5,0]) cylinder(h=20.25,r1=3,r2=2);
```

Place these lines somewhere in the code (albeit not inside a module). This creates two tapered cylinders to support the model's midsection and jaw.

Now, before we print these models, let's look at how to make mashups in a new program called MeshMixer.

Mashups in MeshMixer

MeshMixer (http://meshmixer.com) is still a somewhat experimental application, but what it does for a free and open-source mesh-remixing tool is pretty cool. It is a little quirky though, and things don't always work as expected. In writing this chapter, the application crashed a handful of times, and as far as I can tell, certain features or functions either crash the application or don't do anything in the first place. Regardless of this, we'll go ahead and give it a shot here to see what we can do with it.

To start things off, we need to install the correct MeshMixer for our operating system, being sure to include the library of parts that come with the download. After we have MeshMixer up and running, it's time to make parts for the library, which we will use in our mashup.

Creating Parts

A unique feature of MeshMixer is the ability to turn 3D models into discrete parts that can be manipulated and meshed with other models or parts. Looking at the left-hand side of the main window (see Figure 7-17), you see the parts that come with the standard library.

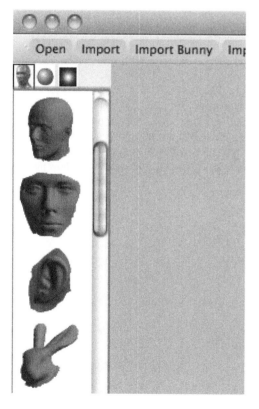

Figure 7-17. MeshMixer parts library

For this mashup, we will use MeshMixer's part-meshing ability to customize our own bizarre action figure, starting with the head of this book's technical reviewer, Tony Buser. Thanks to Tony for being a good sport.

The staff at MakerBot Industries set out to scan just about anyone they could using a very nifty and very expensive 3D scanner. The scan of Tony's head is found on Thingiverse at www.thingiverse.com/thing:10030.

To make this file useable for our mashup, we need to open the file `TonyBuser.stl` in MeshLab and resave it as an OBJ file format. Now, we can import this file in MeshMixer (see Figure 7-18) and begin turning it into a part for the mashup.

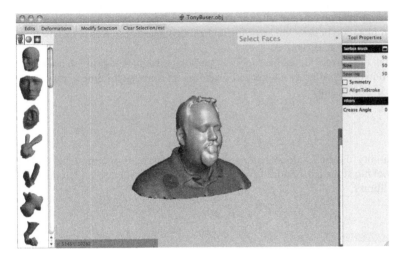

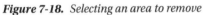

Figure 7-18. *Selecting an area to remove*

All we need for this mashup is Tony's head. We don't want his shoulders, so we use the Select tool to mark the area of the model that we want to remove. With this tool, the selected area changes to an orange color. Deselecting is done by holding the Shift key while selecting an orange area. The Select tool can be enlarged or reduced by clicking Size under the Tool Properties menu, or by using the scroll on your mouse or trackpad. To pan around the model while selecting, you need to hold the Alt or Option key while clicking and dragging.

Once an area is selected (up to the bottom of his chin), we click Edits ➤ Discard. This creates a hollow part, as shown in Figure 7-19.

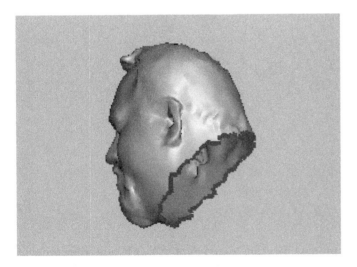

Figure 7-19. *Hollow part*

A hollow model is actually good for creating a part. MeshMixer highlights the boundary loop in blue, letting you know that it is an acceptable edge. Now we need to reselect the model by choosing the Select tool, clicking anywhere on the model, and then choosing Modify Selection ➤ Select All to select the entire model. Now we can choose Edit ➤ Convert to Part to add this model to our parts library. If all goes well, the top of Tony's head should appear in the left-hand window.

Already I feel we will need another part: wings. Going back to Michael Curry's Turtle Shell Racers (www.thingiverse.com/thing:10526), download the file Wings.stl. These wings were made to be attached to the back of a turtle's shell, so, using MeshLab, we need to simplify them a bit for our figure. First, we need to select the second wing and delete it using the method discussed earlier. Then we need to remove a little square bit (highlighted in Figure 7-20), which was used to make the wing print vertically.

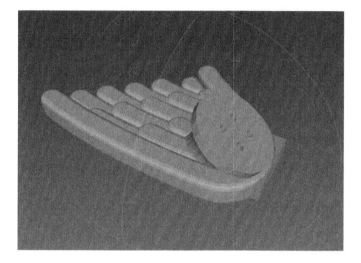

Figure 7-20. *Cleaning STL in MeshLab*

To fix the hole in the edge of the wing, save this file as an STL and upload it to cloud.netfabb.com; the online service will patch the hole for us. Now all we need to do is download and reopen the file in MeshLab, and then resave the file as an OBJ file to bring into MeshMixer. Once inside MeshMixer, we can remove the stand attached to the wing (see Figure 7-21) using the selection tool as before.

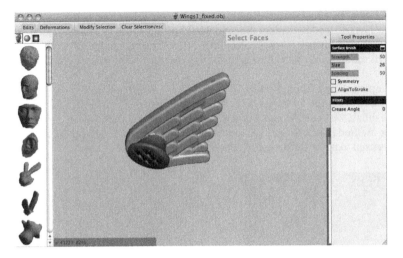

Figure 7-21. *Removing stand from wing*

When the extra bit has been roughly selected, we want to choose Edits ➤ Erase & Fill to not only erase that extra bit but to also fill the gap it leaves behind. This is not too exacting because our next step will mirror the wing. By choosing Edits ➤ Mirror, a nifty grid and arrow setup occurs, as shown in Figure 7-22.

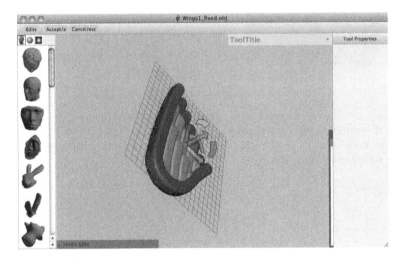

Figure 7-22. *Mirroring one side of the wing*

Mirroring works by moving the gridded plane through the center part of the wing using the three direction arrows—which are colored red, green, and blue—to move the plane in one of three directions or by dragging one of the arc segments to rotate the plane. We should rotate the plane to split the wing down the middle, removing the section that we erased earlier. Once we have a good-looking wing that is evenly split down the middle and of a thick enough width, we can hit Accept.

Before we make a part, we need to select a corner of the wing, leaving a suitable gap to attach to Tony's new shoulders later in the process. The resulting part, made by removing the corner of the wing and creating a new part, is shown in Figure 7-23.

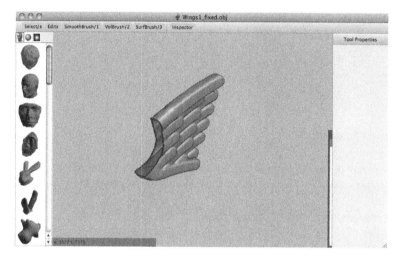

Figure 7-23. *Completed wing part*

I'm sure we will want to make at least one more part to use in this mashup, but let's start with the model that we will base our mashup on.

Mixing Meshes

To start building our action figure mashup in MeshMixer, we need a file that will form the base for the rest of the mashup. Enter Joseph Larson's Minataur Mini (`www.thingiverse.com/thing:16874`), converted in MeshLab to an OBJ file and imported into MeshMixer, as shown in Figure 7-24.

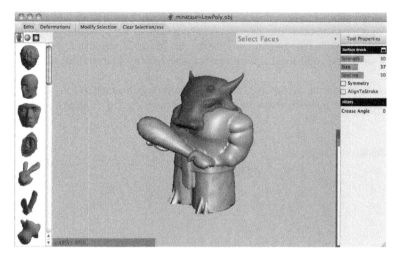

Figure 7-24. *Selecting part of the minotaur for deletion*

Just as before, we need to select the part of the model to remove using the Select tool. When satisfied, choose Edit ➤ Delete & Fill, and then hit Accept. This leaves us with the headless, but smooth, model shown in Figure 7-25.

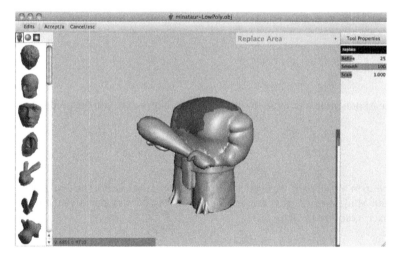

Figure 7-25. *Modified base model*

This gives us a nice base for adding the parts that we created earlier. This is also where MeshMixer is worth its challenges. To add Tony's head to the body of the minotaur, all we need to do is drag the part from the library to any solid surface of the model, as demonstrated in Figure 7-26.

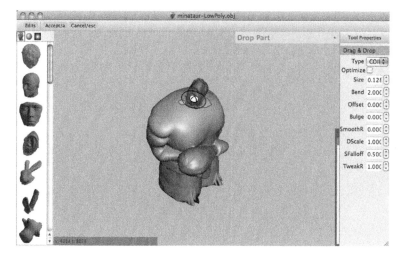

Figure 7-26. *Placing a part from the library*

When a part is dropped onto a model, the part automatically attaches itself, forming a seamless mesh with the new model. To control the shape, size, and orientation of the part, a little widget appears at the base of the part to allow us to fit the part as needed. To better understand the function of this widget, refer to Figure 7-27.

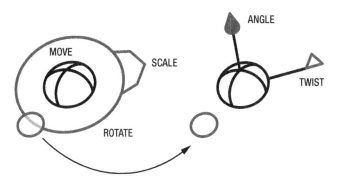

Figure 7-27. *Part manipulation widget*

By using this widget, we can position, scale, rotate, and bend the part until it matches our model in size, direction, and fit. Clicking and dragging the central sphere moves the part around the surface of the model. Rotating is done by clicking and dragging inside the outer ring. Scaling is done with the arrow on the side. Clicking on the outside circle changes the appearance and function of the widget; it also provides the option to adjust the angle of the part relative to the surface of the model or twist the part around a central axis. Figure 7-28 shows the final placement of Tony's head.

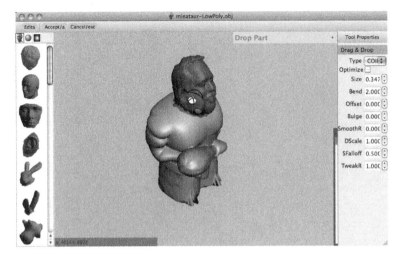

Figure 7-28. *Tony's head meshed with the Minataur torso*

After accepting the final part placement, this process is repeated twice more to add the wings that we made earlier (see Figure 7-29).

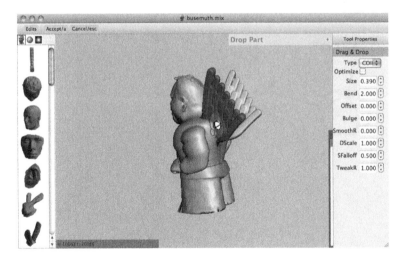

Figure 7-29. *Adding wings to the mashup*

If the notch was cut out of the wings reasonably well earlier in the process, then the wings should sit on top of the model's shoulders at a high enough angle that printing without support material is possible.

The model is still missing something... Horns!

Figure 7-30 shows our final addition.

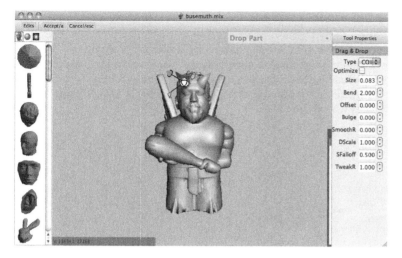

Figure 7-30. *Adding horns to the mashup*

The horn was quickly created from a cone in OpenSCAD, then brought into MeshMixer and made into a part (as previously discussed). Now we have a finished mashup in MeshMixer, shown in Figure 7-31.

I call him Busemuth, Benevolent Dark Lord of MakerBot.

Figure 7-31. *Finished MeshMixer mashup*

To prepare the model for 3D printing, we need to export the mesh as an STL file. It's probably a good idea to run the finished STL file through cloud.netfabb.com before trying to print it.

Before we get there though, let's make one more mashup using OpenSCAD and MeshMixer.

Mashup Bonus Round

So far in this chapter, we have looked at the two best free and open-source applications for creating 3D mashups. Let's bring them together again for one last multipart mashup. Remember that War of the Worlds Playset from Chapter 4? Using the legs from the alien war machine, we could give it a new head to make a fantastic alien-cyborg rabbit overlord. Let's start with the OpenSCAD file for the war machine, available in a ZIP file from www.thingiverse.com/thing:16367, and shown in Figure 7-32.

Figure 7-32. *War machine model*

This image is what is often called a printing plate, where multiple parts have been arranged on a single plane to be printed all at the same time. After printing is complete, the separate parts are then assembled with interlocking slots. While there is nothing stopping you from printing each part separately, this way makes it a little easier to manage. Listing 7-2 shows the code for this file.

Listing 7-2. War machine printing plate

```
%translate([0,0,-0.5]) cube([100,100,0.5]);

translate([25,50,0]) rotate([0,0,30]) import(file="war_machine_body_1.stl");
translate([40,20,0]) rotate([0,0,30]) import(file="war_machine_body_2.stl");
translate([40,50,0]) rotate([0,0,25]) import(file="war_machine_leg_1.stl");
translate([58,60,0]) rotate([0,0,200]) import(file="war_machine_leg_2.stl");
translate([52,50,0]) rotate([0,0,0]) import(file="war_machine_leg_3.stl");
```

This model is fairly straightforward. The first line creates a transparent gray bounding box that defines our 100mm² printing area, a size suitable for most 3D printers. This box will be ignored when generating the STL file—it's just there to help fit all the pieces on the plate. The remaining five lines import the separate existing STL files and positions them in the printing plate to get everything to fit while still providing some space between each part.

For this mashup, we will replace the war machine's head piece with one of our own creation, a cute and slightly disturbing variation, using the adorable Rabbit Habbit (www.thingiverse.com/thing:18350) model by Brian Stamile.

Making a Part in MeshMixer

The first thing we need to do to create a new head for our mashup is to bring our unsuspecting rabbit into MeshMixer by first opening the `rabbit4.stl` file in MeshLab and resaving it as an OBJ file. With this done, we then import the rabbit as before (see Figure 7-33).

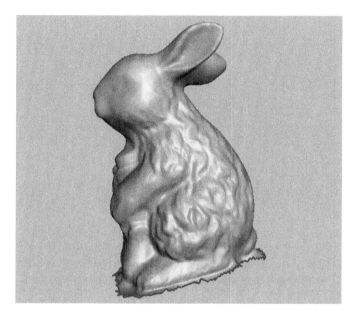

Figure 7-33. *Imported rabbit in MeshMixer*

There will be a blue jagged line at the bottom of the model. This shows that the model is open, or nonmanifold. This might create problems if trying to print this model directly, but since we will be removing the rabbit's body anyway, it shouldn't matter for us here.

To remove the rabbit's body, select it with the Select tool, which colors the entire area to discard in orange. Figure 7-34 shows the selection being made.

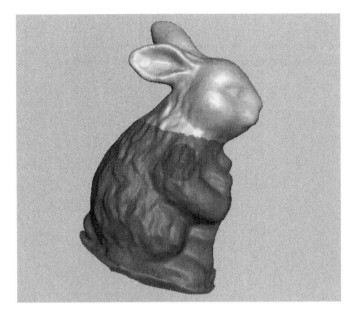

Figure 7-34. *Selecting the rabbit's body*

Once selected, we can choose Edits ➤ Erase & Fill to remove the body and fill the gap left behind. Then click Accept and export the resulting model as an STL. We are now ready to return to OpenSCAD to incorporate the rabbit's head into the rest of our multipart model.

Finishing the Part in OpenSCAD

Since we are adding our rabbit to the war machine printing plate, we will add the following new module, called rabbit_overlord(), to the existing war machine code from Listing 7-2:

```
module rabbit_overlord() {
        difference() {
                translate([04,0,-46]) rotate([0,-7,4]) scale([0.8,0.8,0.8])
                        import(file="rabbithead.stl", convexity=30);
                translate([-20,-20,-5]) cube([40,40,5]);
        }
}
```

The start of this module imports the new rabbithead.stl file that we created in MeshMixer; scales the model to 80 percent of its original size in order to fit the rest of the war machine; then moves and rotates it, through trial and error, to just below the printing plate level; and flattens the bottom of the head using the difference of a cube subtracted from the bottom of the head. Remember, to call this module in OpenSCAD, we need the line rabbit_overlord(); somewhere outside of the module itself, with the resulting model now looking like what's shown Figure 7-35.

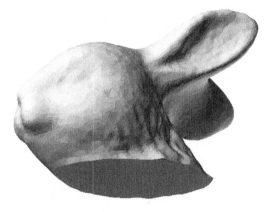

Figure 7-35. *Imported rabbit head in OpenSCAD*

For the new rabbit head to slot in where the old war machine head fit, we need to add some slots to the back of the new model. Through a little trial and error, the thickness of the interlocking parts was found to be 2.25mm thick. Using handy guesswork, we need to position two cubes inside the back of the head so that the top the war machine's back leg can slot into it. The modified module now includes the following two extra lines:

```
module rabbit_overlord() {
        difference() {
                translate([04,0,-46]) rotate([0,-7,4]) scale([0.8,0.8,0.8])
                        import(file="rabbithead.stl", convexity=30);
                translate([-20,-20,-5]) cube([40,40,5]);
                translate([-1.125,2.25,0]) cube([2.25,14,7]);
                translate([-1.125,-8,2.25]) cube([2.25,20,5]);
        }
}
```

When this is rendered and compiled, we end up with what is shown in Figure 7-36.

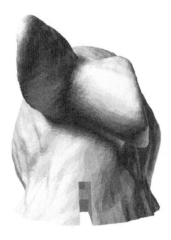

Figure 7-36. *Adding a slot to the back of the head*

Wrapping It Up

After working with this model a little, I'm worried that the lower ear is too low, and as a result, will not print very well. If our slicer has the support option, then this would be one way to solve the issue; but the overhang is so minor that it's really overkill. Instead, we can add a single cylinder that supports the lowest part of the ear during printing. Adding this line to the module and positioning the new rabbit head in place of the war machine head results in the finished code, shown in Listing 7-3.

Listing 7-3. Rabbit Overlord printing plate

```
%translate([0,0,-0.5]) cube([100,100,0.5]);

translate([22,50,0]) rotate([0,0,15]) rabbit_overlord();
translate([40,20,0]) rotate([0,0,30]) import(file="war_machine_body_2.stl");
translate([40,50,0]) rotate([0,0,25]) import(file="war_machine_leg_1.stl");
translate([58,60,0]) rotate([0,0,200]) import(file="war_machine_leg_2.stl");
translate([52,50,0]) rotate([0,0,0]) import(file="war_machine_leg_3.stl");

module rabbit_overlord() {
        difference() {
                translate([04,0,-46]) rotate([0,-7,4]) scale([0.8,0.8,0.8])
                        import(file="rabbithead.stl", convexity=30);
                // flatten the bottom of the model
                translate([-20,-20,-5]) cube([40,40,5]);
                // add slot for attaching to leg 3
                translate([-1.125,2.25,0]) cube([2.25,14,7]);
                translate([-1.125,-8,2.25]) cube([2.25,20,5])
        }
        // add support
        translate([-9.5,15.5,0]) cylinder(h=9.75,r=4);
}
```

Figure 7-37 shows the completed printing plate when it's rendered.

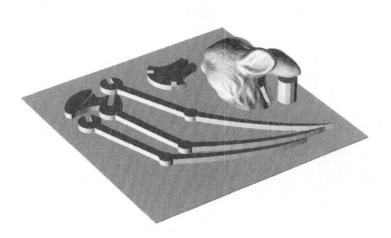

Figure 7-37. *Rabbit Overlord model*

All we need to do from here is compile the model, export the model as an STL, and proceed with printing. When finished, the three legs will attach to the center piece and the head slots into the topmost slot in the tall leg. We now have our complete Rabbit Overlord.

Assembling the Minions

Now that we have an army of rather bizarre minions, we need to get them printed, assembled, and ready for action. If your slicer has the support feature, then using it for all but the first model will most likely help successfully print these models. If not, or if you like to experiment, try using the supports that we have built into the code of these models. Having extra perimeters or shells, as much as three or four, helps to print more solid-looking objects because of these models' organic shapes.

The only model to give me fits was Busemuth the MeshMixer mashup because of its complex shape and overhangs. Using Slic3r's new support feature was a little hit-and-miss. All the same, when printed, the finished army should look something like what you see in Figure 7-38.

Figure 7-38. Printed and assembled minions

Summary

In this chapter, we started to fill our toy box with all manner of fantastical creations that didn't, maybe rightfully, exist before. We used several applications that are useful in one capacity or another for working with STL files; and we recombined them in new ways. Making mashups involves a certain level of curiosity and humor. To look at something in a new way and try to make it a reality is what makes 3D printing such a unique use of technology today. It is a great feeling to hold in your hands something that was only a random thought a few minutes before.

In the next chapter, we will revisit Google SketchUp from Chapter 4 to make a new model entirely from scratch. In this case, it is a robotics platform for tinkering, experimentation, and maybe more importantly, robot combat. The skills that we will learn are useful for making all manner of complex, mechanical models—very handy as your designs and creations increase with your ambition.

CHAPTER 8

■ ■ ■

Mini Sumo Robot

We have used many different applications to create our 3D models in this book, but very few have such an intuitive graphical interface as our next application: Google SketchUp. In Chapter 4, we briefly looked at SketchUp for downloading and converting files found on Google's 3D Warehouse for the purpose of 3D printing. Now we will properly use SketchUp to design a multipart robot platform that can be used for mini sumo robot competitions, as well as other nefarious means.

In this chapter, we will learn the following:

- A little bit about mini sumo robots and how we can design a robot for competition

- How to use Google SketchUp for designing models for personal manufacturing

- How to assemble a complex model using multiple parts, fasteners, and electronics

SketchUp is more suitable for designing architectural models than it is small-scale designs for manufacturing, but there are some tips and tricks that we can use to create reasonably accurate models for our 3D printers. Before we jump into designing models in SketchUp, let's first briefly discuss the sport of mini sumo in order to form a design strategy for our competition robot.

What Is Mini Sumo?

A mini sumo robot competition is a small-scale version of robot sumo, first made popular in Japan in the 1980s and '90s. Like the traditional sport of sumo, two competitors (autonomous robots in our case), enter a ring and attempt to push each other out while themselves trying to stay in the ring. The first robot to be pushed or fall out of the ring loses the match. Figure 8-1 illustrates what a typical mini sumo match looks like.

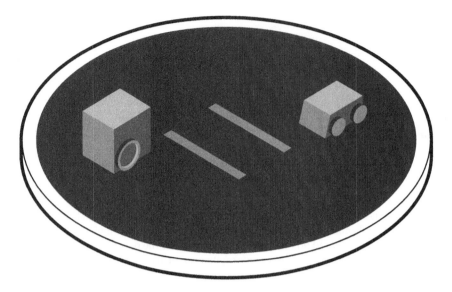

Figure 8-1. *Illustration of a mini sumo robot match*

Here we have two competitors facing off on a regulation competition ring moments before a match begins. The mini-class sumo robots are fairly compact and must conform to a standard size limitation, as shown in Figure 8-2.

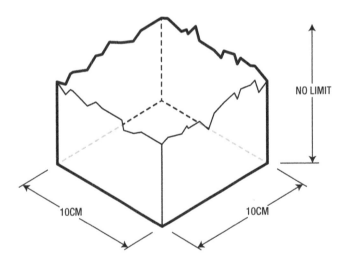

Figure 8-2. *Mini sumo robot size limits*

As seen in this Figure 8-2, the maximum size of a mini sumo robot can be no larger than a square 10 centimeters in depth and 10 centimeters in width. As long as they fit into the building of the competition, these robots can be any height. The weight for these robots is limited to 500 grams(or 1.1 pounds) or less, with some competitions giving an edge in match seeding to the lighter robots. This size scale suits our 3D printers perfectly—just about anything we design with this goal in mind will be printable on just about any 3D printer.

To give us an idea of the robot's environment, the competition is held on a black circular ring, or *dohyo*, as shown in Figure 8-3.

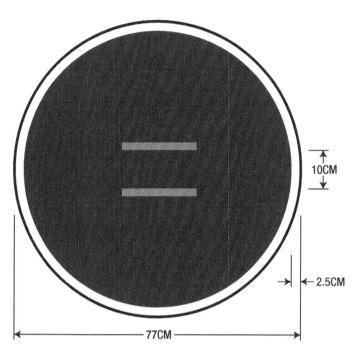

Figure 8-3. *Dohyo competition ring*

This competition ring is 77 centimeters in diameter with a 2.5cm white border called the *tawara*, which circles around the outside of the ring. Two parallel brown starting lines, or *shikiri*, 10cm long and 1cm wide, are painted in the middle of the ring 10 centimeters apart. The contrast between the black field and the white border allows us to build robots that can sense the edge of the ring and attempt to avoid falling out of it.

The sumo match begins with placing the two robots in the ring so that each robot occupies one side of the ring. When the referee, or *gyoji*, declares the start of a match, the two opponents hit a start button on the robot to begin a five-second countdown, giving the team members time to back away from the ring. After this five-second delay, the match begins with each robot attempting to find the other and push the other robot out of the ring within the given time limit. The match is won when only one robot is left in the ring, although a tie is often declared if both robots stay in the ring when time expires. Most competitions have rounds of two or three matches, with robots winning points for each victory.

More information on mini sumo robot can be found on David Cook's Illustrated Guide to American Robot Sumo (www.robotroom.com/SumoRules.html) and the Dallas Personal Robotics Group Mini-Sumo Robot Rules (www.dprg.org/competitions/minisumo.html). Given this brief introduction to the world of mini sumo, let's look at how we can incorporate the rules for this competition into our design considerations for the robot platform. It should be as follows:

- Overall size of less than 10cm width × 10cm depth

- While any height is acceptable, a lower center of gravity might be preferable

- Needs powerful motors for sufficient pushing power

- Tires or tracks need to provide lots of gripping force

- Entire robot to remain under the 500 gram weight limit

With those criteria in mind, we should now turn our attention to the software that we will use for this chapter, and then have a go at the basics of using Google SketchUp. We will return to these design considerations later when we are ready to start modeling our robot platform.

Working with SketchUp

Google's SketchUp 3D modeling application (http://sketchup.google.com) is a little different from some of the other applications that we have put to work in this book. Where other applications allow for parametric designs to exacting tolerances or the direct and sometimes squishy manipulation of 3D model meshes, SketchUp has a more intuitive graphical interface that feels more like sketching a bedroom floor plan than designing a 3D model. In fact, SketchUp is used far more often for architectural models than it is for manufacturing, which means it can present a few challenges when making designs for 3D printing. What makes SketchUp so unique is the push/pull approach to making flat shapes three-dimensional. We will get to how this works very shortly, but for now, download and install SketchUp—if you haven't already—then let's start with setting up our workspace and template.

SketchUp Workspace and Templates

When we first start SketchUp, we are presented with a welcome screen, as shown in Figure 8-4.

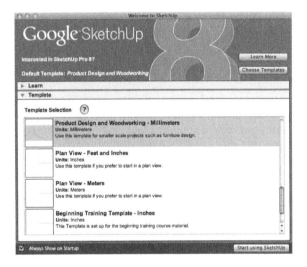

Figure 8-4. SketchUp welcome screen

From here, we can choose a template to work with in our model by selecting the Templates window. For our examples, we will be using the Product Design and Woodworking–Millimeters template, although you are welcome to use another template and adjust accordingly. Once a template is selected, hit the Start using SketchUp button in the lower-right corner to take us to the workspace where we can begin our drawing. Before we start, though, we need to adjust the workspace a little to make things work a bit better for 3D modeling by setting a few options. First, we need to set the precision of our drawing to something more suitable for our smaller-scale designs. Select Window ➤ Model Info from the top menu bar to bring up some information regarding our model (see Figure 8-5).

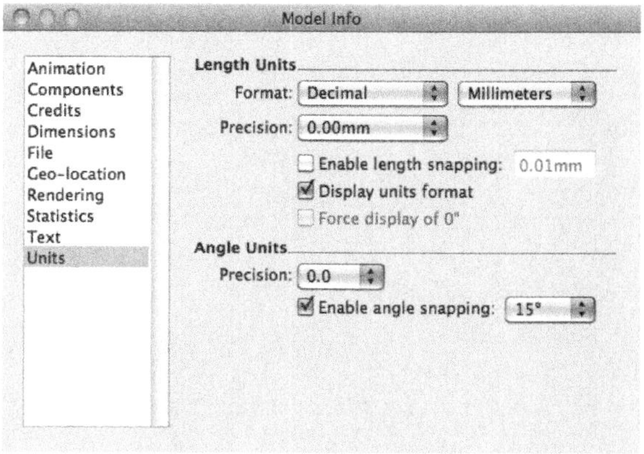

Figure 8-5. *Units options in Model Info*

Select Units from the list on the left, and set Precision under Length Units to 0.00mm. Assuming we are working with the same template, everything else can be left as they are.

Next, we can set some viewing options to help us see the model that we are making. Again, you might prefer another style entirely, although the images in this chapter were created with the following options: from the View ➤ Edge Style menu select Edges, Profiles, and Back Edges. This shows us the edges of the model, outlining the outside perimeters in a darker line and displaying a faint, dotted line for those edges hidden from view. Finally, Under View ➤ Face Style, select Monochrome, and deselect any other of the options. This keeps the appearance simple.

Now we can choose the way we want our toolbars to be set up. I prefer to disable the top toolbar in the window by selecting View ➤ Hide Toolbar. Since we still need access to our tools, I then choose View ➤ Tool Palettes ➤ Large Tool Set. With all of these options set, your workspace should look similar to the images that follow. While the colors in these images have been altered to be more readable in this book, I personally prefer the default blue-gray to all white. With the workspace set, let's look at some of the basic tools and how we can use them to draw shapes.

Drawing Basic Shapes

In order to draw shapes in SketchUp, we need to use a few of the drawing tools in the large toolset, particularly those shown in Figure 8-6.

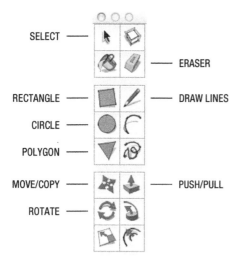

Figure 8-6. *Selected drawing tools*

Start by selecting the Rectangle tool to change the cursor into a pencil icon. Starting at the center axes, click once to define the origin of the shape and then move the cursor outward—as done in Figure 8-7.

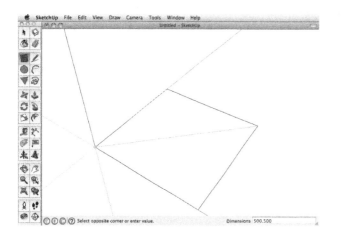

Figure 8-7. *Drawing a square*

Note that unlike many other applications, in SketchUp you will rarely click and drag the cursor while holding the mouse button down. Instead, you click once, move the mouse outwards, enter the values for the shape to be drawn, and then click the mouse again to place the shape. While drawing with the Rectangle tool, SketchUp indicates whether or not you are making a square by showing a red diagonal line (see Figure 8-7). To specify exact measurements in SketchUp, we can enter values into the Measurements Toolbar, found in the right-hand side of the Status Bar at the bottom of the screen.

For this example, enter the values 500,500 into the toolbar (labeled "Dimensions" when one of the draw tools is selected) and hit the Enter key to create a square that measures 500mm wide × 500mm deep, as seen in Figure 8-8.

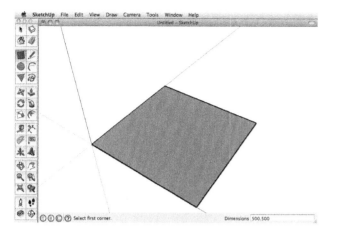

Figure 8-8. *500mm × 500mm square*

To create a cube from our square, we need to select the Push/Pull tool from the toolbar. Click once on the face of the square and, moving the mouse, pull the square upward. Enter the value 250 for distance in the Measurement Toolbar and hit the Enter key to create a cube 250mm tall (see Figure 8-9).

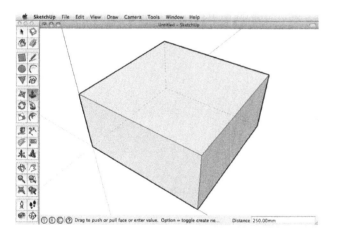

Figure 8-9. *500mm × 500mm × 250mm cube*

With that, we have created a simple cube to the dimensions that we specified. Creating other basic shapes, such as cylinders or polygons, can be done in exactly the same manner using the Circle or Polygon tool to draw a shape, and then pushing or pulling to give it height. Let's see how we can use this technique to make a complex shape.

Drawing Complex Shapes

Building from our first example shape, let's see how we could create a hole through the inside of our cube using the Circle and Push/Pull tools. We can start by drawing a circle with the Circle tool, in the center of the cube. To make this easier, SketchUp provides us with inference points, shown in Figure 8-10, to help us locate points in the drawing.

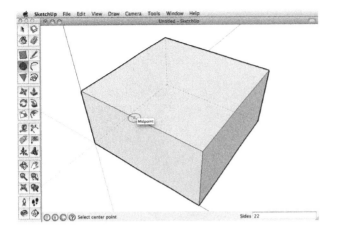

Figure 8-10. *Finding the midpoint inference*

To find the inference point, move the mouse along the edge of the cube until the center of the mouse changes to a bright blue dot, which tells us that we've reached the midpoint inference for that edge. We can use this point to help find the center of the square by first hovering over this point, and then run the mouse over one of the perpendicular edges to locate that midpoint inference. After hovering over that point for a second, we can now move the mouse towards the center of the cube, and when the point gets close to the center, it locks in and shows two dotted lines out to either edge (see Figure 8-11), letting us know that we have found the center.

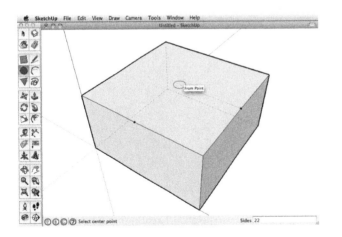

Figure 8-11. *Finding the center*

With the center point found, we can click once to start the circle and, pulling the mouse outward, enter the value 100 in the Measurements Toolbar for the circle's radius. Hit Enter to place the circle (see Figure 8-12).

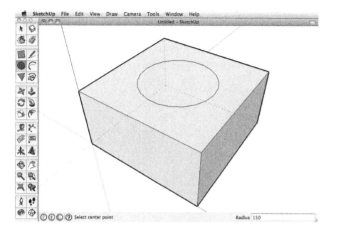

Figure 8-12. *Placed circle in the center of the cube*

You might notice that the circle in Figure 8-13 looks different from the square in Figure 8-8. A shape is purple if it is an open, or a nonmanifold, form, as was the case with the flat 2D square; while if a 2D shape is drawn on a manifold 3D shape, it remains white. As before, we can use push/pull on the circle, except this time we will push the circle into the cube, as shown in Figure 8-13.

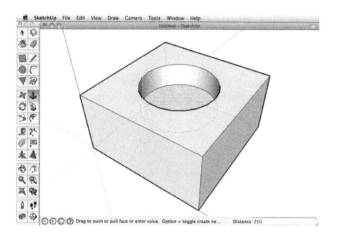

Figure 8-13. *Pushing circle into cube*

To push a shape into another, select the face of the circle with the Push/Pull tool by clicking once, then move the mouse inward and enter the value 250 for the distance to push the circle clean through the cube, as shown in Figure 8-14.

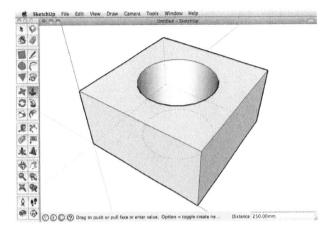

Figure 8-14. *Cylinder negative space*

With that, we have a completed complex shape with a cylindrical negative space. Keep in mind, as powerful as push/pull can be, it only works on surfaces, not edges, and the surface of the object must be parallel and free of extra edges. Push/pull works from the origin point, so each time this operation is performed, the distance starts at 0 from that point. Likewise, it is possible to use push/pull for related actions by double-clicking a surface to push/pull it in the same direction and distance as the last object. With that object created, we should look a little more closely at the navigating tools for viewing our object in the round.

Navigation

Navigating in SketchUp can be a little tricky to get used to, but once you have an understanding of the navigation tools and have mastered the keyboard shortcuts, it becomes second nature. Figure 8-15 shows some of the navigation tools.

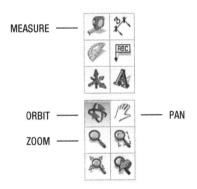

Figure 8-15. *Navigation toolset*

To rotate the workspace, shown in Figure 8-16, we can select the Orbit tool; or hold down the middle key of a three-key mouse on a PC or hit Cmd + Ctrl + left-click on a Mac, and drag the mouse to orbit around the object.

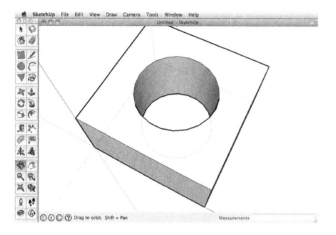

Figure 8-16. *Orbiting the view*

To zoom, we either select the Zoom tool from the toolbar or use the scroll wheel on the mouse to zoom in and out of the model at the point of the cursor (see Figure 8-17).

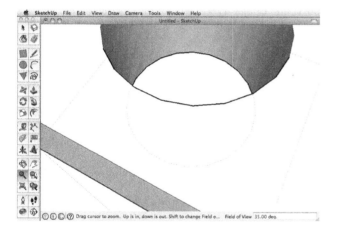

Figure 8-17. *Zooming in the view*

To pan across the object from left to right or right to left, we need to use the Pan tool. You can also hold the Shift key while clicking and dragging with the middle mouse button on a PC or hit Cmd + Ctrl + Shift + left-click on a Mac. Holding these keys while clicking the model moves the point of view, as shown in Figure 8-18.

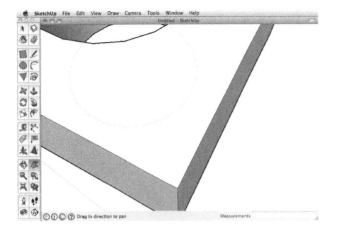

***Figure 8-18.** Panning across the view*

Believe it or not, that is just about everything you need to know about Google SketchUp to complete this project. We will add a few more things to the mix once we get into it, but those basics will serve you fairly well. Remember, there are many great resources on SketchUp if you really get into using it, including Sandeep Singh's *Beginning Google SketchUp for 3D Printing* (Apress, 2010) and Google's very own tutorial video series at `http://sketchup.google.com/training/videos/new_to_gsu.html`.

Now we should switch gears and start designing our project.

Designing a Mini Sumo Robot

For this project, we have numerous considerations to take into account: not only the parts that we will design for 3D printing, but also the motors, wheels, electronics, and other components needed to make our robot platform come to life. We might want to spend some time sketching ideas on what the robot should look like or how the parts that we design will work on the finished platform. While we don't have the space in this chapter to show every nuance of building a mini sumo robot, I can get you started on the right foot by designing a robot chassis that can be customized and reconfigured to suit many different needs.

To begin, let's look at the collected components that are needed to build our robot platform (see Figure 8-19).

***Figure 8-19.** Parts for the mini sumo robot*

Here we have a selection of parts from a few different sources, mostly Pololu Electronics, (`www.pololu.com`), SparkFun Electronics (`www.sparkfun.com`), and the neighborhood RadioShack. These parts range from general prototyping supplies to specialized motors and tracked wheels. Table 8-1 provides a summary of the parts list, not including the printed parts that we will design shortly. As you can see, this is a fairly inexpensive project, totaling just under $75—well under the cost of commercial robot kits. Printing the chassis and other parts helps to make this project all the more affordable.

Table 8-1. *Mini Sumo Robot Supplies List*

Part Description	Supplier	Part Number	Price	Quantity
Tracked wheel set, 22-tooth	Pololu	1415	$13	1
50:1 micro metal gearmotor HP	Pololu	998	$16	2
Baby Orangutan B-328 controller	Pololu	1220	$20	1
170-point solderless breadboard	SparkFun	PRT-08803	$4	1
Momentary pushbutton	SparkFun	COM-09190	$0.5	1
4 AA battery holder	RadioShack	270-391	$2	1
Double-sided foam tape	RadioShack	64-2361	$3	1

In addition to these parts, you will also need a length of wire or preterminated jumper wires to make the electrical connections with the motors and electronics. To assemble the robot, we need a few screws left over from building your 3D printer and a pack of AA batteries to get going. Significant on this parts list are the tracked wheels from Pololu, which will create the unique character of our robot. These wheels are spaced 48 millimeters apart on each side, with the motor wheel mounting to the Pololu 50:1 micro gearmotors and the idler wheel using a special shoulder screw as an axle.

In addition to the way the wheels mount to the robot, we also need to consider in our design that by sticking to the 100mm² size limit, the battery holder is the largest component to work around. This holder measures 64mm wide × 52mm deep—well over half of our allotted space in these directions. Accommodating the size of the battery holder requires careful planning, especially when we start to think about the motor locations and the extra idler wheels that need to screw into the side of the chassis.

When designing the robot platform, we can start with defining the space for the battery holder, and then move on to the motor mounts. After that, we can find space for the wheels and add a dozer blade and other details later. Let's jump in.

Getting Started

To get started, we can consult the specifications for the battery pack and motors, taking note of the dimensions of each item to speed along the design process. We will then work on creating the battery compartment, designing the motor mounts, finishing off any details, adding the dozer blade, and then putting it all together.

Battery Compartment

As mentioned earlier, our battery holder measures a large 52mm × 64mm, so it is a pretty good place to start. The battery holder will be mounted to the bottom of the robot, so we need a few closed sides with an open back to allow the wires to pass through, and an open bottom to replace the batteries. For the top of the chassis, it might be a good idea (for later upgrades) to provide some mounting points using captive nuts, and also provide a space for the breadboard—more on that as we go.

With all that taken into account, we can start with a cube by drawing a square that measures 53mm × 66mm, and then pull it to 12.5mm tall. This will make the compartment larger than the battery holder by 1 millimeter on three sides; and it gives us a nice sturdy top platform measuring 4mm thick. (The height of 12.5 millimeters was chosen somewhat arbitrarily after playing around with the model and figuring out what might work for the battery holder.) With this first cube created, we can draw a square on top of the cube, 1 millimeter from the edges; start with setting two guides on the top surface, as shown in Figure 8-20.

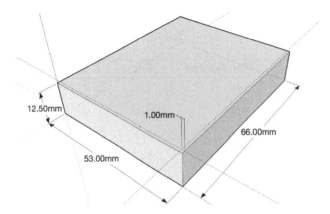

Figure 8-20. *Basic cube with guides inset 1 millimeter*

To find a point 1 millimeter from the outside edges of the cube, we need to set a pair of guides using the Measure tool. Simply click once on the top edge of the cube that you want to measure from, enter 1 into the Length box in the lower right, and then hit Enter. This creates a dotted guideline running 1 millimeter parallel to the edge you selected. After repeating for the other side, we should have a point 1 millimeter inside the corner of our cube. From here, we can draw a square measuring 64mm × 52mm and then push this square inward 8.5 millimeters from the top to create the battery compartment in Figure 8-21.

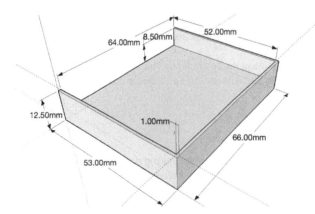

Figure 8-21. *Battery compartment*

With only three sides, the battery holder will stick out the back of the compartment a little bit to allow clearance for the power wires. Now, to finish this part of the design, we can add a cutout for the breadboard to fit inside. Set two more guides as we did on the inside of the compartment, one 3 millimeters from the front corner and another 14.5 millimeters from the side corner. Using these guides, draw a square 46mm × 35mm and push it in 4 millimeters to see the shape shown in Figure 8-22.

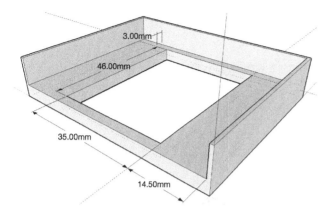

Figure 8-22. *Cutout for breadboard*

With this created, we now have a place to hold the battery compartment, and when the piece is flipped over, the solderless breadboard for wiring up the electronics can fit in the inside indention. Now we can move on to making the motor mounts.

Motor Mounts

Using 3D printing technology, it's possible to make parts that would be difficult or even impossible with other forms of manufacturing. We will take advantage of that when designing a mount for our Pololu micro metal gearmotors, illustrated in Figure 8-23.

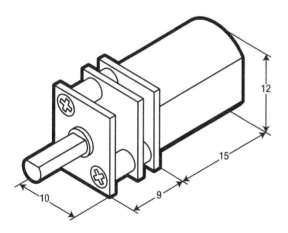

Figure 8-23. *Pololu 50:1 HP gearmotor*

To mount these motors, we can design a simple clip that the motors snap into and be held in place by friction and the pressure of the clip. These mounts will be placed at the front of the robot with the idler wheels in the back. Looking at the dimensions in Figure 8-23, we see that we need to make a cylinder space with flattened sides to hold the main body of the motor. Because the free version of SketchUp lacks the functionality of OpenSCAD's intersection() module, we will need to draw a circle to the proper dimensions on the face of a cube, add lines to modify this shape, and then delete the extraneous lines before pushing the resulting shape into place.

We can start with the basic shape of the motor mount by creating a cube with the dimensions of 14.1mm × 14mm × 14mm, as seen in Figure 8-24.

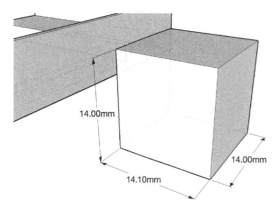

Figure 8-24. *Basic motor mounting block*

With the side that measures 14.1 millimeters in width facing us, we need to set a couple of guides to locate the position of the circle and straight lines to make the profile of the motor shape. First, to match the rest of the platform, a guide is placed 4 millimeters up from the bottom edge. Then a second guide is placed 9.05 millimeters from the bottom edge, with a third guide 1 millimeter from the top edge. Now draw a circle with a radius of 6.05 millimeters on this surface, starting at the midpoint of the center guide (see Figure 8-25).

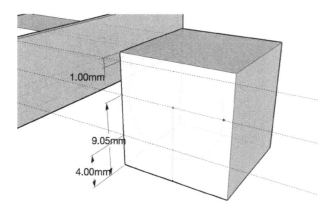

Figure 8-25. *Drawing circle on the face of the motor mount*

Because of a peculiarity with SketchUp that rears its head later on, we need to first specify a 22-sided circle instead of the default 24. With the Circle tool selected, but before drawing the circle, enter the value **22** in the Measurements Toolbar in the lower right and then proceed to draw the circle as normal. This will create a circle that hangs off the top of the cube we drew earlier—but we will fix that later. With a radius of 6.05 millimeters, we are making a circle 0.1mm larger than the diameter of the motor body. This provides a little tolerance for the motor dimensions and is the reason we needed the face of the mount to be 14.1 millimeters wide, giving us at least 1 millimeter on the sides.

Next, we need to draw the flat side of the motor profile by using the Draw tool and drawing a horizontal line that begins with the intersection of the lowest guide and the edge of the circle, ending with the intersection of the lower guide and other side of the circle, as shown in Figure 8-26.

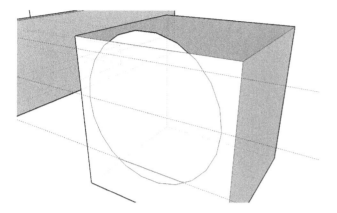

Figure 8-26. *Drawing a horizontal line*

The last things we need to draw are a couple of vertical lines to make the top of the motor mount more printable and reduce the sharp edge. This is shown in Figure 8-27.

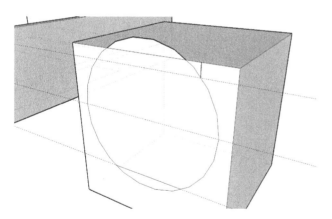

Figure 8-27. *Drawing a vertical line*

In Figure 8-27, I've drawn a vertical line starting at the intersection of the topmost guide and the edge of the circle straight along the blue axis until it hits the top edge of the cube. Once drawn, repeat for the other side of the circle to complete the basic shape for the motor. Now we need to clean up this profile by deleting unnecessary lines using the Eraser tool. This includes deleting the top and bottom arcs of the circle and the little sections of the circles edge that would create an overhang. The end result is seen in Figure 8-28.

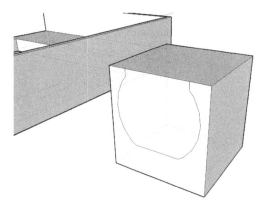

Figure 8-28. *Cleaned up motor profile*

Now we have completed drawing the final motor profile for our motor mount. To create the negative shape inside the cube, all we need to do is push the shape 14 millimeters using the Push/Pull tool. This will give us the finished motor mount shown in Figure 8-29.

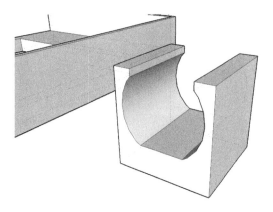

Figure 8-29. *Finished motor mount*

To attach the motor mount to the battery compartment, we need to open some spaces in the front of the compartment that the motor mount will fit into. As shown in Figure 8-30, set a vertical guide 5 millimeters from the front-left corner and draw a square 14mm wide and 12.5mm tall.

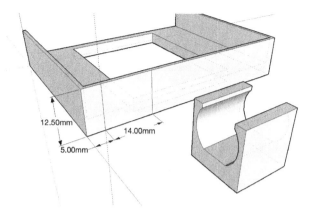

Figure 8-30. *Creating shape for motor mount opening*

Pushing this square into the compartment 1 millimeter will leave a flat, nonmanifold square that can be deleted by using the Eraser tool and clicking on the remaining top edge. This should leave an opening like the one shown in Figure 8-31.

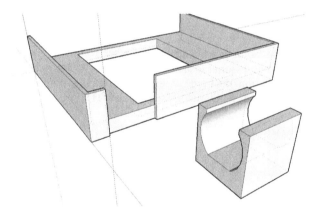

Figure 8-31. *An opening in the battery compartment*

With an opening in the compartment, select the entire motor mount using the Selection tool and then copy it to the clipboard (Ctrl + C on a PC or Cmd + C on a Mac) to add the second motor mount later. Now, using the Move tool, select the lower back corner of the mount and move it into position at the lower back inside corner of the opening we created earlier (see Figure 8-32).

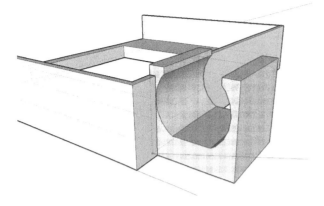

Figure 8-32. *Moving motor mount into position*

If done right, the motor mount should join with the battery compartment, making a single solid object. Repeat these steps for the other side using the copy of the motor mount you placed on the clipboard, and then we can finish up the front of the robot chassis by filling it in with some extra cubes.

Front End

To complete the front end, we need to fill the gap between the motor mount and the edge of the compartment, and add a piece that runs across the entire front end to mount accessories to later. Let's start with the first cube to fill the gap on the side of the motor mount by drawing a square from the front corner of the motor mount to the corner of the compartment, and then pull that square to a height of 4 millimeters (see Figure 8-33).

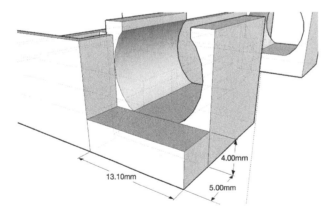

Figure 8-33. *Filling in the front end*

After repeating for the other side of the platform, we will need to create the next cube separate from the existing model and move it into place. (If we drew this cube in place, SketchUp would want to fill in the inner square; however, it's best to leave the square open so that wires can pass through later.) Start with a square 6mm × 66mm and pull it to 4mm tall, as shown in Figure 8-34.

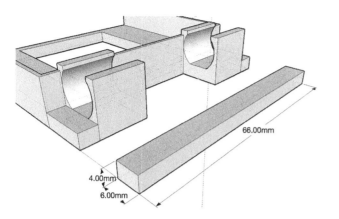

Figure 8-34. *Drawing front bar*

After finishing this front bar, select the entire thing using the Selection tool. Then using the Move tool, click the lower back corner and move the cube so that it sits flush with the front edge of the motor mounts, creating the finished front end shown in Figure 8-35.

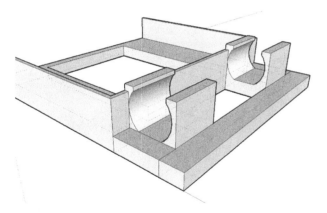

Figure 8-35. *Finished front end*

Wheels and Supports

With the basic platform completed, we now need to turn our attention to where the platform meets the wheels by adding supports for the gear motors and mounts for the rear idler wheel axles.

Motor Supports

To provide a little support for the front wheel motors and to keep them locked into the motor mounts, we need to add a little ledge that supports the gearbox part of the motor. This shouldn't need much more than a square designed to fit inside the brass plates of the gearbox extending upward about0.5 millimeters. We can start by creating an indention like we did for the motor mounts by setting a guide on the side of the platform 1.05 millimeters from the front corner of the battery compartment. Now draw a square 10mm × 4mm, and then push this inward 0.5 millimeter, as shown in Figure 8-36.

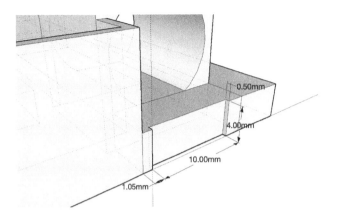

Figure 8-36. *Creating indention for front motor support*

Now starting on the front inside corner of the indention we just made, draw a square 10mm × 4mm, pulling this to 4.5 millimeters in height. When finished, we should have a block that rises above the platform level by 0.5 millimeter, like the one shown in Figure 8-37.

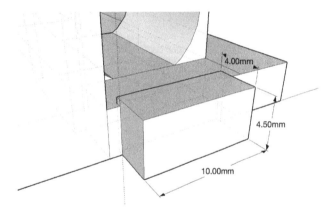

Figure 8-37. *Drawing basic motor support*

While this would almost work, because it extends so far down to what will become the top of the platform, it might catch on the inside of the wheel. To fix this, we could angle the box to provide enough support while staying out of the wheels. If we keep the angle to 45 degrees, then we also keep to a tolerance that is easily printable by most printers. To do this, we can set a guide 1 millimeter from the top of the support and draw a line along the side of the cube from edge to edge using the Draw tool. Then, using the Move tool, select the lower edge and move it inward 3.5 millimeters along the green axis. The final motor support is shown in Figure 8-38.

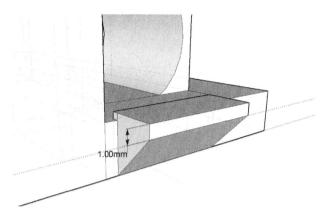

Figure 8-38. *Finished angled motor support*

Repeat this to support the second motor on the other side before continuing on with the rear axle mounts.

Axle Mounts

For the back idler wheels, we need to provide a way for the shoulder screw that comes with the wheels to screw into the platform. One way to do this is to build up a support for the axle mount and then design a space that a hex nut can fit into to give the axle screw something to attach to. We start by setting a guide 38 millimeters back from the edge of the front motor support to ensure the shaft of the motor and the axle are 48 millimeters apart. Then draw a square 10mm × 4mm pulled 12.5mm tall, as shown in Figure 8-39.

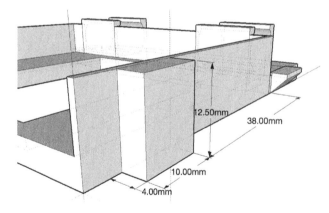

Figure 8-39. *Starting the axle mount*

Just as we did with the motor support, we need to angle the bottom of the axle mount to keep it away from the edge of the wheels. As shown in Figure 8-40, set a guide 4 millimeters from the bottom edge and then draw a line along this guide from edge to edge of the cube, moving the bottom edge inward 4 millimeters.

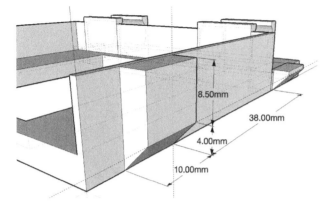

Figure 8-40. *Basic shape of the axle mount*

To create the holes for the axle screw and nut, we need to spin the model around and set a vertical guide along the inside face of the battery compartment 41.05 millimeters from the front inside corner and a horizontal guide 5 millimeters from the bottom inside corner. Now we can draw a six-sided polygon with a radius of 3.2 millimeters, and inside of that, a circle with a radius of 1.5 millimeters, as shown in Figure 8-41.

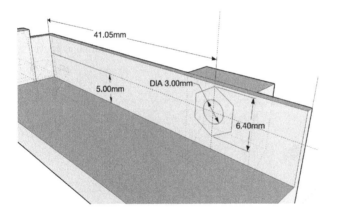

Figure 8-41. *Creating a space for an M3 screw and captive nut*

The 3.2mm radius for the hexagon has been calculated by looking up the width of an M3 metric nut that measures 5.5 millimeters across the flats. This is then divided by the square root of 3, which is 1.73, to calculate the radius of the hexagon from point to center. This way a diameter of 6.4 millimeters will result in a hexagon that is also 5.5 millimeters across the flats. Before we can push this space into the side of the battery compartment, we need to first erase the extraneous line at the top of the axle mount, where the support and compartment meet, so that we can push into it. With the Push/Pull tool selected, click the hexagon and enter 2.5 for the depth. The remaining circle can then be pushed 5 millimeters to create a hole all the way through the axle mount, as seen in Figure 8-42.

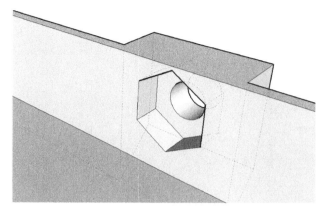

Figure 8-42. *Finished captive nut*

After printing, an M3 nut can be pressed into this space and it will be held firmly enough for the axle to screw into. Once we add another axle support on the other side of the platform, then we are almost done with our design—only a few more little details left.

Battery Clips

Since the battery pack will mount to the platform upside down, we would need to hold it into place with some double-sided tape unless we make some battery clips on the edge of the compartment that would hold the battery pack in place. With a vertical guide set 22 millimeters from the inside corner, we can draw two squares: one measuring 15mm × 1mm along the top and another 15mm × 0.5mm along the side (see Figure 8-43).

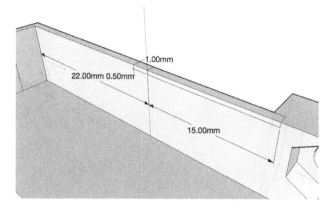

Figure 8-43. *Creating the basic shapes of the battery clips*

From here, we need to pull the top square upward 1 millimeter, and then pull the new square on the side inward 1 millimeter. Now draw a line along the inside face from short edge to short edge0.5 millimeter from the bottom of this new shape. With the Move tool selected, move the lowest edge back 0.5 millimeter. This completes the battery clip shown in Figure 8-44.

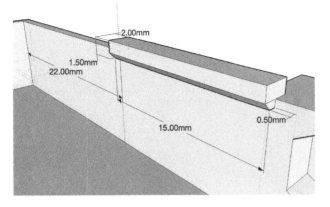

Figure 8-44. *Finished battery clip*

After adding the second clip on the other side of the battery compartment, these clips should provide enough of a ledge to hold the pack in without getting in the way or being too difficult to print. Later on, we might want to use a little double-sided tape to permanently hold the battery pack.

Cleaning and Detailing

Now that we have finished most of the design, all that is left is to clean it up and add some details.

Cleaning Up the Model

As we have been drawing our little robotics platform, we have left all sorts of extra lines in the model that might give us a difficult time when it comes to printing the finished components. Let's take a moment just to clean these up. If we look at Figure 8-45, which shows the other side of the motor mount and front end, we see an example of *coplanar lines*. These are lines that don't define an edge of an object, but instead create shapes that are on the same plane. This might confuse things when we process the model for 3D printing.

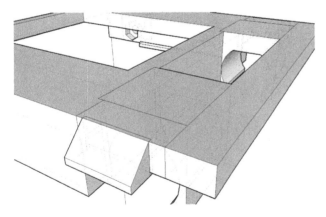

Figure 8-45. *Unnecessary coplanar lines*

To remove these lines, select them using the Eraser tool. If the model turns blue or opens up, you deleted a line that needed to be there. Undo the last operation and think again about deleting that line. If you have Back Edges selected under View options, look for interior lines that don't attach to anything because they can also create problems. When all of the unwanted lines are removed, we should have a clean model with the only visible lines being those that define an edge, like in the image shown in Figure 8-46.

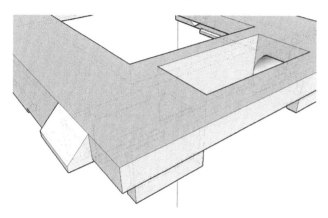

Figure 8-46. *Cleaned up robot platform*

Mounting Points

With our platform design nearly finished, all we need to do is add some mounting points that we can use to mount sensors or other things that we design later. The location of these holes and their shape is chosen pretty much at random. If you have something specific in mind to mount to the platform, you might need to adjust these dimensions. I chose to add four mounting points along the front edge of the platform and an additional six with captive nuts on either side of the battery compartment. Guides were set at 8 millimeters and 24 millimeters from either side of the platform and 3 millimeters from the front leading edge. Starting at the front inside corner of the battery compartment, guides were also set at 9.5 millimeters, 24.5 millimeters, and 39.5 millimeters.

At the intersection of the six guides inside the battery compartment, place hexagons with a radius of 3.2 millimeters. In the center of the hexagons, draw six circles with the radius of 1.7 millimeters. Along the front edge, four circles with a radius of 1.7 millimeters are placed. The six hexagons are pushed 2.5 millimeters through the platform and all circles are pushed 4 millimeters through the platform. This gives us the finished mounting points in Figure 8-47.

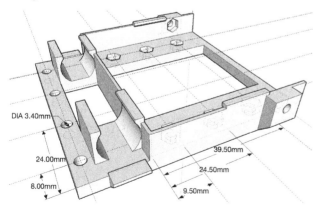

Figure 8-47. *Finished mounting points*

And there we have it: a finished robotics platform. So far, we have been designing it upside down, but if we spin it around, as in Figure 8-48, we can see the finished design.

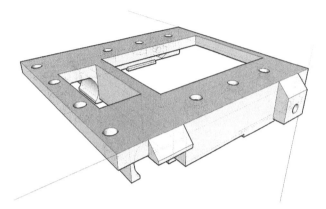

Figure 8-48. *Finished platform design*

While we could just call it a day here, what good is a pushing robot without some sort of dozer blade to push with? Next up is a bonus design for a bolt-on dozer blade.

Dozer Blade

We will keep the design of our dozer blade relatively simple. The blade should bolt on to give us some flexibility in the robot's design. It should reach all the way to the surface that the robot rolls around on and still keep the robot within our 100mm² maximum build dimensions. To get started, we need to draw three cubes (see Figure 8-49), each 4mm thick and 35mm tall, with the two outer cubes measuring 24mm long and the middle cube 44mm long.

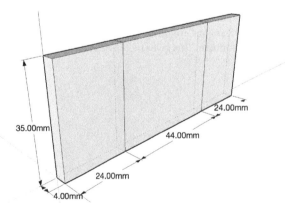

Figure 8-49. *Three cubes for the basic dozer blade*

To create a semicurved blade, we need to add some facets to the faces of these cubes, as shown in Figure 8-50, by drawing lines starting at the outside corners and meeting at the midpoint of the inside lines, and then horizontally across the midsection.

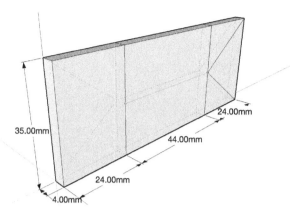

Figure 8-50. *Adding facets to the dozer blade*

These extra lines allow us to move some of the sides around without creating manifold problems. They also help with angling the blade; for example, Figure 8-51 shows selecting the top three faces and using the Move tool to move them forward 8 millimeters along the red axis.

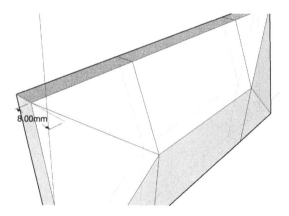

Figure 8-51. *Adding shape to the dozer blade*

Further shaping can be done by moving the edges, corners, or sides until you are happy with the final design. Remember, there is some limitation on the overall dimensions that we are trying to stick to and we need to be sure that the tracks do not rub on the back of the blade when it is mounted.

To create a semicurved blade, I moved the top corners another 5 millimeters along the red axis and the bottom corners 9 millimeters along the red axis, as shown in Figure 8-52.

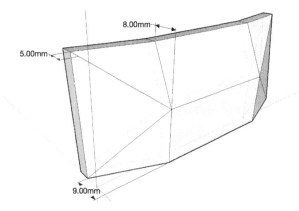

Figure 8-52. *Further shaping the dozer blade*

When we are happy with the design, we need to add a mounting block to the back of the dozer blade. This block should measure 6mm × 28mm, pulled to 4 millimeters in height, as shown in Figure 8-53.

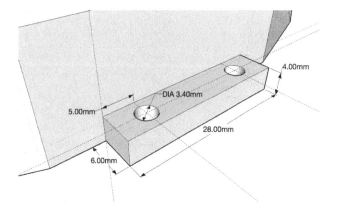

Figure 8-53. *Adding mounting block*

This mounting block, which will be at the top of the blade after printing, has two 3.4mm diameter mounting holes in the middle of the block that are 5 millimeters from each edge to match the front of the platform. When all is said and done, the finished blade should look something like Figure 8-54.

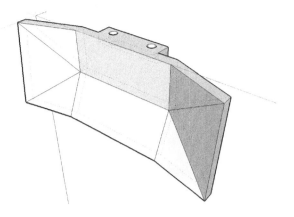

Figure 8-54. Finished dozer blade

With our final part of the mini sumo robot completed, it's time now to print parts, install electronics, and get things up and running.

Wrapping Things Up

This is a fairly complex project, so wrapping things up will involve printing all of the parts that we designed, bolting things together, installing all of the hardware, and then wiring electronics and hooking everything up. We can't spend too much time covering the last half of the project, but hopefully I can give you an idea of how to get going.

Make Ready for Printing

In designing this model, we have made every precaution to make our design manifold a solid shape with no interior lines or holes. The way that SketchUp works by nature, however, means that issues might crop up for no apparent reason. These issues often only become apparent when you slice and print the model, and even then you might not catch the problems before printing.

To get this model out of SketchUp, we need to first export the design using Nathan Bromham's SketchUp to DXF or STL plug-in used in Chapter 4. Head to the menu bar and select Tools ➤ Export to DXF or STL; if nothing is selected, it will ask to export the entire model, so click Yes. Then choose millimeters as the export unit, select STL from the next drop-down menu, and then save the file. With the STL file saved, it's a good idea to process the file through netfabb's web-based file processing at http://cloud.netfabb.com to best prepare your file for printing. After downloading the repaired files, you can slice and print the model as usual.

The finished prints shown in Figure 8-55 were printed with gray PLA set to 2 perimeters, or 1 extra shell, two solid layers, 0.2mm layer height, and 15 percent infill.

Figure 8-55. *Printed models*

Putting It Together

To assemble our mini sumo robot, we should first take a minute to clean up the printed parts with a hobby knife or small needle file, making sure that there are no plastic blobs in the motor mounts or battery compartment, and clearing out the screw holes. Next, we can press fit eight M3 nuts into the spaces we designed earlier (see Figure 8-56).

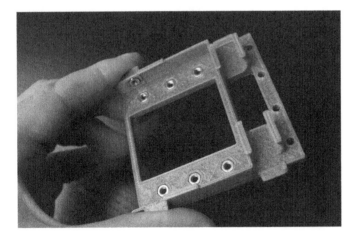

Figure 8-56. *Adding M3 nuts*

Two of these nuts are used to mount the rear axles, while the other six are there for future upgrades. Once the nuts are in place, we can bolt on the dozer blade using spare M3 screws, and then add the wheels, beginning with the front wheels. These wheels press fit on the motor shaft—it can be a little tight so take you time and make sure you have a good fit. Then slide the motor into the front motor mount from the side, as shown in Figure 8-57.

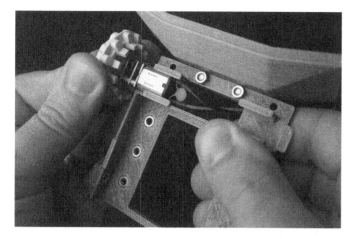

Figure 8-57. *Inserting front motors and wheels*

The motor clicks into place if everything fits as it should. Next, we screw in the rear idler wheels using the shoulder screws provided with the track set (see Figure 8-58).

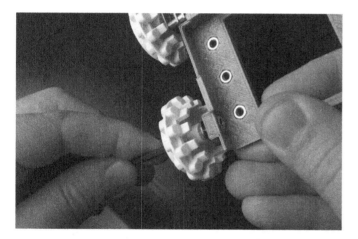

Figure 8-58. *Tightening rear idler wheels*

The shoulder screw inserts into the wheel from the outside. Place an M3 washer over the exposed screw and tighten it into the side axle mount. This hole should be a little tighter than the others, so it might require threading the screw in carefully. If it proves to be too long, you need to cut off some of the exposed screw using a rotary cutoff tool or hacksaw. The screw should fully tighten in the M3 nut, but not extend into the battery compartment.

Now you can slide the battery holder until it clicks into place. Then stretch the tread belts over the wheels, and drop the breadboard into its compartment in the top. With all that in place, we can add the electronics.

Adding Electronics

The electronic brain that I used for my robot was the Baby Orangutan B-328 controller board from Pololu Electronics, which is an Arduino-compatible microcontroller with an onboard dual motor driver. This board was chosen for its low cost, small size, built-in motor driver, and Arduino compatibility. The downside to this controller is that it severely limits the type of sensors available to use on the platform. Other possibilities include SparkFun's Arduino Pro Mini 328 (DEV-11113) and TB6612FNG Motor Driver (ROB-09457), although this solution requires wiring that is more complex. Either way, with a smaller controller you need to solder pins to the board for it to work in a breadboard. This is shown in Figure 8-59.

Figure 8-59. *Soldering pins to the controller*

Insert the male pin headers that came with the controller into the breadboard, placing the controller on top of these pins. Then, quickly solder each pin with a soldering iron and solder, being sure to move swiftly so as not to overly heat the plastic breadboard. Work your way around the board until all of the pins are soldered in place.

Next, we need to prepare the motors by soldering a 0.1uF capacitor (if you have one) and lengths of wire or terminated jumper wires to each lead of the motor, as shown in Figure 8-57. This lets us plug the motors directly into the breadboard to be powered by the onboard motor driver. After that, all we need to do is insert the microcontroller; plug in the motors; add any other components that we might want to use, like a switch or sensors; and then plug in the battery pack. The finished mini sumo robot is shown in Figure 8-60.

Figure 8-60. *Finished mini sumo robot*

Summary

Well, there we have it: probably the most complex project in this book designed with Google's free SketchUp design application. SketchUp may not be the best application for parametric CAD rendering, but it is certainly easy to pick up, and its intuitive interface makes sense to a lot of people.

In this chapter, we learned how to draw basic shapes with a reasonable degree of accuracy and to push or pull those shapes into complex models. The combination of simple objects gave us the power to build a detailed model that works with a vast array of parts, from simple screws to motors and wheels.

Now that our basic robot platform is built, we need to get cracking on programming it using the Arduino programming environment (http://arduino.cc) and a handy guide from Pololu on programming their Orangutan controllers (www.pololu.com/docs/0J17). Once we get our platform rolling under its own volition, we can add sensor arrays to seek and find the competitor robot or detect the edge of the sumo ring to avoid accidentally falling out. And, of course, we will need to build a *dohyo* and a second robot to hold our own matches. As you can see, this chapter is only just the beginning of an interesting fusion of 3D printing and robotics competition.

In the next chapter, we take it down a notch and look at a couple of fun and entertaining projects that I couldn't fit in anywhere else in the book.

CHAPTER 9

■ ■ ■

Bonus Round: More Projects

We have tackled some pretty big projects in this book to get the hang of a handful of 3D applications and utilities that enable us to make new objects on our personal 3D printers. This has allowed us to expand that toolbox that let's us quickly move from a simple idea to holding a finished object in our hands. Hopefully, it has given you the confidence to try new applications and accomplish new ideas as you move onwards from the basic tutorial projects. In this chapter, we will present a couple of additional project ideas to take your 3D design skills even further. We won't dwell on the applications as we talk about these projects; instead, we will focus on how the models are made and why. Consider this a bonus round of new directions to take the skills that you have learned so far.

In this bonus round, we will do the following:

- Model a design using the dimensions and sketches taken from an existing object

- Make derivatives of existing models to fit novelty windup mechanisms

- Create household decor, starting with nothing more than a few squiggly lines

- Hack G-code files to create hollow vessels

This chapter won't require you to wrap your brain around any new applications, so we should be able to move right along and make some cool things. Let's jump right in with our first bonus round project.

Project: Windup Walkers

As hard as it is for me to say, not everything can be 3D printed. Not yet anyway. Sometimes you have a need that can only be met by something you have to shell out cold cash to obtain. Like say, maybe you need a spring-loaded mechanism with a couple of feet, yes feet, to propel printed plastic objects along your desk to do you bidding. In that case, we need to purchase some windup walkers (see Figure 9-1) … and print some things to go on top of them.

Figure 9-1. *Windup walkers*

These walker mechanisms were purchased as a five-pack through MakerBot Industries at http://store. makerbot.com/windup-walkers.html. Similar mechanisms are available with or without things attached to them from toy stores and novelty supply shops.

The goal of this project is to make a shape that approximates the windup body so that we can create a negative space inside a new or existing 3D model—to easily add walking legs to a printed object. To get a leg up on this project, you could use one of the existing models created by our technical reviewer, Tony Buser, including Windup Walker Negative at www.thingiverse.com/thing:14953, Mashup Walker Shell at www.thingiverse.com/thing:14955, or J. Feaver's Windup Walker mechanism model at www.thingiverse.com/thing:17817. While these models will work more or less just fine, it's more fun to walk through how to make these things yourself, so that when some other nifty thing comes along, you'll be able to do something with it as well.

Measuring the Mechanism

To start, we need to take some precise measurements of the windup mechanism, keeping accurate notes that we can design from. For this task, we need our handy digital calipers, which we used in Chapter 3, and some note-taking supplies. Using the digital calipers, we can start recording the various dimensions of the walker, as shown in Figure 9-2.

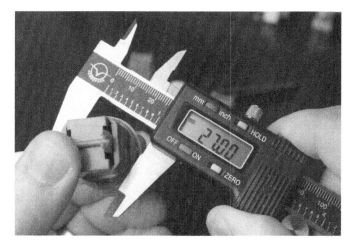

Figure 9-2. *Measuring the windup mechanism*

In this image, I am measuring the diameter of the lower inside ring of the mechanism, which turns out to be 27 millimeters. This measurement will form the bottom of the model that we'll design around the mechanism; and we can work up from there. The mechanism's body measures 30.5 millimeters in height, so we know that when we start to model this in a CAD application, we will want to start with a cylinder that is at least 30.5 millimeters in height and 27 millimeters in diameter, or maybe just a little bigger for an easier fit. As we continue to measure the walker, we want to take detailed notes for each of the dimensions that we record, as demonstrated in Figure 9-3.

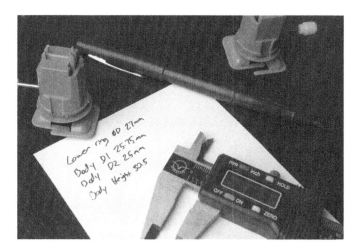

Figure 9-3. *Recording measurements*

Once our list of measurements helps us form a good idea of how this negative shape will look, we are then ready to try our hand at creating the model.

Designing the Windup Model

To create an accurate dimensional model for our windup mechanism we will return to OpenSCAD. You might design using another application, although Google SketchUp may not be the best option because the program needs to support subtracting one model from another.

Since there are models of this windup mechanism already on Thingiverse, the primary design considerations for this version should address the following:

- Take up the least amount of space inside the finished model

- Maintain printability and not require support structures

- Easily fit the mechanism with little to no modification of the printed object

With these criteria in mind, we will try to keep things as simple as we can.

The Basic Shape

To design the basic shape of the windup mechanism, we start by creating a simple cone to represent the basic dimensions of the body of the walker (see Figure 9-4).

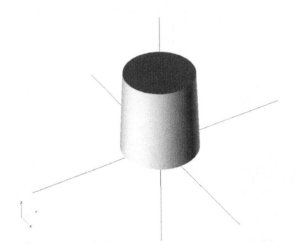

Figure 9-4. *Simple cone for walker mechanism*

This cone (yes, the top is smaller than the base) is created using the `cylinder()` module in OpenSCAD in the following line of code:

```
cylinder(h = 29, r1 = 28/2, r2 = 25/2);
```

In this line, we've created a slightly sloped cylinder using the first diameter of 28 millimeters and the second of 25 millimeters, based on the dimensions that we measured. To make things fit a little easier, these diameters have been increased slightly, by 1 millimeter, from the recorded dimensions. The cone also needs to be a little taller to fully fit the windup mechanism, although while thinking about the fit inside the finished models, it might be helpful to slope the inside of the opening by making another cylinder at the base. Figure 9-5 shows what this looks like.

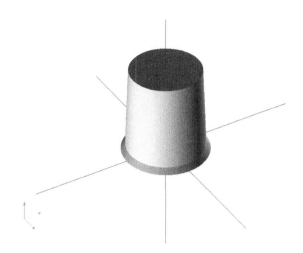

Figure 9-5. *Sloped base for mechanism opening*

The code now includes two lines, as follows:

```
cylinder(h=2,r1=31/2,r2=28/2);
translate([0,0,2]) cylinder(h=29,r1=28/2,r2=25/2);
```

Here we've added a single cylinder, or cone, that is only 2mm tall, and then moved the cylinder from Figure 9-4 up 2 millimeters to sit atop the new cone. This will give us a 31mm total height for the body and should help the mechanism easily pop into the printed model. To fit the little plastic extensions of the legs at the top of the walker mechanism, we could further extend our larger cylinder another6 millimeters, but to make this model as small as possible, we will add another cylinder at the top to slope the negative space inwards without creating difficult-to-print overhangs. By adding the following line of code:

```
translate([0,0,31]) cylinder(h=6,r1=25/2,r2=20/2);
```

We end up with the modified basic form shown in Figure 9-6.

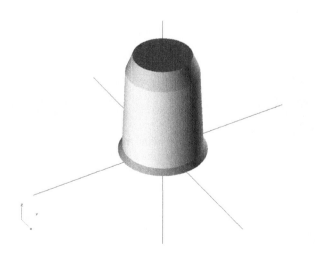

Figure 9-6. *Basic cylindrical form*

Adding the Winder

To complete the basic model, we need to add a space for the winder. At its most basic, the winder is simply a small cylinder for the metal rod that attaches to a larger cylinder for the plastic handle. To fit this in the model, we need to create two slots or grooves that will let the winder slide into the model. Again, we could have simply made a single box for this shape, but by adding the following four lines to our script, we get a slot that better fits the winder and takes up the least amount of space in our finished model.

```
translate([0,10.5,9.5]) rotate([-90,0,0]) cylinder(h=15,r=1.25);
translate([-1.25,10.5,0]) cube([2.5,15,9.5]);

translate([0,10.5+15,9.5]) rotate([-90,0,0]) cylinder(h=12,r=4);
translate([-4,10.5+15,0]) cube([8,12,9.5]);
```

With these lines added to our code, we end up with a form (see Figure 9-7) that works for our windup mechanism.

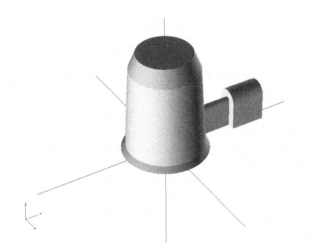

Figure 9-7. *Finished basic mechanism*

While the model, at this point, works for our purposes, it's still a little big. This mean that the models we choose for the windup walkers would also need to be a little bigger than they need to be. Let's modify this design by removing parts that we don't need.

A Little off the Top

To trim this model down, we can start with removing a couple of cubes at the top of the model, leaving just enough room for the top of the leg mechanism to move freely. To accomplish that, the following is the code that we have assembled up to this point, now including additional union() and difference() modules:

```
difference() {
        union() {
                cylinder(h=2,r1=31/2,r2=28/2);
                translate([0,0,2]) cylinder(h=29,r1=28/2,r2=25/2);
                translate([0,0,31]) cylinder(h=6,r1=25/2,r2=20/2);
```

```
            translate([0,10.5,9.5]) rotate([-90,0,0]) cylinder(h=15,r=1.25);
            translate([-1.25,10.5,0]) cube([2.5,15,9.5]);

            translate([0,10.5+15,9.5]) rotate([-90,0,0]) cylinder(h=12,r=4);
            translate([-4,10.5+15,0]) cube([8,12,9.5]);
        }
        translate([-20,-20,31]) cube([16,40,6.5]);
        translate([4,-20,31]) cube([16,40,6.5]);
}
```

When compiled, Figure 9-8 shows that we have removed the two sections at the top.

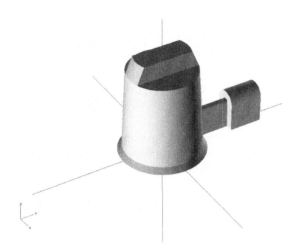

Figure 9-8. *A little off the top*

Finishing It Up

We are almost there, but if we look at the plastic windup mechanism, the front and back have flat areas that would let us get back a little more space in our model. To start, we can subtract two cubes from the front and back of the form using these two lines:

```
translate([11,-20,15.5]) cube([5,40,16]);
translate([-11,-20,15.5]) mirror([1,0,0]) cube([5,40,16]);
```

To make the dimensions a little easier to figure out, I've used the mirror() module to duplicate the second cube in the back of the model. This will give us the form shown in Figure 9-9.

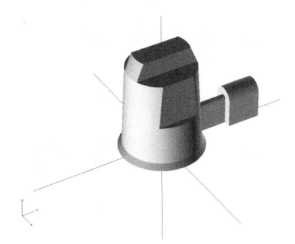

Figure 9-9. *Next to the last step*

That would also work well enough, but just to take out a little more material, I'm going to duplicate these two cubes and rotate them each 3 degrees into the model to get that little bit of space back and to better fit the windup mechanism. When all is said and done, the final code for our walker() module is shown in Listing 9-1.

Listing 9-1. Finished Windup Walker Module

```
module walker() {
        difference() {
                union() {
                        cylinder(h=2,r1=31/2,r2=28/2);
                        translate([0,0,2]) cylinder(h=29,r1=28/2,r2=25/2);
                        translate([0,0,31]) cylinder(h=6,r1=25/2,r2=20/2);

                        translate([0,10.5,9.5]) rotate([-90,0,0]) cylinder(h=15,r=1.25);
                        translate([-1.25,10.5,0]) cube([2.5,15,9.5]);

                        translate([0,10.5+15,9.5]) rotate([-90,0,0]) cylinder(h=12,r=4);
                        translate([-4,10.5+15,0]) cube([8,12,9.5]);
                }
        translate([-20,-20,31]) cube([16,40,6.5]);
        translate([4,-20,31]) cube([16,40,6.5]);

        translate([11,-20,15.5]) cube([5,40,16]);
        translate([-11,-20,15.5]) mirror([1,0,0]) cube([5,40,16]);

        translate([11,-20,15.5]) rotate([0,-3,0]) cube([5,40,16]);
        translate([-11,-20,15.5]) rotate([0,3,0]) mirror([1,0,0]) cube([5,40,16]);
        }
}
```

And when this code is rendered, we have the finished windup mechanism, as shown in Figure 9-10.

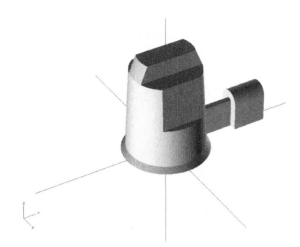

Figure 9-10. *Finished windup mechanism*

This model is a good compromise between being easy to code and easy to print, and still gives us enough room to use a wider selection of models for our windup walkers. When printed, there will be overhangs, but these areas are fairly straightforward bridges that are connected at either side to the rest of the module. While the bridge areas are reasonably easy for printers to print without support material, sometimes, depending on the slicer used, there will be an option to print these bridges with special settings. For example, using ABS, I would set bridges to print a little slower and with the cooling fan, normally turned off for ABS, set to full speed during the bridge.

Now with the completed mechanism drawn up, we need to find a model in need of some legs.

Gargoyle Walker

Our first victim is the great Thinking Gargoyle (`www.thingiverse.com/thing:20634`) by Charles Babbage. This model was created using a new application from AutoDesk called 123D Catch (`www.123dapp.com/catch`), which uses photos of an object to create a 3D model. Before bringing this model into OpenSCAD, I first ran it through MeshLab to reduce the number of faces to about 7,500. I also processed the file through `cloud.netfabb.com`, as discussed in Chapters 4 and 7. The processed model, once brought into OpenSCAD, is shown in Figure 9-11.

Figure 9-11. *Thinking Gargoyle*

We are using the following standard STL import script:

```
import(file="thinkinggargoyle.stl", convexity=5);
```

The added convexity parameter helps display the model when we get to the next part: creating the cavity for the windup mechanism. To do this, we need to use the difference() module to subtract the walker() module that we created earlier. Let's try the following code to do this:

```
difference() {
        import(file="thinkinggargoyle.stl", convexity=5);
        translate([0,3.5,-0.1]) rotate([0,0,90]) walker();
}
```

When this is rendered, we end up with what's shown in Figure 9-12.

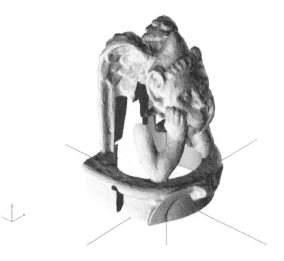

Figure 9-12. *Subtracting the mechanism from the gargoyle*

That didn't exactly work, did it? Part of the problem here is that even though we moved and rotated the walker() module so that the walker would line up and walk in the right direction, the scale of the imported gargoyle STL is a little off. That's an easy fix if we use the scale() module to enlarge the gargoyle to better fit the walker mechanism. It leaves us with the finished gargoyle_walker() module in Listing 9-2.

Listing 9-2. Finished Gargoyle Walker Module

```
module gargoyle_walker() {
        difference() {
                scale([1.35,1.35,1.35]) import(file="thinkinggargoyle.stl", convexity=5);
                translate([0,3.5,-0.1]) rotate([0,0,90]) walker();
        }
}
```

By increasing the size of the gargoyle by 35 percent using the line scale([1.35,1.35,1.35]) in front of the import() module, the gargoyle then fits the mechanism perfectly, as shown in Figure 9-13.

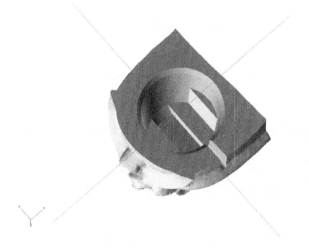

Figure 9-13. *Finished gargoyle walker*

Here you can see the void left behind from subtracting the shape of the walker mechanism from the gargoyle model. When printed, the windup mechanism should slot right in. But before we get to that, let's find another model to try out.

Gnome Walker

Thingiverse is a mystical land full of wondrous and fantastical creatures, including Tony Buser's Gnome Scan #4 (www.thingiverse.com/thing:11506), a 3D scan of a ceramic yard gnome using Tony's DIY Spinscan 3D scanner (www.thingiverse.com/thing:9972). Figure 9-14 shows the gnome entering the matrix.

Figure 9-14. *Gnome being scanned (courtesy Tony Buser, 2011)*

The gnome is a high-resolution file, so the first thing we need to do is bring the model into MeshLab and reduce the number of faces from 72,000 to about 22,000 (see Figure 9-15).

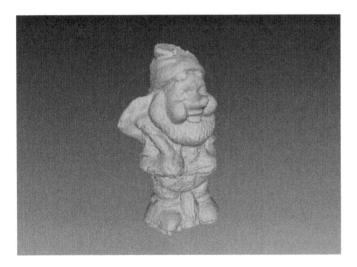

Figure 9-15. *Gnome in MeshLab*

I noticed that there's a little blip on the gnome's hat, likely an artifact from scanning that could give us problems later on. To fix this, we need to export the model from MeshLab as an OBJ file and open the file in MeshMixer, as shown in Figure 9-16.

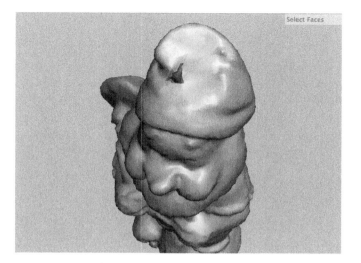

Figure 9-16. *Editing the gnome in MeshMixer*

Once in MeshMixer, we can select the odd little form shown in Figure 9-16 and chose Erase & Fill from the Edits menu. Once we're happy with our edits, we need to save the gnome as an STL and import the file into OpenSCAD using the following line of code:

```
import(file = "gnome.stl", convexity = 5);
```

Because our gnome friend already has a pair of legs, we need to remove them so that he can have bionic versions. To do this, we use the difference() module to subtract a cube from the model, positioning the model as appropriate, as shown in Figure 9-17.

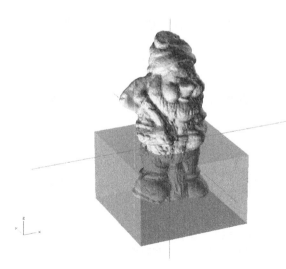

Figure 9-17. *Preparing the gnome model*

The cube is highlighted in Figure 9-17 using the % background modifier, just so that we can see the interaction between these two forms. The code that does this follows:

```
difference() {
        translate([-5,-4,-34]) scale([1.1,1.1,1.1])
                import(file = "gnome.stl", convexity = 5);
        translate([-40,-40,-50]) cube([80,80,50]);
}
```

In this code, we have also scaled the model by 10 percent and positioned it, somewhat intuitively, to be ready for the final step of subtracting the walker() module. Figure 9-18 shows the finished gnome walker model. Listing 9-3 is the finished gnome_walker() code.

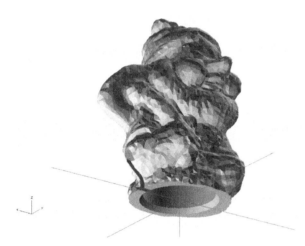

Figure 9-18. *Finished gnome model*

Listing 9-3. Finished Gnome Walker Module

```
module gnome_walker() {
        difference() {
                translate([-5,-4,-34]) scale([1.1,1.1,1.1])
                        import(file = "gnome.stl", convexity = 5);
                translate([-40,-40,-50]) cube([80,80,50]);
                translate([0,0,0]) rotate([0,0,95]) walker();
        }
}
```

Our little gnome had to be difficult about the direction he was facing, so you might notice that rather than rotating the walker mechanism 90 degrees, we rotated it an extra 5 degrees to get the walker to line up with where the gnome was facing. Let's make one more model into a walker before we start printing them out.

Robot Walker

With a gargoyle from the past, a gnome from another realm, we now need a walker from the far future to complete our set. Enter Ed Tekeian's Robot Toy #A (www.thingiverse.com/thing:12180) from a series of robot action figures. This model will form the penultimate of our walkers—it is a multipart model that needs to be assembled after the print. We can even print some of these parts in different materials.

To start, we need to download five files that make up the robot, including RT4Body.stl, RT4Helmet.stl, RT4Hands.stl, RT4Arm.stl, and RT4Bolt.stl. We will layout most of these parts together in a single printing plate, but for now let's start with the body of the robot, shown in Figure 9-19.

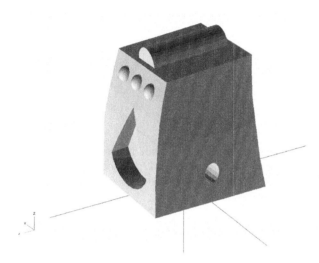

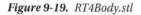

Figure 9-19. *RT4Body.stl*

We don't have quite as much to do to the robot's torso as we did with the gnome, but we still need to spin the model around to make the bottom of the torso flat by removing the bump normally attached to the model's legs. We also need to fill the inside of the torso so that the holes for the arms do not interfere with the walker mechanism. All of that is done in the following lines of code:

```
difference() {
    union() {
        translate([0,0,48]) scale([1.6,1.6,1.6]) rotate([4.25,180,0])
            import(file="RT4Body.stl",convexity=5);
        translate([-15,-10,30]) cube([30,15,15]);
    }
    translate([-50,-50,-10]) cube([100,100,10]);
    translate([0,-3.5,0]) rotate([0,0,-90]) walker();
}
```

All of this may have finished the model in other examples, but this code only completes the torso, shown in Figure 9-20. We still need to do something about the other parts of the model.

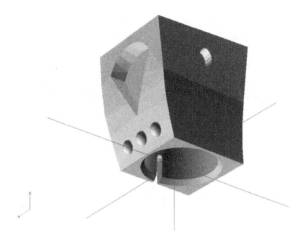

Figure 9-20. *Completed robot torso*

We've scaled the model up 60 percent, rotated it 4.25 degrees to set it flat on our build platform, and then subtracted a cube from the bottom face to make a flat surface. We also subtracted space for the walker mechanism.

The next part to modify is the robot's helmet, shown in Figure 9-21.

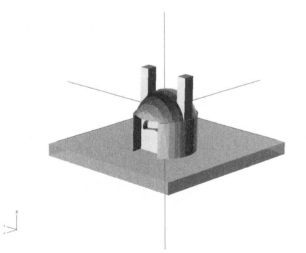

Figure 9-21. *Robot helmet*

The bottom of the helmet has a very small raised bit, almost like a neck, that needs to be flattened to better print. To do this, we subtract a cube from the helmet using the following code:

```
difference() {
      translate([-40,40,-0.25]) scale([1.6,1.6,1.6])
            import(file="RT4Helmet.stl",convexity=5);
      #translate([-70,0,-5]) cube([70,70,5]);
}
```

We also scaled the RT4Helmet.stl file by the same 60 percent that we scaled the torso. We will scale the other parts to match. Now we just need to add the remaining parts, including two copies of the RT4Arm.stl file and the two hands in the single RT4Hands.stl file. This completes the final robot_walker() module, shown in Listing 9-4.

Listing 9-4. Finished Robot Walker Module

```
module robot_walker() {
        difference() {
                union() {
                        translate([0,0,48]) scale([1.6,1.6,1.6]) rotate([4.25,180,0])
                                import(file = "RT4Body.stl",convexity = 5);
                        translate([-15,-10,30]) cube([30,15,15]);
                }
                translate([-50,-50,-10]) cube([100,100,10]);
                translate([0,-3.5,0]) rotate([0,0,-90]) walker();
        }
        difference() {
                translate([-40,40,-0.25]) scale([1.6,1.6,1.6])
                        import(file = "RT4Helmet.stl",convexity = 5);
                #translate([-70,0,-5]) cube([70,70,5]);
        }
        translate([-40,5,0]) rotate([0,0,90]) scale([1.6,1.6,1.6])
                import(file = "RT4Arm.stl",convexity = 5);
        translate([-40,-25,0]) rotate([0,0,90]) scale([1.6,1.6,1.6])
                import(file = "RT4Arm.stl",convexity = 5);

        translate([10,40,0]) rotate([0,0,-90]) scale([1.6,1.6,1.6])
                import(file = "RT4Hands.stl",convexity = 5);
}
```

When compiled and rendered, we have the finished robot printing plate, as shown in Figure 9-22.

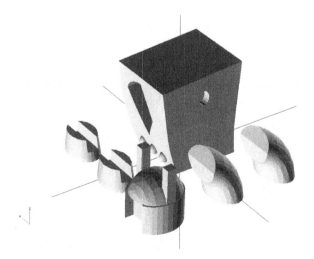

Figure 9-22. *Completed robot walker printing plate*

In order for this robot to be truly epic, however, we need one more element: lightening bolts! The original robot model included a lightening bolt for the robot to carry, presumably to throw at evil rabbits. We would be remiss to not include them.

Because the lightening bolts are too large to fit on the same plate when scaled up 60 percent, and because it might be cool to print them separately in another material, Listing 9-5 shows the code and Figure 9-23 shows the model for the `bolts()` module.

Listing 9-5. Extra Lightening Bolts Module

```
module bolts() {
        translate([0,-10,0]) scale([1.6,1.6,1.6])
                import(file = "RT4Bolt.stl",convexity = 5);
        translate([0,10,0]) scale([1.6,1.6,1.6])
                import(file = "RT4Bolt.stl",convexity = 5);
}
```

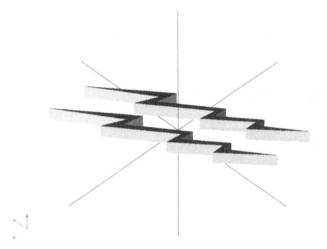

Figure 9-23. *Lightening bolts printing plate*

Now that our robot is complete with a pair of lightening bolts to throw around, let's wrap up this project by looking at the finished code for the Windup Walkers and talk about printing the models.

Wrapping Things Up

Now that we have all the modules created for each of our three walkers, it's time to put it all together in a single file so we can start printing the models. Listing 9-6 provides the completed code for our windup walkers project.

Listing 9-6. Windup Walkers Final Code

```
// disable $fn and $fa, do not change these
$fn = 0;
$fa = 0.01;
```

```
// use $fs to control the number of facets globally
// fine ~ 0.1 coarse ~ 1.0
$fs = 0.8;

walker();
!gargoyle_walker();
gnome_walker();
robot_walker();
bolts();

module gargoyle_walker() {
        difference() {
                scale([1.35,1.35,1.35]) import(file = "thinkinggargoyle.stl", convexity = 5);
                translate([0,3.5,-0.1]) rotate([0,0,90]) walker();
        }
}

module gnome_walker() {
        difference() {
                translate([-5,-4,-34]) scale([1.1,1.1,1.1])
                        import(file = "gnome.stl", convexity = 5);
                translate([-40,-40,-50]) cube([80,80,50]);
                translate([0,0,0]) rotate([0,0,95]) walker();
        }
}

module robot_walker() {
        difference() {
                union() {
                        translate([0,0,48]) scale([1.6,1.6,1.6]) rotate([4.25,180,0])
                                import(file = "RT4Body.stl",convexity = 5);
                        translate([-15,-10,30]) cube([30,15,15]);
                }
                translate([-50,-50,-10]) cube([100,100,10]);
                translate([0,-3.5,0]) rotate([0,0,-90]) walker();
        }
        difference() {
                translate([-40,40,-0.25]) scale([1.6,1.6,1.6])
                        import(file = "RT4Helmet.stl",convexity = 5);
                #translate([-70,0,-5]) cube([70,70,5]);
        }
        translate([-40,5,0]) rotate([0,0,90]) scale([1.6,1.6,1.6])
                import(file = "RT4Arm.stl",convexity = 5);
        translate([-40,-25,0]) rotate([0,0,90]) scale([1.6,1.6,1.6])
                import(file = "RT4Arm.stl",convexity = 5);

        translate([10,40,0]) rotate([0,0,-90]) scale([1.6,1.6,1.6])
                import(file = "RT4Hands.stl",convexity = 5);
}

module bolts() {
        translate([0,-10,0]) scale([1.6,1.6,1.6])
                import(file = "RT4Bolt.stl",convexity = 5);
```

```
        translate([0,10,0]) scale([1.6,1.6,1.6])
                import(file="RT4Bolt.stl",convexity=5);
}
module walker() {
        difference() {
                union() {
                        cylinder(h=2,r1=31/2,r2=28/2);
                        translate([0,0,2]) cylinder(h=29,r1=28/2,r2=25/2);
                        translate([0,0,31]) cylinder(h=6,r1=25/2,r2=20/2);

                        translate([0,10.5,9.5]) rotate([-90,0,0]) cylinder(h=15,r=1.25);
                        translate([-1.25,10.5,0]) cube([2.5,15,9.5]);

                        translate([0,10.5+15,9.5]) rotate([-90,0,0]) cylinder(h=12,r=4);
                        translate([-4,10.5+15,0]) cube([8,12,9.5]);
                }
        translate([-20,-20,31]) cube([16,40,6.5]);
        translate([4,-20,31]) cube([16,40,6.5]);

        translate([11,-20,15.5]) cube([5,40,16]);
        translate([-11,-20,15.5]) mirror([1,0,0]) cube([5,40,16]);

        translate([11,-20,15.5]) rotate([0,-3,0]) cube([5,40,16]);
        translate([-11,-20,15.5]) rotate([0,3,0]) mirror([1,0,0]) cube([5,40,16]);
        }
}
```

To see the model of your choice, place the root modifier, or ! symbol, at the beginning of the code; this will display only that module and ignore the others. For example, Listing 9-6 enables only the gargoyle_walker() module and ignores the other four. From here, you can compile and render the design, and export each module as a single STL file.

When exported as STLs, sent to the printer, and assembled with the windup walker mechanisms, we should have a series of windup walkers like those shown in Figure 9-24.

Figure 9-24. *Finished windup walkers*

For my three walkers, I used blue ABS and printed with 3 perimeters or shells, 2 solid layers, and a 10 percent infill. I wouldn't print these any more solid than that because the walker mechanism might not be able to move if the print is too heavy. In fact, these objects could possibly work fine printed with a 0 percent infill.

The robot's lightening bolts were printed using clear PLA with 1 perimeter, 20 percent infill, and 2 solid layers; they are pressed into the robot's hands when finished. The rest of the robot, which is printed from ABS, is glued together using a little acetone applied to the plastic surfaces. Acetone works very well to bond ABS plastic because it dissolves a small amount of the plastic, fusing pieces together when dry. If you print these walkers from PLA, you want to use superglue to assemble the robot.

Now that our first bonus round project is complete, let's head to a bonus project for our homes.

Project: Squiggle Vases

At the time of this writing, Spring is in full effect so for this project we will make something for our homes by revisiting some of the techniques that we used in Chapter 5 to take a 2D drawing and make a 3D object. Specifically, we will make a simple shape from a squiggle line that we draw in Inkscape, extrude this shape into a radial volumetric object, and then re-mesh the model to make a faceted polygonal vase suitable for 3D printing. And holding flowers. To illustrate how this basic principal works, let's look at the following simple circle in OpenSCAD:

```
circle(r=5);
```

It creates a 2D circle with a radius of 5 millimeters. Now, let's say we add a new module in front of this circle, like so:

```
rotate_extrude() circle(r=5);
```

With this modification, we will end up with a 3D sphere because OpenSCAD takes the 2D shape and extrudes it around a central axis. The result is illustrated in Figure 9-25.

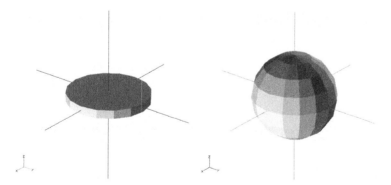

Figure 9-25. *Extruding a circle into a sphere*

This is just like the linear_extrude() module we used in Chapter 5, except this time it spins the shape as it extrudes it. Let's make our own interesting shapes, starting with some squiggles in Inkscape.

Drawing Some Lines

We start this project innocently enough in Inkscape, the open-source vector drawing application touched on earlier in this book, to make a few vector lines. We will use two primary drawing tools, shown in Figure 9-26, to draw freehand and straight lines.

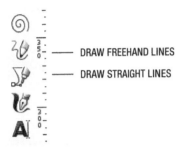

—— DRAW FREEHAND LINES

—— DRAW STRAIGHT LINES

Figure 9-26. *Inkscape drawing tools*

With the freehand drawing tool selected, draw a series of squiggly lines that are generally somewhat vertical. This is meant to be a gestural and intuitive mark, so experiment freely to see what happens. Figure 9-27 shows a few of the lines that I created this way.

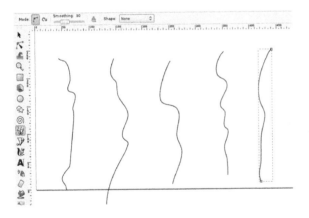

Figure 9-27. *Drawing random, freehand lines*

To make your lines a little less ragged, it's possible to use the smoothing feature in the toolbar options, shown in Figure 9-28.

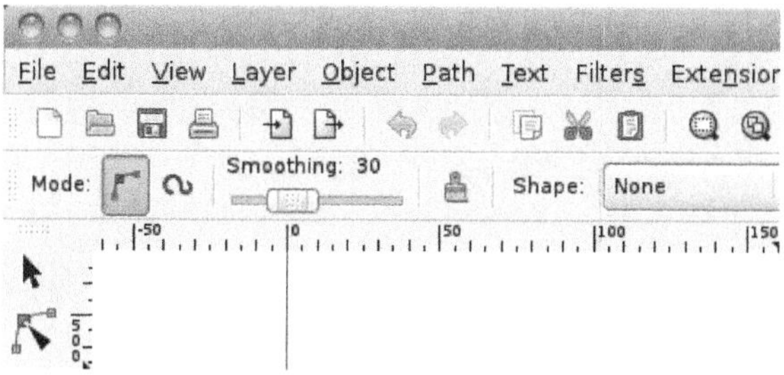

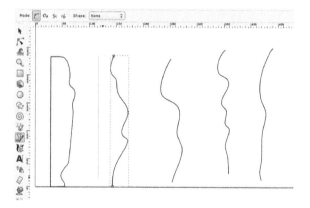

Figure 9-28. *Drawing tool options*

I have smoothing set to 30 for a good balance between detail and smoothness.

Completing the Profiles

Once we have some basic profile lines created, we want to turn them into a solid shape by completing the profile with some straight lines. This should start to make sense once we extrude these drawings, but for now, we are only looking for a shape a little more complex than our sample circle. Figure 9-29 shows the Straight Line tool being used to draw, well, straight lines extending from our freehand lines.

Figure 9-29. *Completing the shape with straight lines*

First, click the freehand line with the Nodes tool to view the end nodes of the line. Then, with the Straight Line tool selected, click one of the nodes to start the line and then, while holding down the Ctrl key, click somewhere to the left of the line to establish the width of the vase. Complete the rest of the shape by connecting the straight lines back to the end of the freehand line.

Making Straight-Line Segments

When the shape profile is completed, we need to make straight-line segments by selecting all of the nodes of the shape with the Nodes tool, as shown in Figure 9-30.

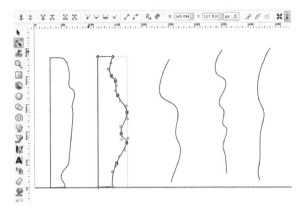

Figure 9-30. *Selecting nodes*

Now as we did in Chapter 5, we need to add nodes to this path using the Insert New Nodes button (see Figure 9-31). Then click Make Selected Segments Lines (Figure 9-32).

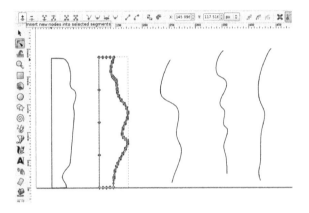

Figure 9-31. *Insert new nodes*

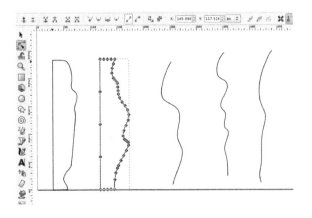

Figure 9-32. *Make selected segments lines*

Now we should have a series of profiles to experiment with. But first, we need to prepare our design for export by creating some layers and saving the file.

Creating Layers

Once we have completed drawing a series of profile shapes that started as nothing more than scribbles, we should place each shape on its own layer to make things a little easier later on. I've used the layer names line1, line2, and so on, as shown in Figure 9-33.

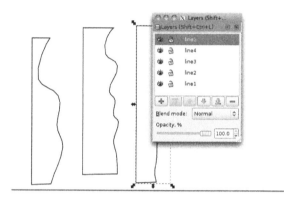

Figure 9-33. *Placing shapes on layers*

Once all the shapes are drawn and placed into their own layers, we might want to stack them all up in the corner of the page, as shown in Figure 9-34. While not absolutely necessary, this will help when we get around to making a 3D shape out of these profiles.

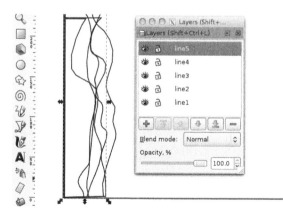

Figure 9-34. *Stacked up shapes in the corner of the page*

At this point, we have five different shapes, each made up of straight-line segments and placed in its own layer. We can now save the file in DXF format. I've saved my file as lines.dxf. We are now ready to import this file into OpenSCAD.

Extruding the Profile

So far, we have drawn arbitrary squiggle lines using the freehand tool in Inkscape and then made these lines into closed-shape profiles. After saving the collection of shapes as a DXF, we can now bring these line drawings into OpenSCAD. Using the following line of code, we end up with our drawn shape, shown in Figure 9-35.

```
import(file = "lines.dxf", layer = "line2");
```

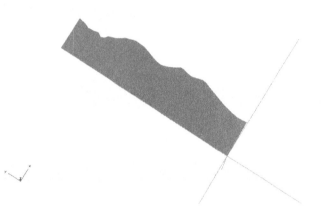

Figure 9-35. *Imported DXF line drawing*

With the basic profile now imported, in this case from the layer line2, we can use the rotate_extrude() module to extrude a given 2D shape into a circular or cylindrical 3D model, as shown with the circle to sphere example. By modifying our line of code as follows:

```
rotate_extrude() import(file = "lines.dxf", layer = "line2");
```

We end up with the model shown in Figure 9-36.

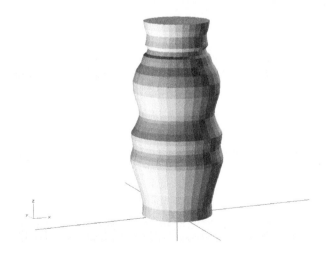

Figure 9-36. *Extruded profile*

Pretty nifty feature, right? Starting with just a simple little squiggle line, we have now created a 3D object. We are not done with our vase just yet though, because we can push the design even further and make a more abstract form using MeshLab.

Remeshing in MeshLab

To take our vase a little bit further, let's export the extruded form as an STL and open the file in MeshLab. As shown in Figure 9-37, all we are going to do is remesh the model using MeshLab's Quadratic Edge Collapse Decimation feature, located under Filters ➤ Remeshing, Simplification and Reconstruction. We've used this option to reduce a model's file size, but this time we will use it for artistic means.

Figure 9-37. *Remeshing the extruded form*

Pick a suitably low number for a target number of faces, let's say 42, to reduce the smooth, rounded vase form to a more geometric and polygonal object. Resave the model under File ➤ Export Mesh As... and be sure to select STL file type. We are now ready to bring the model back to OpenSCAD and clean it up for printing.

Cleaning Up the Vase

To bring the file back into OpenSCAD, we will need to reimport the file as an STL. While we are at it, we need to clean up the top and bottom surfaces to make them flat for printing. We can even play around with the scale of the vase to get it just the right size. Listing 9-7 provides the final code that makes this happen.

Listing 9-7. Cleaned Up Vase Code

```
difference() {
        translate([0,0,-5.5]) scale([1.5,1.5,1.6])
                import(file="squigglevase.stl",convexity=5);
        translate([-50,-50,-5]) cube([100,100,5]);
        translate([-50,-50,112.75]) cube([100,100,30]);
}
```

In this code, we've imported from MeshLab the vase with the low polygon count, scaled it up, and made it a little skinnier. We then subtract a cube from the bottom and top of the model to make these surfaces flat. When this is compiled, it should look something like what's shown in Figure 9-38.

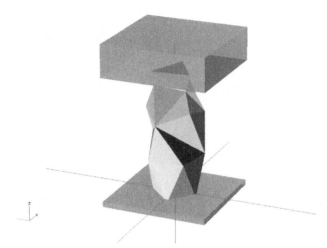

Figure 9-38. *Cleaning up the top and bottom*

To make a flat enough base for printing, we have to play around with the numbers a little until everything looks good. When settled on the finished design, we are ready to export the final model, shown in Figure 9-39, and prepare for printing.

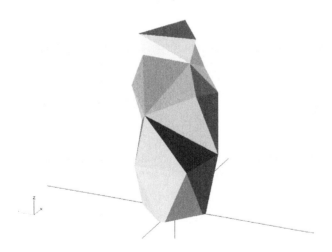

Figure 9-39. *Finished squiggle vase design*

One Last Thing

You might be wondering how I plan to turn a solid model into a hollow vase able to hold water. If your slicer, such as Skeinforge or SFACT, supports the option to slice to a certain layer using the Carve module, you can choose to slice to the layer just below the top of the model. That way, when we slice the model with 0 percent infill and 3 solid layers, the model is built hollow from the bottom up and the topmost layers are skipped, leaving an open vase.

If your slicer does not support this feature, then another trick is to either simply stop the print before it reaches the last solid layers, or better yet, go back and edit a little of the G-code generated when we slice the model to remove those layers. So for example, I've sliced this model with three solid layers and I know that the total height of the model is 112.75 millimeters and that my layer height is set for0.25 millimeters. That means that the final three layers begin at 112 millimeters.

With that in mind, let's open the G-code file of the sliced model—I saved mine as `squigglevase.gcode`—in a text editor such as TextEdit or Notepad. This file can be intimidating because it's just one long list of letters and numbers, so let's do a search for Z112 to find the layer that begins the uppermost solid layers. This small little section of code should look similar to the following:

```
...
G1 X84.444 Y68.360 E12.91013
G1 X49.617 Y81.498 E14.50664
G1 X49.014 Y78.408 E14.64171
G1 X52.119 Y45.521 E16.05851
M106 S253
G1 F1200.000 E14.55851
G92 E0
G1 Z112.000 F3600.000
G1 X52.771 Y46.697
G1 F1200.000 E1.50000
G1 X83.825 Y66.509 F1800.000 E3.07990
G1 X85.106 Y66.925 E3.13764
G1 X84.493 Y67.447 E3.17218
G1 X50.027 Y80.450 E4.75217
G1 X49.729 Y78.923 E4.81888
...
```

We need to select all of the text, beginning with the line G1 Z112.000 F3600.000 in the middle, and scroll all the way down, nearly to the bottom of the file, to the line before the command G92 E0 that precedes any of the end G-code placed in the file by your slicer. This is done to turn off your motors or similar commands. Once the last three layers have been selected, we can simply delete this chunk of G-code from the file and resave it. Now we're ready to print the file.

Wrapping Things Up

After drawing up another one or two squiggle vases, you will undoubtedly want to get them printed. As mentioned earlier, I've sliced mine with 3 perimeters, 3 solid layers, and 0 percent infill, although you might get away with less with some experimentation. In Figure 9-40, I've used clear PLA filament because these vases really do look good in translucent plastic, and PLA is food-safe as well. After that, all the vases need are some flowers.

Figure 9-40. *Finished squiggle vases*

Summary

Using the tools and techniques we have already learned, in this chapter we added a couple more project ideas to the list: from mashing up existing models to create cool windup toys and collectibles, all the way to making something nice for the home—and score points with the significant other. Once you've started to expand your 3D modeling toolbox, the more you look at things differently. Suddenly, you move from "I can't do this because it's too hard," to "How hard would it be to make this…?"

Now that you've put your printer through its paces, in the next chapter we are going to tackle some common printer upgrades to make the printing experience more enjoyable. The more you improve your printer, the better the chance your prints will work—and have better quality. And that makes us happy.

CHAPTER 10

■ ■ ■

Bonus Round: Upgrades

By now, you have run your new 3D printer through its paces as you learned a handful of applications and put together the projects from the previous chapters. Inevitably, there will be things about your printer that can be or need to be improved to make your 3D printing experience more reliable and enjoyable. The great thing about these predominately DIY-centered fabricators is the general sense of openness, both in design and philosophy, which allows us to make and share these improvements on our printers. In our last chapter, we take a broad survey of the various electrical and mechanical upgrades that we can buy, print, and make to improve a few different aspects of our personal 3D printer.

Our second bonus round will cover the following:

- The mechanical upgrades that we can build to make the printer run smoother and keep it running more reliably

- Upgrades of computerless printing electronics and improving the quality of prints using different materials

- Suggestions for handing your filament spools with ease and upgrading that junk-drawer extruder to something classy

Not all of the upgrades in this chapter will work for all printers, so skim through the parts that may not apply to your printer, or look for ways that those upgrades might be modified to work. For example, if you have a new MakerBot Replicator, there may not yet be much out there to improve the printer; whereas if you own a RepRap, then there are many things that we can do with it. So, let's start with the nuts and bolts of the mechanical upgrades.

Mechanical Upgrades

Our personal 3D printers are mechanical machines. They rely on motors, bearings, rods, pulleys, belts, and other mechanical components to work reliably up to a surprisingly high degree of accuracy. As you know, mechanical machines are often prone to failure—cars, lawn mowers, and blenders all have days when they refuse to do what they are intended to do. Your sub-$2,000 3D printer is no different. Depending on the printer, and factoring how it was built and the type of parts used in its construction, invariably, there are things that either need to be replaced for the printer to function or there are things we can do simply to improve the printer's day-to-day operation.

The mechanical aspects of a 3D printer are never noticed when the printer is working well, but are a constant thorn in your side when things don't work well. We start this section with a look at arguably one of the best mechanical improvements that you can make on your 3D printer: timing belts and pulleys.

Timing Belts and Pulleys

To move the three axes of a Cartesian robot, your 3D printer will use at least a pair of timing belts attached to the motors on both the x- and y-axes. The belts, essentially flat belts with evenly spaced teeth that mesh with a pulley to provide a positive grip similar to that of a chain or gear, are responsible for translating the rotational movement of the motor to a linear movement for that axis. The possibilities for types of timing belts and pulleys are countless, but upgrading the belts and pulleys might have a measurable effect on the printing quality of your printer.

Tooth Profiles

All timing belts are characterized by their tooth profile, or the shape of the individual teeth found on both the pulley and belt. This profile needs to match on both the pulley and belt, and are defined by the shape of the tooth and the pitch, or spacing between each tooth. Figure 10-1 provides a comparison of two common tooth profiles.

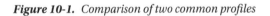

T5 TOOTH PROFILE   GT2 TOOTH PROFILE

Figure 10-1. *Comparison of two common profiles*

In this illustration, we are comparing the shape and size of a T5 timing belt with that of a GT2. These are two common timing belt profiles used in 3D printers. Historically, T5 timing belts have been used in RepRap-style machines because the larger tooth profile, and a pitch of 5 millimeters between teeth, means that it is technically possible to print the timing pulleys needed to use these belts on a 3D printer. This reduces the amount of mechanical parts that must be purchased and saves a little on the overall cost. The problem with this strategy is that even the most precisely calibrated 3D printer cannot produce a timing pulley to the same tolerances of those that have been manufactured. The T5 tooth profile is also not a suitable profile for linear motion, like that used in a 3D printer, because the square shape of the tooth causes backlash in the axis of movement, creating sloppy and inaccurate prints.

The GT2 profile—which are gaining popularity and are used by several kit-based machines, like the MakerBot and Ultimaker printers—features a rounded tooth profile that better fits the matching pulleys to reduce the amount of backlash in linear movement systems. The GT2 profile also has a much finer tooth pitch (generally 2 millimeters, although 3 millimeter pitches are available), giving a greater degree of accuracy at the cost of a more difficult-to-print pulley. Since it is often a good idea to buy manufactured pulleys anyway, the benefits of the GT2 profile more than make up for any additional upfront expense.

Timing Belts

There are many different types of timing belts that might be used in a 3D printer, two of which are shown in Figure 10-2.

Figure 10-2. *A pair of timing belts*

As with the earlier comparison, Figure 10-2 shows timing belts in both the T5 and GT2 profiles. Belts are made from several different materials, such as polyurethane or neoprene, with tensile strings, such as steel or fiberglass, running through the belt to add strength. When upgrading the belts on your printer, you will mostly likely move from a T5, XL, or similar large tooth profile to a GT2, MXL, or another smaller tooth profile to increase the resolution of the axis and decrease backlash during printing.

Timing Pulleys

There is even more variety among timing pulleys than there is with timing belts. A small selection is shown in Figure 10-3.

Figure 10-3. *Assorted timing pulleys*

When upgrading your timing belts, you will have already chosen a tooth profile, so the next step is to find a pulley that matches. You need to decide on the type of material the pulley is made from; the diameter of and the number of teeth on the pulley; the number of flanges on the outside of the pulley; and the type of hub that the pulley will use to attach to the motor. When selecting a manufactured pulley, you want a pulley that has enough teeth to engage at least six teeth on the belt at any time, illustrated in Figure 10-4. At the minimum, I would start looking for 14-tooth pulleys and limit the search to no more than 36 teeth at the maximum to retain decent resolution.

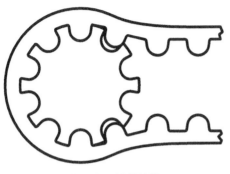

GT2 BELT AND PULLEY

Figure 10-4. *Belt and pulley meshing*

The material that a pulley is made from is limited to plastic, usually polycarbonate, or metal, usually aluminum. Metal timing pulleys are more precise and will last longer although cost significantly more. You can also select from a single- or double-flange pulley to either make the belt easier to put on or to keep the belt on, respectively. Finally, the hub should most likely be metal if the rest of the pulley is plastic with at least one setscrew for tightening against the motors shaft. Hubs that are more exotic also exist, which promise a more secure hold.

If we look at Figure 10-3, on the left we see a plastic T5 profile timing pulley that has a single flange and metal hub with a setscrew; in the center there is a pair of plastic GT2 36-tooth plastic pulleys with two flanges; and on the right there is a pair of GT2 18-tooth metal pulleys that have a special hub design for a tight hold. When all is said, upgrading your timing belts and pulleys is mostly a personal preference, although some consideration for the specific printer needs to be taken.

Generally, I would recommend upgrading to GT2 belts and either 36-tooth plastic pulleys for RepRap Prusa printers (see Figure 10-5), or 14-tooth metal pulleys for Mosaic, Huxley, and other small printers.

Figure 10-5. *Upgraded GT2 timing belt and pulley on a MakerGear Prusa Mendel*

The GT2 profile and machined pulleys often have an immediate and significant effect on the quality of your prints. New belts and pulleys can be purchased through major vendors such as SDP/SI (www.sdp-si.com) or Misumi (http://us.misumi-ec.com), or smaller vendors like TechPaladin (http://techpaladin.com) or Aleph Objects (www.lulzbot.com/en).

After replacing your timing belts, remember to recalibrate the number of steps per millimeter for each axis, as this will change sometimes significantly.

Linear Bearings

Next to replacing the timing belts and pulleys, upgrading the linear bearings that each axis slides on can also have a significant impact on the print quality of your printer and reduce any binding that might occur over an axes movement. Most 3D printers have a carriage or sled for each axis, which attaches to bearings that slide along a pair of smooth rods. The smoothness and accuracy of your prints are directly related to the precision of your linear bearings. There are several different types of linear bearings; a couple are shown in Figure 10-6.

Figure 10-6. *Examples of linear bearings*

Figure 10-6 shows two types of linear bearings: a linear ball bearing, inside a printed bearing holder, is on the left; a pair of self-aligning bronze bushings are on the right; and centered between them are three loose linear ball bearings. Another common type of linear bearings not shown in this image are Igus bushings, a high-tolerance plastic bushing. Some have even experimented, with mixed results, using printing PLA bushings. If your machine was built with printed PLA bushings, then you will definitely want to look at upgrading to a better bearing system. Of course, your results may vary. For example, a MakerGear Prusa that we use at my university needed to be upgraded from self-aligning bronze bushings to more tolerant linear ball bearings to improve some problems with poor print quality.

Linear ball bearings, like the LM8UU bearings shown in Figure 10-6 for 8mm metric smooth rods, have gained popularity recently. They come standard on the RepRap Huxley, MakerBot Replicator, and Ultimaker printers. Similar to radial ball bearings, linear ball bearings have an outer stainless steel shell and an inner plastic ring that holds tiny ball bearings in a horizontal arrangement along the length of the bearing. At the cost of a slightly louder movement noise, this makes a linear ball bearing system move fairly smoothly and is more tolerant of variations in the smooth rod used on the axis. Bronze and plastic bushings offer a potentially smoother and quieter operation, but require the smooth rods to be of higher tolerance; although even then, I have found that they tend to bind during movement much more than linear ball bearings.

The best place to find linear ball bearings is VXB (`www.vxb.com`), although many have had luck prowling eBay (`www.ebay.com/sch/i.html?_nkw=lm8uu`) for the best prices. Igus bushings are available from SDP/SI or Aleph Objects, while self-aligning bronze bushings can be had at TechPaladin.

If your printer doesn't already use linear ball bearings, upgrading is not that difficult to do. Figure 10-6 also shows a printed linear ball bearing holder (`www.thingiverse.com/thing:16158`) from Jonas Kühling that is designed to mount to the bottom of the y-axis sled on a RepRap Prusa Mendel. Similar holders or redesigned carriages are available for the x-axis and new x-axis ends can be fitted with linear ball bearings on the z-axis of a RepRap Prusa Mendel.

MakerBot Thing-O-Matic users can upgrade to SW06UU linear bearings on all axes, although the older MakerBot printers use imperial smooth rods rather than metric, which cost a little more to upgrade overall. These upgrades include Christian Hinna's Z-Axis Linear Bearing Space for the z-axis platform (`www.thingiverse.com/thing:14548`), shown in Figure 10-7, along with Jeremy Green's Y-Axis Bearing Holder (`www.thingiverse.com/thing:18457`) and Mark Durbin's Linear Bearing X-Axis Carriage (`www.thingiverse.com/thing:9420`).

Figure 10-7. *Linear bearing installed on a Thing-O-Matic z-axis (courtesy Tony Buser, 2012)*

Navigating all of the diverse options for linear bearings can be daunting at first, but the best place to start is a Thingiverse search for the words "linear bearing" and the type of printer you own. Check out what people have had success with, and give the upgrade a shot to see what it can do for you.

Leadscrews and Shaft Couplers

Our last mechanical upgrades are primarily for the multitude of RepRap Prusa Mendel owners out there, but it might be helpful for other printers with similar linear movement on the z-axis. Typical of these RepRap machines, the z-axis is driven by threaded rods attached to the shaft of the z-axis stepper motors using some form of coupler. Often these couplers are printed or make use of nylon tubing in some form to grip the shaft of the motor and the threaded rod connecting the two together. Improperly aligned couplers or couplers that lack a degree of flexibility might cause the z-axis rods, and by extension the entire x-axis that rides on it, to wobble as the axis moves up and down. This side-to-side movement can create pronounced layers in your printed objects. In some cases, printed couplers might even give way completely, dropping the axis in midprint. Some RepRap owners have tried to fix this by overly constraining the z-axis; conversely, I have found that having a little more tolerance in your z-axis, such as that provided by the helical shaft couplers shown in Figure 10-8, provides slightly better performance overall.

Figure 10-8. *Aluminum helical coupler on a RepRap z-axis*

Here we have a machined aluminum helical coupler with a 5mm bore on one end to mount to the motor shaft and an 8mm bore on the other for attaching to the threaded drive rod. In the middle of the coupler is a helical or spiral cut, somewhat like a spring, which decouples each end of the coupler to allow for and smooth out slight misalignments between the motor and drive rod. This simple upgrade often has a noticeable impact on the alignment and smoothness of vertical layers in a print caused by z-axis wobble and generally makes printing more reliable.

Even so, this is not exactly a prescribed practice because the coupler is not meant to support the entire weight of the x-axis as it does on the RepRap Prusa Mendel. Ideally, the motors for the z-axis would be reversed, placed at the bottom, and pointing up to reduce the axial force applied to the motors—a design that is starting to make ground in the MendelMax and AO-100 designs similar to the z-axis shown in Figure 10-9.

Figure 10-9. *MendelMax z-axis with spider coupler (courtesy Tommy Cheng, 2012)*

In this example we have the latest MendelMax design with an inverted z-axis, where the stepper motors are mounted at the bottom of the printer instead of at the top. Rather than a helical coupler, this setup uses a spider coupler that consists of two metal parts, one attaching to the motor and another to the leadscrew. These two parts are separated in the middle by a cross-shaped silicone piece called the spider. The spider provides a tight enough fit to accurately move the leadscrew while at the same time allowing flexibility in the axis to make smoother prints and prevent binding. Because the three parts are not actually attached to one another, this setup only works with the weight of the x-axis bearing downward on the coupler and motor.

Tommy Cheng's updates to the MendelMax design (`http://www.thingiverse.com/thing:23842`) also include the use of proper CNC leadscrews as opposed to the more typical hardware-grade threaded rod found in the Prusa Mendel. Precision leadscrews like that in Figure 10-9 provide a much higher degree of accuracy in the z-axis and, like machined timing pulleys, reduce the overall amount of backlash. This will increase the quality of your prints even more. Machined leadscrews are a little tricky to upgrade your printer with because of the matching leadscrew nuts that differ from the typical metric hardware. This means that more often than not you will need to print new parts that work with that leadscrew and nut.

Currently, the best place to find helical couplers is through TechPaladin at `http://techpaladin.com` or UltiMachine at `http://ultimachine.com/content/motor-shaft-coupling-5mm-8mm`. TechPaladin also has some economy leadscrews available although Misumi (`http://us.misumi-ec.com`) has the best selection of precision leadscrews, nuts, and couplers regardless of cost.

Electronics Upgrades

In addition to the mechanical aspects of your 3D printer, we also have the electronics systems used to interface with and operate our 3D printers. In this section, we will look at a few upgrades that you can make to your 3D printer's electronics to improve the quality of your prints or simply make printing easier and more rewarding. Some of these upgrades are not really replacing anything as much as they are installing something that might not have been there in the first place. Let's start with those.

Mechanical Endstops

Not all printers come equipped with endstops, those useful devices that let the printer know when it has reached the limit on a particular axis. Endstops are not strictly necessary, but they can be helpful and prevent printing accidents that occur when a printbed or extruder is not where it should be. Endstops come in several varieties, including optical sensors, magnetic sensors, and mechanical switches (see Figure 10-10), which are favored for their simplicity and reliability.

Figure 10-10. *Y-axis minimum endstop on a MakerGear Mosaic*

Most 3D printers that you buy come with endstops included in the kit or preinstalled (although the MakerGear Mosaic, for example, only includes the z-axis endstop; but two extra switches are included in the kit). If you built your own RepRap, you might have forgone endstops in favor of getting up and running a little quicker. Now is a good opportunity to take a little time to find an endstop holder design that works for your printer and wire up some endstops.

Figure 10-10 shows an endstop holder of my design (www.thingiverse.com/thing:21487) for the MakerGear Mosaic, although a quick search on Thingiverse for "endstop" will yield hundreds of designs for every imaginable printer. After printing the endstop holder, the switch can be wired one of two ways, but either way they will need to be configured properly in the controller's firmware. By way of example, Figure 10-11 provides a wiring schematic for one way to wire your endstops.

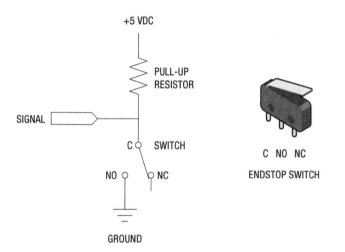

Figure 10-11. *Endstop wiring schematic*

A wiring schematic is a simple diagram showing where connections are made in a circuit. As shown in Figure 10-11, the endstop switch has three possible connections: C for common, NO for normally open, and NC for normally closed. Wired in this way, the switch will normally connect the common and normally closed pins when at rest; but when the switch is triggered, the common is connected to the normally open pin. MakerGear printers on the other hand are typically wired so that the normally closed pin of the switch is not connected to anything; while the normally open connects to ground and the common connects to the signal pin of the controller board. Also shown in this schematic, a resistor needs to be connected to the signal pin, pulling the signal up to +5 volts DC when the switch is not triggered; although this pull-up resistor is usually enabled on the Arduino board and so an additional resistor is not needed.

For this type of endstop wiring, the firmware will need to be configured to enable endstops and the logic level needs to be inverted. First, we should look for the following line that enables endstop pull-ups:

```
#define ENDSTOPPULLUPS
```

Make sure this line has not been disabled; remove the comments or // mark if found in front of this line. Next, we need to look for the following three lines of code to invert the endstop directions:

```
const bool X_ENDSTOP_INVERT = true;
const bool Y_ENDSTOP_INVERT = true;
const bool Z_ENDSTOP_INVERT = true;
```

Setting these values to true will tell the controller that a low-level logic signal means that the endstop has been triggered. Either way you wire the endstops, however, be sure to check these three lines in the firmware if you have any problems with an axis not moving properly. With the endstops installed, wired correctly, and configured in the firmware, you should be able to use the homing feature in your printer interface software to automatically set the starting point before a print begins.

Heated Printbed

Just as with endstops earlier, not all printers come with a heated printbed. The Ultimaker does not currently ship with a heated printbed; and if you've built a RepRap, you might not have purchased one due to the cost or time hooking it up. Figure 10-12 shows a heated printbed installed on a MakerGear Prusa Mendel with a mirror printing surface.

Figure 10-12. *Heated printbed on a Prusa Mendel*

Using a heated printbed is not absolutely needed when printing with PLA, but it makes life that much easier if you have one; whereas printing in ABS without that heated surface is simply a nightmare. Commonly, a heated printbed consists of a specially design printed circuit board, or PCB, that an electrical current runs through. The resistance of the copper traces on the circuit board creates heat, and the entire circuit board heats up. A sheet of aluminum or glass (that is ideally layered with Kapton tape) is usually placed on top of this circuit board; although some have had success with printing PLA on clean, uncoated heated glass or using hardware store-variety blue painter's tape with both PLA and ABS. This additional aluminum or glass surface helps to distribute the heat evenly across the print and provides a smooth, level surface to print on. It is possible to build a heated printbed using specialty Nichrome wire or power resistors as heating elements mounted to an aluminum surface, although this takes some entrepreneurial experimentation and research.

Printbeds for RepRap Mendel sized machines can be found at LulzBot (`www.lulzbot.com/en/14-heated-print-bed.html`) and UltiMachine (`http://ultimachine.com/content/prusa-pcb-heated-bed`). For the Huxley or smaller machines, you might try eMAKERshop at `www.emakershop.com/browse/listing?l=175`. When upgrading to a heated printbed, be sure that your electronics and power supply can handle the additional load needed by the heater. A Prusa heatbed, for example, can draw upwards of 9 amps or more than 100 watts. That's a lot of power, so be prepared.

One last thing about printbeds that is not exactly related to the electronics. A lot of work has gone into finding the ideal surface to print various materials on. Through this research, two characteristics are important: using a very flat surface that retains heat well and a surface that secures the hot printed object during printing. Aluminum, glass, or mirror of about 5 millimeters in thickness has been found to be ideal surfaces for their flatness. On top of this, a layer of polyamide, PET, or blue painter's tape is usually applied so that the extruded plastic will stick to the print surface. Recently, I have been using a mirror (see Figure 10-13) as a print surface covered in polyamide tape with great effect.

Figure 10-13. *Mirror print surface on a MakerGear Mosaic*

So far, the advantage over using glass or aluminum seems to be that the mirror is a more rigid material than glass alone. It also provides an extremely flat surface, while at the same time the metal coating on the back of the mirror better distributes heat and heats up faster than normal glass. As far as upgrades go, running down to the local hardware store to have a piece of mirror cut to your printbed's dimensions is about as easy as it gets—and it is well worth it.

Cooling Fan

This upgrade is for all of you that enjoy printing in PLA as much as I do. PLA is a fantastic material: it prints very smoothly, has a smell that is much more pleasant (it reminds me of waffles), and it prints at lower temperatures, reducing the print times. One of its bigger drawbacks is that PLA tends to cool very slowly so that in the middle of a print, it is possible for PLA to slump, pool, or otherwise distort during the print. To fix this, we need a cooling fan attached to our printer, as shown in Figure 10-14.

Figure 10-14. *Additional cooling fan on MakerGear Prusa Mendel*

In Figure 10-14, I've installed a 40mm fan on the x-axis carriage using a pair of clips designed by Jake Poznanski for the MakerGear Prusa Mendel (`www.thingiverse.com/thing:13343`), which points the fan at an angle to where the plastic exits the nozzle. This fan is then connected to the output labeled D9 on the RAMPS controller board and enabled both in firmware and in the cooling options for the particular slicer. This allows the fan to be controlled by G-code as needed, although you could just as easily connect the fan to a +12 volts DC source and leave it running. Keep in mind, this additional cooling fan is mostly for use with PLA. Large objects printed in ABS will crack if they are allowed to cool too quickly, so the fan should be kept off during most ABS prints (although it can be helpful when printing small parts or detailed areas). The print in Figure 10-15 shows two calibration towers, 10mm square and 40mm tall, printed in red PLA with the cooling fan enabled only on the left tower to illustrate the benefits of cooling PLA during printing.

Figure 10-15. *Comparison of prints with (left) and without a cooling fan*

When comparing these two prints, the cube on the left is much straighter and has tighter, more defined layers and corners; whereas the cube on the right exhibits a little more sagging in the layers and much less definition in the corners caused by the filament not cooling fast enough. Moral of the story: use an external cooling fan when printing with PLA!

There are hundreds of cooling fan solutions on Thingiverse, from Jake Poznanski's simple parametric fan mount shown in Figure 10-13, to Richard Gain's cooling fan for the eMaker Huxley (`www.thingiverse.com/thing:15899`), and even Tony Buser's Dual Extruder Fan Shroud (`www.thingiverse.com/thing:16071`). Find something that work's for you and give it a try the next time you print in PLA.

SD Card

This upgrade will allow for a *mostly* computerless printing experience by uploading a sliced file onto an SD memory card and then allowing the controller electronics to print directly from this file rather than waiting for commands to be sent from your computer. After uploading the file and starting the print, you can disconnect your computer from the 3D printer and off you go.

To get started, you need an additional SD card breakout board for the electronics controller used on your printer, such as SD RAMPS for RAMPS 1.3 and higher (`http://reprap.org/wiki/Sdramps`) shown in Figure 10-16; SDSL for Sanguinololu (`http://reprap.org/wiki/SDSL`); or if an SD card reader doesn't already exist for your controller electronics, you might use one of the available breakout boards from Adafruit (`www.adafruit.com/products/254`) or Gravitech (`www.gravitech.us/sdcaad.html`) with a little creative wiring.

Figure 10-16. *SD RAMPS breakout board*

Some controllers, such as MakerBot's newest controller (www.thingiverse.com/thing:16058), and the new board from Printrbot (http://reprap.org/wiki/Printrboard), already come with built-in SD card support. Other setups, like RAMPS and Sanguinololu, might need some additional wiring and updated firmware to enable SD card support. To give us a computerless experience using the RAMPS controller, we need to set up RAMPS to power the Arduino from the +12 volts supply normally used to power the stepper motors.

Setting Up RAMPS

Starting at Figure 10-17, we will walk through the steps needed to install an SD card on a RAMPS controller for computerless printing. The process is somewhat similar for other controllers.

Figure 10-17. *Locating empty part D1*

Begin by finding the usually empty part labeled D1 located underneath the x- and y-axis stepper drivers. This is an optional diode that, if installed, allows the Arduino electronics to run on the motor supply rather than from USB, letting us disconnect our PC while printing. The tradeoff is that we can no longer use more than +12 volts to power the stepper motors. For most of us, this is not really a problem.

Once we've found the location for D1, we need to install a 1N4001 or similar diode, often included with the electronics (although usually not preinstalled) through the two holes so that the silver line on the diode matches the line on the circuit board. This is shown in Figure 10-18.

Figure 10-18. *Diode D1 installed through the matching holes*

Once the diode has been installed properly, it is time to solder the legs to the pads on the bottom of the circuit board, as shown in Figure 10-19.

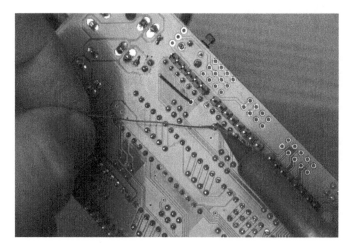

Figure 10-19. *Soldering diode to circuit board*

Using a soldering iron, heat both the pad and leg of the diode, and apply a little solder to the spot where the leg touches the pad. The solder should form a smooth, clean, and shiny mound that fully adheres to the pad and pin. After both legs are soldered, clip them smooth using a pair of flush cutters, as shown in Figure 10-20.

Figure 10-20. *Clipping legs from diode*

With the diode D1 soldered in place and its legs clipped even with the rest of the pins on the back of the circuit board, we can now reinstall the stepper drivers, mount the RAMPS shield back on the Arduino, and then connect the SD Ramps add-on board, as shown in Figure 10-21.

Figure 10-21. *Installed SD RAMPS*

With the SD adapter installed correctly and the controller powered up, we should have a glowing red indicator light on the SD board, which lets us know that it is ready. Now we need to make sure that SD is enabled in our firmware, properly format the SD card, place a file to print on the card, and start a print from the card using our printer interface.

Enabling SD Support

To enable SD support in our firmware, we need to open our firmware in the Arduino development environment, as demonstrated in Chapter 3, making sure we use a firmware such as Sprinter or Marlin that supports SD cards. In the configuration.h file, we will look for a line such as this:

// #define SDSUPPORT

The two slashes, //, in front of the line have disabled SD support. To enable, all we need to do is remove those two slashes, like so:

#define SDSUPPORT

Once saved and uploaded to the controller board, we are good to go on the next step: formatting the SD card to work with our controller.

Formatting the SD Card

The Arduino uses an older method for reading files from the SD card, so the first thing we need to do is format the card to work with the FAT-16 file system. The obvious thing here is that we need a way to read the SD card on our computer using either a built-in SD card reader or an external card reader that plugs into USB. Once the computer recognizes out card, we can format the card on the Mac using the Disk Utility application (see Figure 10-22) or on the PC by right-clicking the drive and choosing Format (see Figure 10-23).

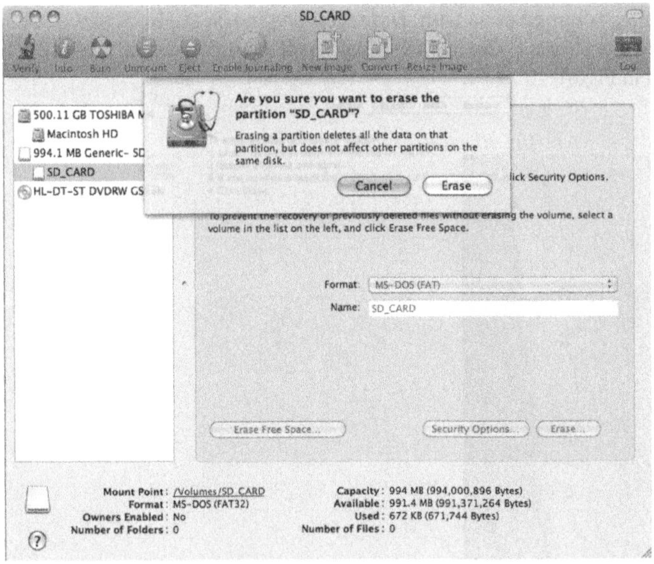

Figure 10-22. *Formatting an SD card on a Mac*

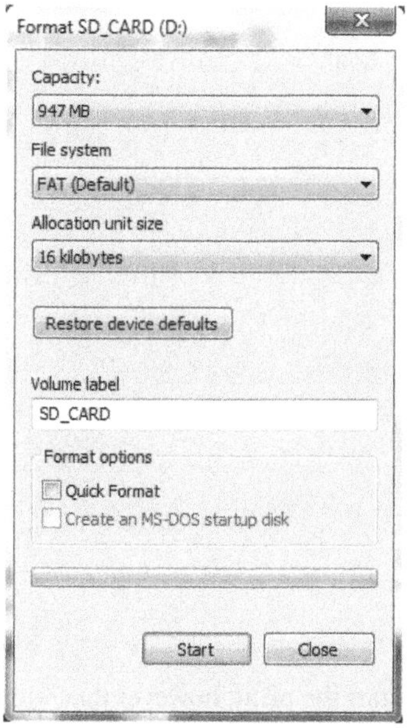

Figure 10-23. *Formatting an SD card on a PC*

When formatting the SD card, choose the option FAT or MS-DOS (FAT) to format using FAT-16 and select a name for the volume that is no longer than 11 characters with no spaces in the name.

Printing from SD

After formatting the card, we need a G-Code file on the card to print from. We could send the file to the SD card using the printer interface, but this takes forever and a day, so I recommend copying any G-code file to print using your computer, just as you would copy a file to any other drive. This file is just like any other file that is generated from our slicer application and that we would process using our printer interface. When we have a file to print, we can eject the SD card from our computer and insert it into the SD breakout board. With that installed, open the printer interface application, connect to the printer as normal, and then look for the SD button shown in Figure 10-24.

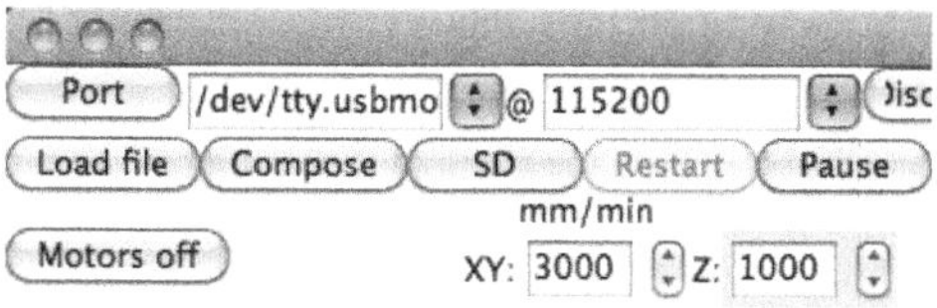

Figure 10-24. *SD button in Pronterface*

Clicking this button gives you the option to open the SD card and see the files available to print. In the file menu shown in Figure 10-25, we can choose one of the files to load.

Figure 10-25. *SD file menu*

Once a file has been selected, hit the Print button as you would normally to start the print; however this time, once the print is underway, you can disconnect the USB cable from your printer, freeing you from the clutches of that four-hour print you just launched!

Even More Upgrades

So far, we have looked at upgrades for your printer's mechanical systems and the printer's electronics. This section offers a few more upgrades that are neither mechanical nor electronic.

Filament Spool Holder

Increasingly, filament suppliers are providing filament on spools rather than in loose coils. All it takes is ordering a big coil of filament and having it get all tangled up in the middle of a print to figure out that spools are a good thing. A spool keeps the filament contained, straight, and wrapped in the right direction to easily feed into your printer. Even so, you are not out of the woods, so don't leave your printer running a four-hour print without first building a spool holder of one variety or another.

Do a quick search on Thingiverse for "spool". At last count, I found 263 related filament spool holders for every conceivable printer found on Thingiverse, and in a number of styles and designs. Figure 10-26 shows my Mosaic Feet & Spool Holder (`www.thingiverse.com/thing:21446`).

Figure 10-26. *Filament spool holder*

This style of spool holder has been a favorite of mine recently. It uses four printed plastic components tied together with four lengths of threaded rod to make a simple frame. Four radial ball bearings are bolted inside of the frame that the spool sits on and rolls over. The weight of the spool keeps it balanced on these four bearings; the frame keeps the filament from unraveling.

Other variations of this design include Nathaniel Graham's derivative of Filament Spooler (www.thingiverse.com/thing:12102), a single printed part holder that uses four bolts and bearings; and Cory Daniel's Simple Prusa Spool Holder (www.thingiverse.com/thing:17473), which perches a spool on top of the RepRap's frame. For one of the more iconic spool holder's on Thingiverse, be sure to check out Charles Pax's MakerBot Filament Spool Holder (www.thingiverse.com/thing:7105). This one-piece design is intended to bolt onto the side of the MakerBot Thing-O-Matic and holds the spool by friction alone, yet still allows it to spin as needed.

Replacement Extruder

Depending on of the model or manufacturer of your printer, you might have a rock-steady extruder that performs every time you throw a print out to be fabricated. If your extruder works reliably every time, count yourself lucky. If you are less fortunate and deal with an unreliable extruder that jams frequently, feeds filament inconsistently, or produces prints that are impossible to calibrate, then you might want to consider upgrading to a better extruder. Figure 10-27 shows the MakerGear Plastruder (www.makergear.com/products/plastruder), arguably one of the best, long-standing plastic extruders on the market today.

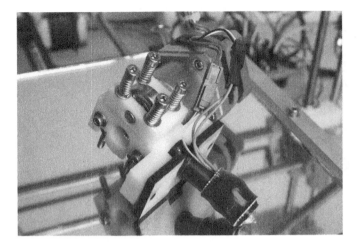

Figure 10-27. MakerGear stepper extruder

What makes this extruder work so well is the use of an extremely high-torque stepper motor with an integrated planetary gearbox mounted to a dead-simple filament driver with a spring-tensioned ball bearing idler combined with a very accurate and very reliable hotend. This extruder design works equally well with ABS or PLA and comes in varieties designed for either 1.75mm or 3mm filament with nozzle diameters that range from 0.25 millimeters to 0.5 millimeters. Simply investing in a new, quality extruder such as this to replace the janky or worn-out extruder that came with your machine—or that you built yourself—can make it seem as if you have a brand-new printer.

If you currently own a MakerBot Thing-O-Matic or Replicator and only have one extruder, or have the older Mk5 or Mk6 extruder design, you might want to consider upgrading to a Mk7, Mk8, or even Dual Extruder setup available from MakerBot (http://store.makerbot.com/toolheads.html) and seen in Figure 10-28.

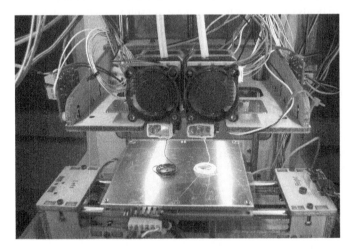

Figure 10-28. Mk7 Dual extruders on a MakerBot Thing-O-Matic (courtesy Tony Buser, 2011)

If replacing the entire extruder is not an option, you might try simply upgrading the filament driver. As an example, there are many replacements for the filament driver in the MakerGear stepper extruders, such as Tommy Cheng's (www.thingiverse.com/thing:13628), or even the minimalist MakerBot Mk7 filament driver by Whosawhatsis (www.thingiverse.com/thing:15718), pictured in Figure 10-29, to replace the filament driver in a MakerBot Mk7 extruder.

Figure 10-29. *Minimalist Mk7 filament driver*

This design by Whosawhatsis improves on the standard MakerBot design by replacing the Delrin plunger that pushes the filament into the drive gear with a proper ball-bearing idler, which is held firm against the drive gear using a spring-loaded arm. This allows for filament that is not consistent in diameter to be fed through the extruder at a steady rate; and it makes changing filament out a little easier. Once the replacement parts are installed, the rest of the extruder goes together as normal. Through this simple upgrade, many have reported significant improvements right away.

If, however, your existing filament driver pushes the filament through just fine, but something is not working well with your hotend, then those can be upgraded as well. The MakerGear hotend for example is available as a separate item at www.makergear.com/products/operators-pack. (It is well worth the extra cost for the fully assembled option.) Alternatively, you might try the J-Head hotend from https://www.hotends.com, or the newcomer by Aleph Objects called the Budaschnozzle, available at www.lulzbot.com/en/96-budaschnozzle-11.html and shown in Figure 10-30.

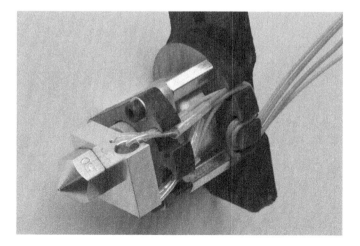

Figure 10-30. *Aleph Object's Budaschnozzle hotend (courtesy Aleph Objects Inc., 2012)*

The combined efforts of the filament driver and the hotend to make a complete extruder forms the most critical element in your successful 3D prints. It simply does not make sense to scrimp even a little bit on this important part of your printer. Invest wisely in this upgrade, and you will be rewarded with consistently beautiful prints from your 3D printer.

Summary

In this chapter, we took a few steps back to see what we could do to improve the operation of our 3D printer and the overall quality of our printed 3D objects. We did this through a few (mostly) simple enhancements, from upgrading the timing belts that came with our printer to mounting a secondary cooling fan for printing with PLA. All of these upgrades will hopefully have a positive impact on your 3D printing experience and make it more rewarding.

Personal 3D printing is still an emerging, engaging, and sometimes moderately challenging hobby. It can be a lot of fun when things go right and provide hours of entertainment when it doesn't. With any luck, this book offered some useful tips and tricks—from buying your first 3D printer all the way to making crazy multipart projects—so that things go right more than they go wrong. Stick with it and you'll enjoy having your very own factory on your desktop. Eventually, you won't be able to imagine your life without it.

Before we go, we have a few more things in store, including helpful advice on troubleshooting various aspects of the 3D printing process and how to perform maintenance on your printer to make it work better and produce better prints. We follow this with a collection of resources for finding information, including that one silly part that you might be looking for.

APPENDIX A

Printing Tips

Whenever your car needs its routine maintenance and oil change, or your inkjet printer needs servicing, chances are you take it in to some sort of service center. When your personal 3D printer needs a little work, *you* get to be the service technician. Don't worry. For the most part, servicing it is not all that hard, and there is an active online community that can help you. This appendix shares some general printing tips for maintaining your 3D printer to keep it running smoothly for a long time to come. We'll also look at how to troubleshoot some of the more common problems that you might have with your printer, as well as a few more tips for finishing your 3D printed objects.

Maintenance

As a mechanical machine, your 3D printer needs regular maintenance to perform at the top of its game. This includes cleaning or replacing your print surface, cleaning your extruder's drive gear or nozzle, and lubricating your printer's slides or rods and leadscrews.

Lubrication

Every month or so, or whenever your printer starts to become a little squeaky, it's a good idea to clean and lubricate the smooth rods or slides and the leadscrews, where appropriate. To clean these components, I generally use acetone on a clean paper towel or cloth rag, paying attention not to get any acetone on any plastic components—for reasons you will see later in this appendix. You might instead try rubbing alcohol to avoid any potential problems. When the bearing surfaces and leadscrews are shiny clean, you'll need to apply some form of lubrication to these surfaces. For linear slides, I generally use a PTFE-based grease applied with a cotton-tipped swab (see Figure A-1). I use general machine oil or 3-IN-ONE oil for leadscrews, although others have reported success with PTFE-based spray-on dry lube.

Figure A-1. *Applying PTFE grease to a linear slide*

In Figure A-1, I'm applying grease to the bearing surfaces on the linear slides of a MakerGear Mosaic. All it takes is a little grease rubbed into the grooves along the slide, moving the axis carriage back and forth a few times to spread out the grease, and then cleaning up any excess grease. This grease works really well on our 3D printers and it can be used on other bearing surfaces, such as smooth rods and leadscrews. Rather than grease, I often use 3-IN-ONE machine oil for leadscrews and smooth rods (see Figure A-2).

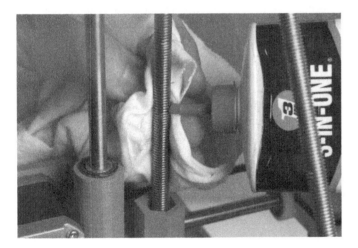

Figure A-2. *Applying machine oil to a Prusa Mendel leadscrew*

Using a rag to soak up any excess oil, squeeze out a little oil from the container into the threads of the leadscrews and then run the axis up and down to even out the oil. If you're particularly adept, you can apply the oil while the axis is moving, rubbing the oil into the leadscrew with the rag. Just be careful not to get caught on anything.

When it comes to lubricating your 3D printer, it takes a little trial and error to find what works best for you and your printer. 3-IN-ONE or other machine oil works great on many parts of a printer, although it needs to be applied more frequently than other forms of lubrication and can discolor plastic parts of the printer. PTFE grease works really well for anything with ball bearings in it, like those slides on the Mosaic, but it can be a little tricky to find locally. You could even use a silicon-based grease, especially if your printer has printed PLA bushings.

Whatever you do, there are a couple things to avoid. First, never use WD-40 as a lubricant in your 3D printer. The primary ingredients in WD-40 are kerosene and mineral spirits, which can be corrosive and are otherwise not suitable for mechanical lubrication. I would also avoid lithium grease. Unlike the nonlithium-based PTFE grease, this lubricant is not as slippery and can dry out quickly, potentially damaging the rubber seals in your bearings.

Printbed Surfacing

If you are printing straight onto a bare glass or aluminum print surface, then all you need to do is properly clean the surface with acetone every day or so to continue printing. Most people use a print surface such as blue painter's tape or polyimide tape (Kapton) to print with a wider variety of materials. If this is the case, then about every week or two, or if the first layer of your prints stops sticking, it's a good time to change the tape on your printbed. This is fairly easy to do with blue painter's tape, but polyimide tape can be a little tricky. Rather than avoid using polyimide, I have a nifty way to easily replace the tape on your print surface using a technique very similar to applying tinting film on windows.

▪ **Note** Acetone is a flammable chemical, so it is best to turn off your heated printbed, if you have one, and let it cool before cleaning the print surface.

To replace the tape print surface, the first thing we need is the polyimide tape that fits our printbed dimensions. I like to use wide rolls of tape that fit my printbed using only a single piece of tape. Fortunately, ProtoParadigm offers polyimide in rolls up to 330mm wide (www.protoparadigm.com/products-page/polyimide-tape). In the following images, I'll be using 130mm wide tape for the printbed on a MakerGear Mosaic. With the tape in hand, we need the following supplies to apply the tape:

- Container of soapy water
- Clean kitchen sponge
- Acetone
- Clean paper towels or rags
- Kitchen towel
- Small squeegee or plastic card
- Hobby knife with a new blade

While it is possible to unroll a length of your new tape and stick it on the print surface, I have never once successfully done this without creating wrinkles and air bubbles in the tape. Although this is not disastrous, having a perfectly smooth print surface will make your prints more successful. It's not too hard using this method, but there are a few steps that we need to follow to make it work.

1. Peel off the old tape from the printbed and clean the printbed with acetone.
2. Wet the surface with soap and water.
3. Cut a length of polyimide tape and apply it to the soapy printbed.
4. Squeeze the water out from the tape using a small plastic card.
5. Trim the edges of the tape flush with the printbed.
6. Clean the new tape surface with acetone.

We start with Figure A-3: gathering our supplies together, peeling the old tape off the printbed, and cleaning the printbed with acetone to remove all the adhesive left behind after removing the tape.

Figure A-3. *Cleaning the printbed surface*

Since I am using a mirror on my Mosaic, I can easily remove the surface for this process, placing it on top of a kitchen towel to keep my desk clean. If your printbed is nonremovable, it's still possible to do this, but it makes it a little more challenging. Now with the surface clean of any adhesive or oil, we can cover the surface in soapy water, as shown in Figure A-4.

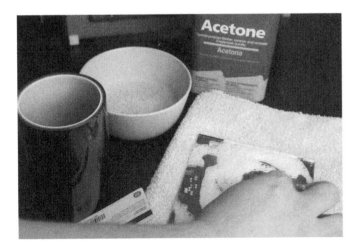

Figure A-4. *Wetting the surface with soapy water*

The soap helps with surface tension when we stick the tape on, so make sure there are lots of bubbles. Now we can peel off a big length of polyimide from the roll and cut it longer than is actually needed for the bed. I kind of overdo this part, but the tape will last forever and the extra length means that I am sure to find a section that hasn't stuck to itself by the time I get it on the printbed. Now we simply lay the tape across the soapy glass surface, as shown in Figure A-5.

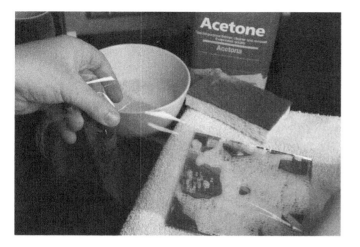

Figure A-5. *Applying polymide tape to soapy surface*

We should get the tape reasonably flat, but don't worry about the bubbles at this stage. Right now, the tape should slide around on top of the soapy water and not stick to anything permanently; if it does, then you might need more soap. Once the tape is lined up, you can squeeze the water out from under the tape, as in Figure A-6, using a small squeegee, or in this case, a spare grocery store card.

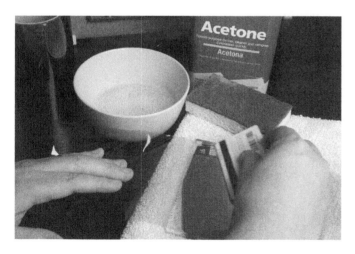

Figure A-6. *Removing soap and water from underneath the tape*

Starting in the middle, use the card to squeeze the water out toward the edge of the platform, repeating for the other half as well. This part of the process is where the towel is handy to soak up all that water. While there is still a little water underneath the tape, it will continue to slide on the glass or pull up on the corners. Carefully continue to rub the edge of the card across the surface, removing as much water as possible. When you have it reasonably flat, you can trim off the edges of the tape using a hobby knife with a fresh blade, as shown in Figure A-7.

Figure A-7. *Trimming polymide tape with a hobby knife*

Here, I am simply running the blade of the knife along the edge of the glass to get a somewhat smooth cut, being mindful to not pull the tape off the wet platform. After trimming the tape, run the squeegee or a clean towel over the surface a couple more times to try to remove more water. After that, we need to clean the soap residue off the tape using a little acetone on a paper towel (see Figure A-8) so that plastic will once again stick to the print surface.

Figure A-8. *Cleaning new tape with acetone*

At this point, you should have a mostly clean new print surface, but there might still be water in there; so what we need to do is replace the platform in the printer, heat it up to temperature, and let the surface break in for a little before we next print. It's during the first heating that little bubbles might appear under the tape—don't worry about these, they will work their way out after a little while.

With the new print surface in place, it's time to start up a new print and see how it does. If we look at Figure A-9, the first layer of our print should now uniformly stick to the printbed. Make sure the perimeters are not curling up and that the solid infill is flat and smooth, rather than looking like bacon.

Figure A-9. *First layer of a new print*

It might take a little practice to get this down, but a clean and smooth print surface that gives you great prints is always worth a little extra work.

Cleaning

These little 3D printers have a habit of leaving little blobs of plastic all over the place, making a mess of everything. Periodically, it makes sense to do a little housekeeping on your 3D printer, removing any stray plastic or debris that might have built up in all your 3D printing adventures. I've seen axes stopped in their tracks because of a stray piece of plastic. Just keeping things a little tidier could have prevented this.

Nowhere else is this more a problem than inside your filament driver. The filament driver uses some form of a feed gear, like the one shown in Figure A-10, to grip the filament and feed it into the extruder's hotend. This gear can become quite clogged up over prolonged use.

Figure A-10. *MakerGear plastruder drive gear*

Depending on your printer's extruder design, you might need to open the driver. In this case, I removed the four screws and springs that held the idler bearing in place. With the drive gear open, inspect the teeth for any plastic remnants in and around the drive gear. You can clean any plastic you might find there with a toothpick or stiff brush until the gear is all shiny again. If you have an air compressor available, you can blow out these teeth with an air nozzle, advancing the motor a bit to get around all the teeth. If it gets really bad, say from using very poor-quality filament, you might need to completely disassemble the extruder to remove the drive gear. With the drive gear pulled out, you can clean or soak the gear with acetone to remove any stubborn bits of plastic. In extreme situations, you might even need to replace the drive gear if the teeth are completely worn out.

Other Maintenance

For the most part, these three things—lubrication, printbed surfacing, and general cleaning—are all that you will need to worry about for periodic maintenance. Once in a while, however, there might be additional steps that you need to take to keep your printer running in top shape. If you own one of the Box Bots, you might want to tighten all the screws that hold the printer together because they can work their way loose due to all the vibrating. Even on RepRaps and other machines that use threaded rod frames, it's a good idea to tighten up all those nuts once in awhile.

After running your printer for some time, certain parts are bound to start to wear out. If your printer uses PLA or Igus bushings, you might eventually find that the axes of your printer are not running as smoothly or as quietly as they once did. It might be time to inspect your bearings and replace them if they show signs of wear or have flat spots. Your 3D printer's timing pulleys and belts can also wear out over time. If this happens, your printer might skip steps in one of its directions, making prints that shift as they print. To fix this, simply take off the belts and pulleys from your printer, inspect for missing teeth or signs of wear, and replace parts as needed. I have also seen the nuts used on the z-axis leadscrews of some Prusa Mendels wear out to the point of skipping steps vertically. Replacing these with stainless steel or brass nuts can improve reliability and performance over the long term.

Your 3D printer's extruder is also under a lot of stress from dealing with molten plastic at high temperatures. When the plastic stops flowing like it should, it might be time for a little cleaning and overhaul of the extruder's hotend. Sometimes, simply replacing the nozzle can breathe new life into a tired extruder, although in extreme cases you might have to rebuild or replace the entire hotend.

Troubleshooting

Keeping your personal 3D printer clean and well-maintained will prolong its life and make your 3D printing experience all that more productive. Invariably, though, there will be times when things don't go exactly according to plan. This section provides a few examples of things not working out—and what we can do to fix them.

Print Curling

Figure A-11 shows an example print in which the lower corners of a large object peeled up from the surface of the printbed.

Figure A-11. *Curling corners*

This problem happens when the printed object does not firmly stick to the print surface, which could be caused by a temperature problem or something being out of adjustment in your printer. In order of most likely to least likely, the following are some things to check:

- If you forgot to clean the print surface with a swab of acetone, clean it and try the print again.

- If the print surface is clean but you haven't replaced the tape in awhile, you might want to resurface with new tape and try again.

- If the tape is somewhat new and clean, double-check your temperature settings to make sure they are at the correct temperature. If the settings are correct, raise the temperature in 5°C increments to see what happens. Do not exceed 225°C on the hotend and 115°C on the printbed.

- Next, double-check that the z-axis endstop has not come out of adjustment; otherwise, lower the endstop by a small amount to decrease the height of the first layer to better squish the first layer into the printbed. You can take this too far, though, so be careful not to crash the extruder into the printbed.

- Finally, re-level your printbed, as discussed in Chapter 3, to make sure that the print surface is level to the nozzle across the entire platform.

Thin Layers and Layer Splits

Figure A-12 shows an unhappy cephalopod with pronounced gaps in its printed layers.

Figure A-12. *Thin layers during a print*

This problem might happen somewhat randomly throughout a print. Several layers print just fine, but then one or two layers are either very thin, completely disappear, or split apart. You might be able to solve this problem by trying the following steps:

- First, check the filament diameter setting in your slicer utility. I almost always forget to check the filament diameter when I change filament, and this is often the cause of the problem. If your filament diameter is set to a higher number than the actual filament measures, then not enough plastic will be extruded.

- Next, check the extrusion temperature to make sure the filament is heated to the right temperature. If it is and you're still having problems, you might try raising the temperature in 5°C increments to see if it improves.

- If the filament diameter and temperature settings fail to make a noticeable improvement, your filament driver might not be consistently feeding the filament into the extruder, so you might need to clean your drive gear.

- If you are using ABS, the layers of a print can split apart if the ambient air temperature is too cool or if there is a cold draft that blows across your printer. You might try heating the nearby space or reducing drafts to improve this condition. (PLA does not suffer from this problem as much.)

- If none of these potential solutions provide improvement, then it is very likely that you have poor-quality filament. Filament that fails to maintain a consistent diameter through the spool can cause areas to thin out, and there is not much to do about it other than try a different supplier.

Poor Infill

If we look at the top of our cephalopod (I just like writing that word) in Figure A-13, we see significant holes in the top surface of the print.

Figure A-13. *Gaps in a print*

This type of problematic printing often happens in organic or curved shapes with a gentle slopping top surface. While it might be caused by some of the same issues outlined in the thin layer example, it is most likely caused by one of the following print settings:

- The probable culprit of this poor print is not enough perimeters or shells outlining the object. If the object slopes inward too much as the subsequent upper shells are printed, then these shells have nothing supporting them underneath and will either stretch or collapse during printing. Increase the number of perimeters or shells and try again.

- To help support the perimeters as the object is built up, you might try increasing the infill percentage. This will only work up to a point; if the slope is too flat, then the infill will still show through the layers. For this object, you might try 25 percent or more infill.

- If this object was printed with three or four perimeters (two or three extra shells) and 25 percent infill, and it still exhibits a similar problem, then you might want to increase the number of solid layers to something around five, or even six. While this increases print time, it makes the uppermost surface far more solid.

- The last thing to check is the cooling settings. If you have a fan, then try setting the fan to come on with these smaller layers. If you don't have a cooling fan, then consider getting a fan upgrade to help these prints turn out better.

More Tips

This final section provides extra tips that might prove helpful.

ABS Cement

This tip comes from the filament guys at ProtoParadigm (`www.protoparadigm.com`). If you are using ABS filament in your 3D printer and want a great way to stick two (or more) printed objects together, or a way to smooth out the surface of an object, then consider making your own ABS cement. With this tip, it is possible to make your own plastic glue that matches the color of your specific filament, using acetone's ability to dissolve

ABS with ease. ABS sticks well to a polyimide print surface that has been cleaned with acetone. All you need is the following:

- Nail polish container or similar

- Acetone

- Filament clippings

- Clippers or wire cutters

You will need a small glass container for the cement, ideally a new bottle with a brush in the lid—although in a pinch, an empty bottle of nail polish will work. As shown in Figure A-14, start with an empty nail polish bottle that has been cleaned with a little acetone to dissolve and remove any remaining nail polish.

■ **Caution** Handle acetone with extreme care, avoid prolonged skin contact, use in a ventilated area, and whatever you do, do not wash acetone down your sink. The primary material for modern plumbing is ABS, for which acetone is an extremely effective dissolvent.

Figure A-14. *ABS cement supplies*

Take the empty container and fill half the bottle with acetone, keeping the lid on the container as much as you can. Acetone is extremely volatile and evaporates very quickly if left uncovered. Next, drop a pile of filament clippings into the bottle until the bottle is about three-quarters full. Swirl the filament-acetone mixture a bit and then leave it over night. When you come back to it in the morning, the finished cement should look something like what's shown in Figure A-15.

Figure A-15. *Finished ABS cement*

With your new color-matching ABS glue, you can weld together separate objects, like the cubes in Figure A-15; brush it on an object to smooth printed lines; or create textures with it. Depending on the consistency that you need, you can either add more acetone to thin the mixture, or add more ABS to thicken it. When dry, your new ABS cement will form a very permanent bond between the two plastic parts. Just don't mistake it for nail polish!

■ **Note**   This might sound obvious, but ABS cement only works on ABS. Acetone, MEK, and other plastic solvents have little to no beneficial effect on PLA. To glue PLA, use cyanoacrylate, generally known as superglue, instead.

Changing Filament

If you're like me, the more you print, the more you look at all those shiny, many-colored spools of filament and can't help picking up a new color here or there. Changing out filament from one print to the next is not all that difficult to do when following these simple steps:

1. Preheat the extruder to extrusion temperature.

2. Reverse the filament out of the extruder.

3. Insert new filament and test the extrusion.

The first thing we need to do is to preheat our extruder to the temperature that our filament extrudes at. For PLA, this might be around 185°C; while ABS might be as high as 220°C. When the extruder reaches temperature, we need to reverse the filament out of the extruder. To do this depends on the type of extruder you have. If you have a quick-release filament driver like the Minimalist Mk7 by Whosawhatsis (discussed in Chapter 10), then all you need to do is push down on the lever of the extruder to release the idler pressure—holding the filament tight to the drive gear—and then simply pull the filament straight up and out of the extruder.

If your filament driver has a more closed idler, like the original MakerBot Mk7 or the MakerGear Stepstruder, then it makes sense to back out the filament using your printer's control panel. In Pronterface, I often reverse the extruder about 35 millimeters at 200mm/s. In ReplicatorG, you need to set the extrusion speed to about 3RPM and reverse the extruder for about 30 seconds or so. The trick here is to make sure that all of the plastic comes out of the extruder and that a small chunk of plastic is not left behind.

If you have one of the Bowden-cable style extruders, like those on the Huxley and Ultimaker, filament changing is a little more difficult. You might want to check with the manufacturer for specific instructions.

With the filament removed, it's time to feed in the new filament. Make sure that the hotend is at the highest temperature for your filament. So if changing from PLA to ABS, be sure to heat the nozzle to the higher 220°C temperature; or if changing from ABS to PLA, keep it at 220°C until you have removed all the ABS from the nozzle. To feed in the new filament, simply reverse the steps to remove the filament and either push the filament into the extruder manually with a quick-release filament driver or with a closed idler. Then feed the filament by extruding somewhere between 30 and 50 millimeters of filament.

If feeding filament through your printer's control panel, be sure that the filament drive gear properly grabs the filament and continuously feeds the filament into the machine. If the filament hangs somewhere in the extruder, then the drive gear might strip the filament; this makes for a bit of a mess.

With the new filament installed, continue to extrude plastic until the nozzle is clear and the filament fully changes color. At this point, if switching from ABS to PLA, you can set the temperature back down to 185°C and start printing with your new filament. Be sure to measure the diameter of your new filament and adjust your slicer settings accordingly before you make that first print.

APPENDIX B

■ ■ ■

Resources

This appendix contains a collection of resources that you might find helpful to refer to occasionally. I've provided a list of places to discuss all things 3D printing; sources for 3D models and 3D modeling applications; suppliers of the printers, parts, and materials used in 3D printing; and the models featured throughout this book, as well as many other models that are worth checking out.

Additional Resources

Despite only being a few years old, the world of personal 3D printers is so vast that there is no way to cover everything in just one book. In this section, I've provided a list of resources that include: forums, groups, web chat, wikis, and blogs; useful calculators and helpful data and information; the main sources for locating 3D models; and some great free and/or open-source software for 3D modeling.

Forums and Groups

eMakershop Forum (www.emakershop.com/forum): Discussions on RepRapPro Mendel and Huxley printers

Freenode IRC (http://webchat.freenode.net): Try #reprap, #MakerGearv2, #slic3r, among others

MakerBot Industries (http://wiki.makerbot.com/forum:start): The official MakerBot forum

MakerBot Operators Google Group (https://groups.google.com/forum/#!forum/makerbot): Discussions about MakerBot printers

MakerGear Google Group (https://groups.google.com/forum/#!forum/makergear): MakerGear extruders, nozzles, Prusa Mendel, and Mosaic

MendelMax Google Group (https://groups.google.com/forum/#!forum/mendelmax): Discussion about the MendelMax printer

RepRap Forum (http://forums.reprap.org): Discussions on all RepRaps, development, electronics, and software

Printrbot Forum (www.printrbottalk.com/forum): Unofficial forum for the Printrbot series of printers

Ultimaker Forum (http://forum.ultimaker.com): All things Ultimaker

Wikis

Printrbot Wiki (www.printrbottalk.com/wiki): Assembly, getting started, and troubleshooting for the Printrbot series of printers

RepRap Wiki (http://reprap.org): The definitive source for all RepRap-style 3D printers

Ultimaker Wiki (http://wiki.ultimaker.com/Ultimaker_wiki): Assembly and guides for the Ultimaker printers

Blogs to Follow

Brazen Artifice (http://brazenartifice.wordpress.com): Information about MakerGear Prusa Mendel printers and firmware settings

Dust's RepRap (http://dustsreprap.blogspot.com): Building RepRaps

HydraRaptor (http://hydraraptor.blogspot.com): The legendary blog of Nophead

MakerBlock (http://makerblock.com): Drawbots, MakerBots, and Doctor Who

MakerBot (www.makerbot.com/blog): 3D modeling and MakerBot

ProtoParadigm (www.protoparadigm.com/blog): Printer theory and general information

RepRap (http://blog.reprap.org): Developments in the RepRap world

RepRap Log Phase (http://repraplogphase.blogspot.com/): The personal blog of Neil Underwood, aka Spacexula

RichRap (http://richrap.blogspot.com): RepRap development and DIY printing

Other Information

G-Code (http://reprap.org/wiki/G-code): Useful G-Code information that can be added to sliced models or even sent to a printer directly to control the printer

MakerBot Documents (www.makerbot.com/docs): Information on the Replicator, Thing-O-Matic, and other MakerBot products

Metric Screw Dimensions (www.numberfactory.com/nf_metric.html): Useful dimensions for metric nuts, bolts, and screws

OpenSCAD User Manual (http://en.wikibooks.org/wiki/OpenSCAD_User_Manual): Resource material for working with OpenSCAD

RepRap Calculator (http://calculator.josefprusa.cz): Calculator for print and mechanical settings brought to you by Josef Prusa

Sources for 3D Models

Google 3D Warehouse (http://sketchup.google.com/3dwarehouse): 3D models for the Google SketchUp 3D modeling application

Thingiverse (www.thingiverse.com): "Digital designs for physical objects"

3D Modeling Software

3DTin (www.3dtin.com): Web-based 3D voxel modeling

Google SketchUp (http://sketchup.google.com): 3D modeling application featuring push/pull designs

MeshLab (http://meshlab.sourceforge.net): 3D model processing and editing

MakerBlock (http://makerblock.com): 3D mesh manipulation

netfabb Cloud Service (http://cloud.netfabb.com): Online model processing

netfabb Studio Basic (www.netfabb.com/basic.php): Mesh editing and repair

OpenSCAD (www.openscad.org): Script-based 3D solid modeling

Tinkercad (https://tinkercad.com/home): Web-based 3D solid modeling

Selected Suppliers

Personal 3D printers come from a long line of industrial supplies for hardware, parts, and materials. Here are a handful of useful suppliers to consider.

Printer Suppliers

Aleph Objects, Inc. (www.lulzbot.com): Prusa Mendel and AO-100 3D printers and parts

MakerBot (www.makerbot.com): MakerBot Replicator 3D printer, parts, and filament

MakerGear (www.makergear.com): Prusa Mendel and Mosaic 3D printers, MakerGear plastruders, and hotends

MixShop (http://store.mixshop.com): Prusa Mendel kits, parts, and electronics

Printrbot (http://printrbot.com): Printrbot 3D printers, hotends, and electronics

RepRapPro, Ltd. (http://reprappro.com): RepRapPro Mendel and Huxley kits

TrinityLabs (http://store.mendelmax.com): MendelMax kits

Ultimaker (https://shop.ultimaker.com): Ultimaker 3D printer and upgrades

Parts and Filament Suppliers

Faberdashery (www.faberdashery.co.uk): PLA by the meter

ProtoParadigm (https://www.protoparadigm.com): High quality filament and polymide tape

RepRapSource (www.reprapsource.com): Hardware and kits for RepRap printers

TechPaladin (http://techpaladin.com): Select hardware for 3Dprinters

UltiMachine (http://ultimachine.com): RAMPS electronics, hardware, and filament

XYZ Printers (http://xyzprinters.com): Electronics, 3D printer hardware, and kits

Hardware Suppliers

Amazon Supply (www.amazonsupply.com): Fasteners, pneumatic fittings, and tools

McMaster-Carr (www.mcmaster.com): Screws and bolts, threaded and smooth rods, springs, and general hardware

SDP/SI (www.sdp-si.com): Timing belts, timing pulleys, and Igus bushings

The Big Bearing Store (www.thebigbearingstore.com): Mostly radial ball bearings

VXB Ball Bearings (www.vxb.com): Linear and radial ball bearings, linear motion systems, and smooth rods

Models Used in This Book

A book about 3D printing just wouldn't be that good if it didn't use a multitude of different models. Table B-1 is a listing of all of the models we printed or referenced in this book.

Table B-1. *Models Used in This Book*

Model Name	URL	Author	Chapter
Stanford Bunny	www.thingiverse.com/thing:3731	Stanford Computer Graphics Laboratory	2
The Essential Calibration Set	www.thingiverse.com/thing:5573	Coasterman	3
Minimug	www.thingiverse.com/thing:18357	Sebastien Bailard	3
Build Platform Level Test Pattern	www.thingiverse.com/thing:15709	Ed Nisley	3
Circle Calibration Set	www.thingiverse.com/thing:12259	Whosawhatsis	3
Hollow Calibration Pyramid	www.thingiverse.com/thing:8757	Scott Pierce	3
OpenSCAD Pirate Ship	www.thingiverse.com/thing:12856	MakerBlock	4
War of the Worlds Playset	www.thingiverse.com/thing:14657	Drew Petitclerc	4
Pony Creation Kit	www.thingiverse.com/thing:6123	Allan Ecker	7
Creatures of Thingiverse	www.thingiverse.com/thing:12652	Hillary Brosnihan	7
Turtle Shell Racers	www.thingiverse.com/thing:10526	Michael Curry	7
Hipsta	www.thingiverse.com/thing:13468	Pomalin	7
Gangsta	www.thingiverse.com/thing:5367	Yvo Waldmeier	7
Walnut	www.thingiverse.com/thing:17235	Siderit	7
Tony Buser	www.thingiverse.com/thing:10030	MakerBot Industries	7
Minotaur Mini	www.thingiverse.com/thing:16874	Joseph Larson	7
Rabbit Habbit	www.thingiverse.com/thing:18350	Brian Stamile	7
Thinking Gargoyle	www.thingiverse.com/thing:20634	Charles Babbage	9
Gnome Scan #4	www.thingiverse.com/thing:11506	Tony Buser	9
Robot Toy #A	www.thingiverse.com/thing:12180	Ed Tekeian	9
Slim LM8UU Holder	www.thingiverse.com/thing:16158	Jonas Kühling	10
Z-Axis Linear Bearing	www.thingiverse.com/thing:14548	Christian Hinna	10
Y-Axis Bearing Holder	www.thingiverse.com/thing:18457	Jeremy Green	10
Linear Bearing X-Axis Carriage	www.thingiverse.com/thing:9420	Mark Durbin	10
MakerGear X-Carriage Fan Mount	www.thingiverse.com/thing:13343	Jake Poznanski	10
Birdstruder for MakerGear Plastruder	www.thingiverse.com/thing:13628	Tommy Cheng	10
Minimalistic Mk7 Replacement	www.thingiverse.com/thing:15718	Whosawhatsis	10

Cool Things to Print

We've designed and printed a lot of cool things in this book, but there are still so many more cool things to make, some of my favorites are listed in Table B-2. Give one of these a try the next time you need something fun to print.

Table B-2. *Cool Things to Print*

Model Name	URL	Author
Tornado	www.thingiverse.com/thing:7519	Martijn Elserman
Bucket o' Octopi	www.thingiverse.com/thing:7900	Brian Emerson
Stegosaurus - sliced	www.thingiverse.com/thing:12246	RichRap
Screwless Cube Gears	www.thingiverse.com/thing:10483	Emmett Lalish
Mr. Alligator	www.thingiverse.com/thing:13612	Randy Jamison
Sappho's Head	www.thingiverse.com/thing:14565	Luke Chilson
Miniature Castle	www.thingiverse.com/thing:7013	Tony Cervantes
Yoda - Lite	www.thingiverse.com/thing:10752	Clare Cunningham
Spidersaur Printing Plates	www.thingiverse.com/thing:9646	MakerBlock
Mars Exploration Rover	www.thingiverse.com/thing:10057	Tony Buser
Random Vase V2	www.thingiverse.com/thing:12105	Hrvoje Cop
GearVase	www.thingiverse.com/thing:19031	Jelle
Owl Statue	www.thingiverse.com/thing:18218	Tom Cushwa
Companion Cube	www.thingiverse.com/thing:13588	Andrew Diehl
Treefrog	www.thingiverse.com/thing:18479	Morena
Beethoven Bust	www.thingiverse.com/thing:1178	Dino Girl
Gothic Cathedral Play Set	www.thingiverse.com/thing:2030	Michael Curry
Starfish	www.thingiverse.com/thing:11349	Steven Conine

Index

CPSIA information can be obtained at www.ICGtesting.com
Printed in the USA
LVOW03s2149160914

404441LV00008B/110/P

9 781430 243922